POLITE LANDSCAPES

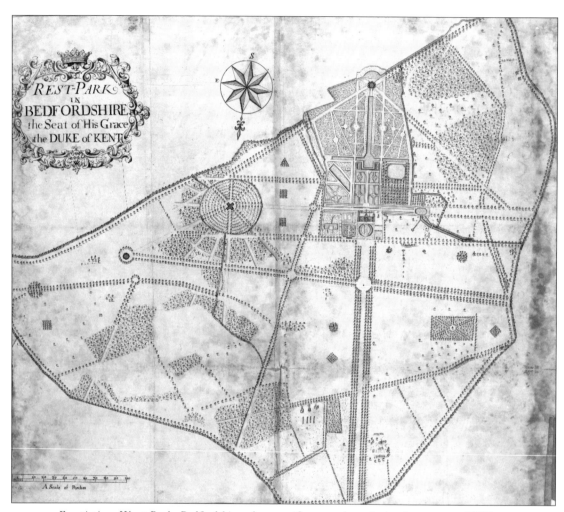

Frontispiece:Wrest Park, Bedfordshire: the magnificent gardens, depicted on a map of 1719.

POLITE LANDSCAPES

GARDENS AND SOCIETY IN EIGHTEENTH-CENTURY ENGLAND

TOM WILLIAMSON

THE JOHNS HOPKINS UNIVERSITY PRESS
BALTIMORE, MARYLAND

Printed in Great Britain

First published in the United States of America by
The Johns Hopkins University Press
2715 North Charles Street
Baltimore, Maryland 21218-4319

ISBN 0-8018-5205-6

LC 95-79552

A catalog record of this book is available from the British Library.

Contents

List of Illustrations

Acknowledgements

Many people have helped with this book, by providing information, ideas or inspiration. I would like to thank, in particular: Liz Bellamy; David Brown; the Marquess of Cholmondeley; Viscount Coke; T.R. Cubitt; Stephen Daniels; John Dye; Paul Everson; Jon Finch; Penny Fogg; Edward Harwood; Peter Holborn; Rosemary Hoppitt; John Dixon Hunt; David Jacques; David Lambert; Mark Laird; Mark Leoni; Beverley Peters; John Phibbs; Monica Place; Chris Ridgeway; Judith Roberts; Kate Skipper; A. Hassell Smith; Keith Snell; Anthea Taigel; Chris Taylor; Lord Walpole; Mr S.C. Whitbread; Robert Williams; Jean Williamson; and Richard Wilson. Particular thanks are due to Stephen Daniels, who read and commented on the text; and to Liz Bellamy, who compiled the index.

This book would not have been possible without the help of the staff of the following institutions: the Norfolk, East Suffolk, West Suffolk, Bedfordshire, Berkshire, Buckinghamshire, and Hertfordshire Record Offices; the John Innes Foundation; Cambridge University Library.

I would also like to thank the following individuals and organizations for permission to reproduce illustrations: Bedfordshire Record Office (Frontispiece, 4); Michael Brandon Jones (1, 2, 10, 11, 17, 20, 21, 25, 57, 58, 59, 60, 61, 62, 63, 64, 65, 66, 67, 68); Buckinghamshire Record Office (37); Viscount Coke (24, 41); *Country Life* (49); Derek Edwards and the Norfolk Air Photography Library of the Norfolk Museums Service (3, 69); Jon Finch (15, 40, 44); Herefordshire and Worcestershire Record Office (14); Hertfordshire Record Office (29); Brian Horne (7, 9, 32, 48); Ipswich Museum (47); David Jacques (34); Sir Berwick Lechmere (14); The Duke of Marlborough (56); Richard Muir (5, 6, 16); National Gallery, London (26); National Trust (22 and 33); Lord Shuttleworth (38); Staffordshire Record Office (34); Anthea Taigel (13, 39, 43, 46); Lord Walpole (67 and 68); Weidenfeld and Nicholson (42, 45); Mr S.C.Whitbread (4). My thanks also to anyone who has been inadvertently omitted from this list.

CHAPTER ONE

Gardens and History

INTRODUCTION

This book is about garden design in eighteenth-century England, and in particular about the origins of the landscape park – that uniquely English contribution to the arts which we now normally associate with the name of Lancelot 'Capability' Brown. The great aesthetic landscapes established by wealthy landowners in this period are still cherished as part of our heritage, and they remain a central part of contemporary cultural experience. They are worthy of serious historical enquiry: they demand investigation. Yet this book is not, and could not be, *just* about gardens. In order to explore why tastes in landscape design changed in the course of the eighteenth century we shall look at many other topics: at politics and economics, at farming and forestry, at changing patterns of social organization. For eighteenth-century parks and gardens fulfilled many different roles and expressed many aspects of the lives of their owners. Their history is as complex as that of society itself, and as a result this book can do no more than introduce a fascinating subject.

An earlier and perhaps more fortunate generation of garden historians did not really feel the need to explain the changing styles of garden design in these wide terms. Gardens just changed. Fashions were formulated in part by influential writers such as Alexander Pope, Joseph Addison, William Mason, or Horace Walpole, and influenced to some extent by the availability of new plants introduced from distant lands. For the most part, however, it was original artists such as Charles Bridgeman, William Kent, 'Capability' Brown, and Humphry Repton who set the pace, each developing in turn the styles created by his predecessors. Their own styles, in turn, became a fashion, eagerly sought after by landowners and copied by inferior designers.[1] There was, however, a dominant trend, running throughout the period, towards ever more irregular, asymmetrical, 'natural' forms of gardening.

Seventeenth-century and earlier gardens had been highly artificial environments: enclosed by high walls, geometric in design, dominated by bushes clipped into pyramids and globes and by patterns defined by low box hedging and the like. Gradually, inexorably, the popularity of such features declined in the course of the eighteenth century. Horace Walpole described in the 1760s how, spurred on by the writings of Pope and Addison, Charles Bridgeman and William Kent made progressively closer approximations towards a 'natural' form of landscape. Geometric layouts were simplified: the wall was replaced by the sunken fence or ha-ha, and:

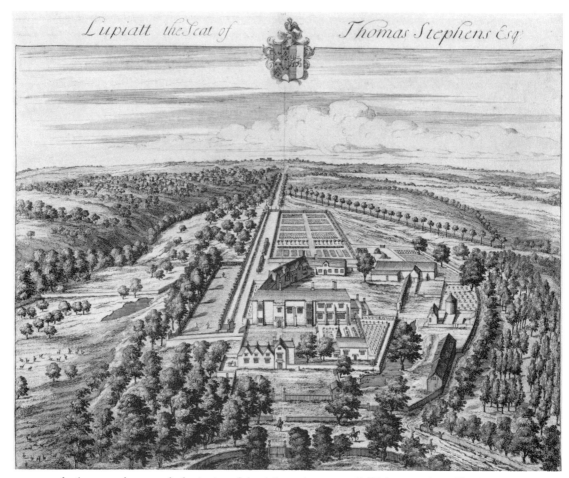

1. A country house at the beginning of the eighteenth century. J. Kip's engraving of Lypiatt Park, published in Sir Robert Atkyns' Ancient and Present State of Glostershire *in 1712. The hall is surrounded by garden enclosures and yards, many of them walled.*

The contiguous ground of the park without . . . was to be harmonised with the lawn within; and the garden in its turn was to be set free from its prim regularity, that it might assort with the wilder country without.[2]

This process culminated in the decades after 1760: nature finally triumphed in the casual, irregular, sweeping scenery of the landscape parks created by 'Capability' Brown and his imitators. Walls, gardens, order and regularity were banished. The mansion was left standing, as Repton was later to put it, 'solitary and unconnected' in the boundless sea of turf.

In so far as earlier garden historians attempted to explain the apparently inexorable advance towards naturalism they generally did so in terms of philosophical ideas: they searched for answers in the texts produced by contemporary intellectuals. Some modern historians still emphasize the importance of such things as the eighteenth-century rejection of Cartesian systematism in favour of empiricism.[3] As we shall see, changing philosophical ideas were an important factor in the development of garden design, but this kind of explanation should not be pushed too far. Letters and diaries make it clear that in the eighteenth century, as now, abstract philosophy was of little or no concern to the vast majority of people, who needed to cater for and express a broader (if shallower) range of interests in their gardens and grounds. We should be wary of explanations produced by contemporary intellectuals and aesthetes; they will always be partial, highlighting those aspects of reality and experience which most interest them, and ignoring others.

A rather different explanation for the particular evolution of the English landscape garden has been advanced both by some eighteenth-century writers and by certain modern scholars.[4] By the start of the eighteenth century the frontiers of cultivation in England were being pushed to their limits: subsequent enclosures and reclamations removed the last vestiges of wilderness. Nature was now tamed, wildness no longer a threat, and as a result the old popular aesthetic preference for fertile, tamed and cultivated scenes was in retreat. More natural landscapes were increasingly valued, and thus became the model for the pleasure grounds of the wealthy. As the early nineteenth-century designer John Claudius Loudon put it:

> As the lands devoted to agriculture in England were, sooner than in any other country in Europe, generally enclosed with hedges and hedgerow trees, so the face of the country in England, sooner than in any other part of Europe, produced an appearance which bore a closer resemblance to country seats laid out in the geometrical style; and, for this reason, an attempt to imitate the irregularity of nature in laying out pleasure grounds was made in England . . . sooner than in any other part of the world. . . .[5]

We will return to this argument later on, but it is worth noting at this stage that eighteenth-century writers on gardening were for ever advocating the development of *more* naturalistic forms of design. This should immediately alert us to the fact that nature is not some unchanging objective concept but one defined in different ways by successive generations. After all, there is nothing obviously natural about the contrived serpentine meandering of the paths in early eighteenth-century shrubberies, still less in the manicured simplicity of Brown's parks. These did not resemble the open heaths, fens, or coppiced woods which by the eighteenth century were the last – and much altered – vestiges of wilderness in England.

Such explanations accept that there was indeed a real sense in which gardens became, decade by decade, ever more 'naturalistic'. While this may be true it is as well to be aware of the dangers involved in such a reading of landscape history. This approach encourages us to concentrate only on those aspects of the designs of a given period which appear to be in the main flow of stylistic development,

2. Isolated in a sea of open turf: a country house in the late eighteenth century. Copped Hall, Essex, as illustrated in William Watts' The Seats of the Nobility and Gentry *(1779).*

and to play down or ignore more 'conservative' features which might, in fact, have been more noticeable on the ground. It may be better, perhaps, to take each phase of garden design on its own terms, and study it in its own context, than to look at it simply as a stage on a path leading to something else.[6] On closer inspection, moreover, some developments, widely accepted as continuities, may not be quite what they seem. In particular, I shall argue in the chapters that follow that the landscape *gardens* designed by William Kent and others in the 1730s and '40s – relatively small areas of grass, shrubbery and ornamental buildings – were quite distinct from, and served rather different functions to, the more extensive landscape *parks* created by Brown and his contemporaries in the second half of the century.

THE NEW GARDEN HISTORY

The stories told by garden historians have, traditionally, focused not only on the great designers who forged the main lines of stylistic development but also on the 'key sites' where new ideas were first put into practice. Places like Stowe,

Rousham, Stourhead, or Painshill repeatedly appear in books on garden history, like so many rabbits out of a hat. It is only in the last few decades that historians have begun to examine a wider range of texts, including diaries and letters from a broad spectrum of landowners; and a wider range of landscapes, including those created by the mass of the local gentry. Their often long and complicated histories have been studied through documents, illustrations and maps kept in both public and private archives. Increasingly, too, garden historians have turned their attention away from the dry and dusty documents.[7] Armed with the tools of the archaeologist and others, the earthworks remaining from earlier phases of garden design have been assiduously traced and – where resources have allowed or the imminence of destruction has demanded – excavations have been conducted. Aerial photography has revealed the traces of long-lost terraces and parterres, while ancient garden walls and buildings have been measured and analysed.[8] At many places the surviving pattern of planting has been rigorously examined, the trees classified and mapped according to age, species and variety.

Such detailed analyses of the physical fabric are necessary because illustrations and maps can be misleading. Some exaggerated the size or sophistication of gardens in order to flatter the owner. Others represent ambitious proposals which were never executed. Survey evidence can, more importantly, be used to fill in the many gaps in what is all too often a highly fragmentary documentary record. I do not mean to suggest here that the physical, archaeological evidence is necessarily 'true', the documentary information false or misleading. All the sources used to study the history of a landscape will mislead in their own particular way. The art is to test one against the other, combining and recombining the various threads until a coherent story emerges. Of course, in most cases the history of a particular garden can only be very imperfectly recovered. But when a large number are studied the gaps in the individual *biographies* become less important, as the framework of a coherent *history* begins to emerge.

The recent increase in research has made garden history both more interesting and more problematic. It seems at times as if the more we find out, the less we know. Indeed, even when all phases in the development of a landscape are reasonably well understood, certain things remain unknowable. We are often, for example, in the dark about precisely what the designers envisaged as the finished product of their labours. An architect designs a building, a builder puts it up, and there it stays: time will mellow it but, within the lifetime of the owner and his progeny, it will not materially change. The same might be true of the most formal and artificial forms of garden design, at least for as long as the labour is available to trim and weed them. But with the kinds of larger ornamental landscape that emerged in the period under discussion here, the situation is different. Deciduous trees reach a reasonable stage of growth in forty or fifty years, enough to make a tolerable avenue or clump. Did owners or designers think much beyond this stage, and if so, how far ahead did they think? The question is important because increasing age radically changes the structure of a design: sharp lines soften, vistas are closed; the Scots pine changes from something like a Christmas tree into a romantic and twisted head of foliage. Unless we have design drawings rather than – as is usually the case – planting plans, the eventual intention will

3. *Warham, Norfolk: soil marks of a formal garden destroyed in the eighteenth century. Archaeological techniques such as aerial photography have contributed a great deal to the study of garden history.*

often elude us. Today, if 'Capability' Brown could wander through the vast beeches he had planted at Blenheim or Longleat, he would surely have difficulty in recognizing what has become an over-mature landscape on the point of terminal decay.

Two clear and striking things have, however, emerged from the spate of recent studies. The first is that the 'key sites' which loom so large in the literature are often a poor guide to the gardens created by the majority of landowners. These places were often described *ad nauseam* precisely because they were innovative and unusual: almost by definition, different from ordinary gardens, idiosyncratic or even odd creations. Moreover, such gardens were generally laid out around the homes of the greatest landowners in the land: men of national importance, owners of great estates of 500 hectares or more, who often drew on income from government office, mineral leases, or urban rents as well as from their agricultural estates. The fortunes, lifestyles and political and intellectual horizons of such men were quite different from those of the far more numerous local gentry, men with estates of a few hundred hectares, economic interests limited to a small group of parishes and political horizons circumscribed, as often as not, by the county boundary. Such men were, almost by definition, slow to follow élite fashions: not so much because they were ignorant of them, or even because they lacked the necessary resources (although this was often the case), but rather because they had different lifestyles, and made different requirements on their immediate environment.

The second crucial fact to emerge is the importance of the owner in the creation of particular gardens. Many landowners, of course, designed their own grounds and we encounter their pleasure, pain and frustration in doing so again and again in diaries and letters. 'I am scratching out upon Paper ten thousand Designs for the other parts of the Garden', wrote one gentleman from his half-completed grounds at Marston in Somerset in 1733, '& my Plans commonly come to the same Fate . . . they are flung into the Fire and forgot.'[9] Many of the most famous and most visited eighteenth-century gardens were designed by such enthusiastic amateurs. But even when professional designers were employed it is a mistake to believe that their plans were simply adopted wholesale by the client. In practice, most designs seem to have developed through a series of compromises; and the final decision about what was or was not to be implemented lay, naturally enough, with the landowner. He who pays the piper calls the tune, and even the 'great names' had to create landscapes which suited the needs, and pocket, of the landowner. Otherwise, famous or not, the client would go elsewhere. As Repton put it:

> Among the most painful circumstances attending the Professor's life, [are] the time and contrivance wasted to produce plans although highly approved; yet from vanity, from indecision, or from the fickleness of human nature, not infrequently thrown aside . . .[10]

Such slights had to be borne stoically. This was, as we shall see, an increasingly commercial age – when advertisements and newspapers began to reach a relatively wide audience. But social connections, personal recommendations and outright patronage continued to be of fundamental importance in furthering the career of the designer.

All this allows us to focus more sharply the questions we need to ask about eighteenth-century gardens. If the role of the individual landowner was crucial in the evolution of a particular design, then the needs and interest of landowners as a group must have been the determining factor in the more general development of style. Gardens need to be explained in terms of the lives and lifestyles of their owners. Such a suggestion is not particularly remarkable, nor in itself new. In particular, a number of modern writers have sought to explain eighteenth-century landscape design in terms of the changing relationships between the gentry and their social inferiors. Some, such as Ann Bermingham, have suggested that the naturalistic landscape garden, as this developed in the middle and later decades of the century, was a form of *legitimation*, which served to make the increasingly hierarchical nature of English society appear natural and inevitable.[11] In Bermingham's words,

> As the real landscape began to look increasingly artificial, like a garden, the garden began to look increasingly natural, like the pre-enclosed landscape. Thus a natural landscape became the prerogative of the estate . . . so that nature was the sign of property and property the sign of nature. . . . By conflating nature with the fashionable taste of a new social order, it redefined the natural in terms of this order, and vice versa.[12]

And so vast social inequalities were made to appear normal and unchanging, rather than arbitrary and perhaps temporary. Now these are important arguments, but we must recognize their limitations. While social relations between rich and poor might be the most important concern for some modern scholars, we cannot simply assume that the same was true of the people who created the landscapes in question. Individual landowners were, it can be argued, more concerned about the impression their gardens made on neighbours of similar social rank than with the impact they had on the local poor, who were anyway kept firmly in place with a wide range of economic and coercive sanctions. Gardens, like houses, were certainly expressions of wealth and status and, to some extent, instruments of social control. But the social realities they expressed, or concealed, were highly complex, for eighteenth-century England was a complex society, and was not composed simply of two opposed groups, the landed rich and the landless poor. Instead it was – or was becoming – a competitive, commercial, capitalist society with a whole range of social groups: merchants, financiers, industrialists, an urban middle class.

Such a society had not developed overnight. Its origins lay in Tudor and Stuart England. In the fifteenth and sixteenth centuries the traditional structures of feudal society had begun to disintegrate. The agrarian economy had become more market-orientated, and more regionally specialized, as a rising class of yeoman farmers began to engage in the production of those commodities (grain, sheep, cheese, etc.) to which the local conditions were particularly suited. There were also fundamental political changes. The power of central government grew under the Tudor dynasty at the expense both of the great feudal families in the provinces and, with the Reformation, of the international Catholic Church. A new kind of gentry emerged, profiting from the Dissolution of the Monasteries and internal peace. Wealth was now to be made from careful estate administration, farming, government service and the law; and power came from having influence at Court rather than a band of armed retainers. The Tudor age saw internal peace, demographic growth and economic expansion.

In the sixteenth century economic and social change had served to bolster the power of the monarchy, but in the seventeenth century they began to threaten it. For a truly capitalist economy to emerge, absolute rights of private property were required, protected from the arbitrary power of the Crown by a parliament representing the propertied. Charles I, however, not only resisted this but attempted to extend the powers of central government into the provinces, which brought him into conflict with a local gentry jealous of their own influence in their 'countries'. Royal claims to power were bolstered by reference to religion but a substantial number of Puritan Englishmen wished to take the Reformation further and reject the half-hearted compromise of the Church of England. Combined with the personal incompetence of Charles I and various short-term economic problems this array of tensions exploded in the 1640s and '50s in civil war, regicide, the establishment of a republic and, finally, political chaos.

The Restoration of 1660, and the Glorious Revolution of 1688, restored the monarchy but confirmed the principal gain of the war: the supremacy of parliament. Yet, as we shall see, ideological tensions remained, and new social strains emerged, as the new political dispensation allowed the unrestricted development of a capitalist economy. Beneath the surface, eighteenth-century England seethed with contradictions and conflicts. Gardens and parks played an important part in their resolution. But the emerging forms of social and economic organization also provided new possibilities for landscape design, for the development of capitalism had a fundamental effect on the structure of the vernacular countryside.

THE CONTEXT OF THE GARDEN: LANDSCAPE AND LANDOWNERSHIP

Garden historians tend to ignore the development of the wider working landscape of fields and woods, hedges and lanes, village and farmstead, but when eighteenth-century writers urged garden designers to consult the 'genius of the place' it was this essentially man-made framework to which they were referring. The eighteenth-century landscape varied in innumerable ways from place to place and region to region; but to the garden historian the most important variations relate to the ways in which, and the times at which, it was enclosed.[13]

In medieval England much arable land had consisted of 'open fields', in which the property of landowners and tenants lay intermingled in a myriad of tiny strips, the exploitation of which was regulated by village communities. Large areas also consisted of heaths, moors and greens, grazed in common by the animals of the community. Such landscapes were well suited to a society of small-scale peasant producers but not to the needs of the new market-orientated agriculture. Enclosure was the process by which they were replaced by a patchwork of hedged fields, held as private property by individuals who could do what they pleased with them. Enclosure was the subject of much discussion in eighteenth-century England, when large areas of open fields and commons were removed by parliamentary acts. Yet the magnitude of a process is not easily measured by the number of words written about it, and it is probable that less than a quarter, and possibly little more than a fifth, of England was affected by enclosure in the period between 1750 and 1840. Some parts of England had never possessed open fields, or had lost them before the start of the eighteenth century. These regions were principally located in the south and east (the Home Counties, much of East Anglia) and in the west (the west Midlands, the Marches, the West Country). They shared other distinctive features: in particular, a generally

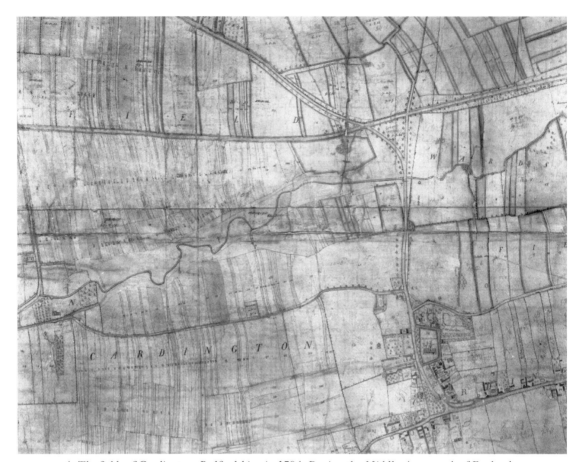

4. The fields of Cardington, Bedfordshire, in 1794. During the Middle Ages, much of England was farmed as open fields. Although enclosure had made much progress before 1700, many areas continued to be dominated by open-field farming until the end of the eighteenth century, or even beyond.

dispersed pattern of settlement with many isolated farms and hamlets as well as – or in some districts, instead of – nucleated villages. The layout of boundaries and lanes in these areas was not rigidly rectilinear. Instead, they were characterized by a degree of picturesque irregularity born of their often considerable antiquity.

These anciently enclosed regions contrasted markedly with what early topographers termed 'champion' areas, concentrated in the Midlands of England and the north-east: countrysides which conformed to the traditional image of a pre-enclosure landscape, with nucleated villages and boundless, treeless prospects. Even in these areas, however, enclosure had made great strides during the fifteenth, sixteenth and seventeenth centuries. Sometimes this was because all the land in a parish had fallen into the hands of a single proprietor (who sometimes then depopulated the village). More often it occurred through

5. *Panorama of fields, Hembury, Devon. Not all areas of England have landscapes created by post-medieval enclosure. In much of the south and east of England, and in the west, the essential framework of roads and boundaries was created in the Middle Ages, or earlier.*

agreements between several proprietors, often ratified by a case brought in the Court of Chancery. Early enclosure was a particular feature of the heartlands of the great estates: for no man of wealth or taste would, by 1700, have relished a prospect across the unbounded, archaic landscape of open fields.

The parliamentary enclosures of the later eighteenth and early nineteenth centuries thus represented the tail end of a long process:[14] and this casts some doubt on the arguments discussed above, which relate the increasingly enclosed nature of the countryside to the growing irregularity of gentlemen's pleasure grounds. The chronology doesn't quite fit: most of England had been enclosed long before the advent of 'Capability' Brown. Yet an understanding of enclosure is, nevertheless, crucial for our enquiry into the development of landscape design. Firstly, as already noted, the 'genius of a place' was largely the consequence of its enclosure history. In areas enclosed since ancient times, the designers of the mid- and late eighteenth century worked with more amenable terrain than those in areas more recently enclosed, for they had the advantage of landscapes in which mature trees, woods and copses existed in abundance. Secondly, there was a clear link between the increasing scale of landscape design during the seventeenth and eighteenth centuries, and the increasingly enclosed nature of the landscape. Enclosure was the *sine qua non* of large-scale landscaping. This was partly because

6. *Henlow, Bedfordshire. This detail from the enclosure map of 1798 shows surveyors busy in the open fields.*

a landowner required a compact block of land, rather than a property splintered and scattered in a myriad of small fragments, in order to create an extensive design – whether this was geometric or naturalistic in character. But it was also because open fields and commons were subject to seasonal or permanent access by the community, for grazing and other purposes. Until they were enclosed it was impossible to establish trees on them, for these would either be eaten by livestock or removed for firewood.

However, enclosure cannot be studied in isolation from another key process. From late medieval times small freeholders gradually but inexorably lost more and more of their share of the national land 'cake': a process once again related to the development of a more capitalist, market-orientated economy, and to the comparative advantage within this enjoyed by larger units of agrarian production.[15] This development was most marked in the grain-producing areas of England, where the small landowner was in almost continuous decline in the early modern period. It was most marked of all in areas of especially light, poor soil: on

7. The landscape of parliamentary enclosure: straight boundaries with flimsy hawthorn hedges in Ickleton, Cambridgeshire.

the dry heaths of eastern England, or on the Yorkshire and Lincolnshire Wolds. Here great landowners invested in large-scale capital-intensive land improvement schemes, especially in the second half of the eighteenth century. The naked opulence of the Coke's Holkham (Norfolk), or the Yarborough's Sledmere (Yorks), stood at the centre of landscapes more widely transformed, 'improved', by aristocratic endeavour. In contrast, the development of such estates was more muted and gradual in areas devoted to livestock rearing and dairying. In the uplands of England, over much of the moist and warm West Country, and on the heavier soils of the south-east and East Anglia, small family farms remained viable well into the eighteenth and nineteenth centuries and small freeholders and lesser gentry maintained a significant stake in the property available.

By and large the second half of the seventeenth century and the first half of the eighteenth were difficult times for the small freehold farmer, and to some extent for the local squire. The fortunes of both were dependent on agricultural prices which, after a century of buoyancy, now slumped. A long period of demographic increase was followed by one in which the population grew slowly or even declined, increasing real wages and keeping agricultural prices low. These problems were exacerbated by the imposition, in 1693, of the Land Tax. Many small freehold farmers were obliged to disinvest themselves of land, and even some of the gentry were forced to sell up. Many of the greater landowners, in contrast, did not do so badly in this period, and systematically bought up the holdings of their less fortunate neighbours. Many could capitalize on other forms of income, from the ownership of urban property or mines, from membership of government and the spoils of office.

But there were other, more fundamental reasons why large landed estates tended to grow ever larger in this period. Now that the arbitrary power of the Crown had been curtailed, as a result of the gains of the Civil War and the Revolutionary Settlement of 1688, the great landowners were more secure in their possessions. Political rivalries were now conducted through the medium of parliament, and families were less likely to lose their possessions by backing the wrong side in Court intrigues or – as in late medieval times – in dynastic warfare. Moreover, this period saw the elaboration of the practice of the *strict settlement*, a legal device which ensured that most large estates were 'entailed', tied up in such a way that the owner was obliged to pass on his inheritance intact to the next generation (except for the various portions and jointures to other members of the family stipulated in the agreement). Under such arrangements it was difficult for estates to fragment, for owners to sell off a few farms to cover their gambling debts, for example. They often became increasingly mortgaged and indebted, but they seldom decreased in extent.

Large estates were not only growing in size. They were also becoming more consolidated. The ideal was to own a single coherent block of land, and to this end peripheral properties would be sold off in order to acquire areas nearer the estate heartlands. In part such consolidation was intended to ensure the more efficient management of estates. But it also enabled large landowners to concentrate their political influence, and to increase the opportunities for manipulating the appearance of the landscape to display the extent of their possessions.

Some of the factors encouraging the growth of large estates at the expense of smaller landowners began to change in the second half of the eighteenth century.[16] Population growth began to pick up again after 1740, leading to a fall in wages and a steady rise in agricultural prices and agricultural rents, which produced a revival in the fortunes of the local gentry. At the same time the Land Tax, while it continued to be levied, represented (like other forms of direct taxation) a decreasing part of the fiscal burden. Indirect taxation – especially customs and excise – became increasingly important in the State finances, and thus spread the tax burden on to a wider and poorer section of the population. This period did not, however, see much of a recovery in the fortunes of the small freehold farmer. The greatest profits could be made by men with capital, men who could invest in the techniques, equipment, stock and plant required to make the large efficient farms necessary to remain competitive in this age of 'Agricultural Revolution'.[17] Such men were more likely to be tenants than freeholders: men who could share the burden of investment with an estate owner. Thus it was that the second half of the century saw the continuing prosperity of the great landowners, a revival in the fortunes of the local gentry, but a continued decline in those of the small freeholder.

The fortunes of the principal landowning groups in society, summarized briefly here, are important because parks and gardens existed in a real world, not just in one of abstract ideas: a world in which land and money needed to be found for their creation, in which wages had to be paid for their maintenance. The changing distributions of land and wealth constituted the necessary, indispensable background to the developments in garden design which we shall examine in the chapters that follow.

THE SOCIAL AND POLITICAL CONTEXT

Enthusiastic supporters of the settlement of 1688 endlessly vaunted the virtues of England's 'balanced constitution' which, it was said, combined the principles of democracy (in the form of the House of Commons) with those of aristocracy (the House of Lords) and monarchy. The suggestion that the Commons represented democracy needs, however, to be taken with an enormous pinch of salt. The vote in county elections was restricted to freeholders owning property worth £100 per annum, no small sum, while in many boroughs still more restrictive franchises existed. Often, for example, only members of the unelected, self-selecting corporations had the right to vote. Such anomalies, being ancient, were regarded as part of the liberties of England.

As a result of the 1688 settlement the power of the monarch was limited in significant ways, but he or she remained a vital player in the political game. He or she was no mere figurehead, but was consulted regularly by ministers, would call elections and dismiss administrations, and was generally involved in the process of government. Nevertheless, in the final analysis real power now lay with the great landowners and aristocrats. As in the previous century, these were separated by a great social gulf from the mass of the local gentry, their wealth and power bringing deference and respect. Elections in the counties (and in some boroughs) were in effect struggles between territorial magnates backed by their respective interests – local clients, dependents, freeholders of the locality who often offered their political support in return for favours or preferment in the gift of the candidate.[18] In some seats – smaller or decayed boroughs – aristocratic dominance was more straightforward: roughly half of the seats in the Commons were, in the middle decades of the century, occupied by members whose electorate was so small that they had almost certainly gained their seats by outright bribery.[19] Indeed, eighteenth-century politicians railed endlessly against 'corruption'; but all practised it. It took many forms. MPs in the Commons could themselves be bribed, rewarded for their faithful support of the governing administration by grants of offices, posts and pensions to themselves or – where this was forbidden by law – to their brothers, sons, cousins, or friends. The pool of such rewards was larger than it had ever been before, due to the expansion of the government machine (especially in the field of customs and excise) and the existence of a standing army. To some extent, the great political struggles of the early eighteenth century were about control of this reservoir of patronage. But there were real ideological issues as well, and in the first half of the century these were usually framed in terms of a contest between Whigs and Tories. Put simply, the former were supporters of the 1688 settlement and the Hanoverian succession, of a measure of religious toleration, and (at least after 1722) of a foreign policy geared to peace. They were (again to oversimplify) the party of the groups who had benefited most from the new political dispensation: the greater landowners, powerful city interests, wealthy merchants. The Tories, in contrast, were the party of the High Church, of old-fashioned, non-commercial, paternalistic values. They had originally supported the Stuart succession, although this predeliction became ever less evident with the passing decades. In essence, their leaders were – of necessity – drawn from the disaffected among the great landowners, but the core of their support lay with the provincial local gentry, the backwoods squires. We need, however, to be wary of these labels, and of the neat allegiances which they imply. The changing political circumstances of the 1730s and '40s brought new constellations of interests, and new political groupings, and the old terms increasingly served to mask or confuse the real issues and struggles.

English political activity in this period had significant repercussions on the design of gardens. Landscapes, like houses, were important instruments in the political game. They could be used to proclaim the wealth and power, and thus by implication the continuing political success, of great landowners: overawing the local population and attracting the undecided to their 'interest'. They could be used to demonstrate a governing élite's particular beliefs and ideology and also – as advertisements of its taste and knowledge – its fitness to rule. But they could also be used by excluded groups, as symbols of *their* ideas, programmes and philosophies.

For much of the first half of the eighteenth century England was controlled by the Whigs. Indeed, for a relatively long period – from 1714 until 1742 – it was dominated by one man, the extremely able (if extremely corrupt) Robert Walpole. Whig rule in this period was, at least in part, a reflection of the underlying economic realities of the time, of the comfortable circumstances of the greater landowners.

But this élite lived within a changing world, its traditional assumptions increasingly challenged. The political changes brought by the Civil War had allowed a competitive, and increasingly complex, market economy to develop apace in England. Such an economy encouraged people to think in terms of individuals rather than in terms of groups or abstract entities such as 'the Commonwealth'. Moreover, by the early eighteenth century patterns of economic organization and interdependence had begun to develop which seemed so complicated that it was difficult to comprehend their totality. Educated people were alarmed: it was becoming impossible to understand society as a whole.[20] Intellectuals were vexed by a whole raft of related issues concerning the relationship between private selfishness and the public good, or (in more basic terms) between the individual and society; indeed, concerning the very nature of individuality and personal identity. These issues were central to many of the principal philosophical texts of the age: Mandeville's *Fable of the Bees*; Locke's *Essay Concerning Human Understanding*; Hume's *Treatise of Human Nature*.[21] As we shall see, they also had some impact on the design of gardens in the first half of the eighteenth century.

The progress of this more sophisticated economy was at first retarded by depression and slow demographic growth. But from around 1740 there was rapid expansion. This period saw both the slow beginnings of large-scale industrialization, and the 'consumer revolution': that is, the development of a society geared, as never before, to the production and consumption of a whole range of fashionable, mass-produced (and as often as not essentially unnecessary) goods and services. The new leisure facilities – spas, resorts, assemblies; the rapidly changing fashions in clothes; the mass-produced yet elegant pottery of Josiah Wedgwood – all were symptoms and symbols of this new order.[22] This general economic expansion brought about, as we have seen, a recovery in the fortunes of the local gentry. But it also led to an increase in the size and affluence of what we may call (with some reservations) a 'middle class', a somewhat amorphous group, ranging from wealthy merchants and prominent professionals down to larger-scale farmers and shopkeepers.

All this burgeoning economic activity, in turn, transformed the nature of political and social relations. The role of parliament began to alter in the decades after 1750. More and more it was used by landowners to promote local economic improvements: it was inundated with private bills to create or improve navigations and turnpike roads, to enclose open fields and commons, and in general to do everything necessary to pave the way for further economic growth.[23] And the local gentry were actively involved in promoting economic improvements in their communities, armed with new political powers. With the passing of the County Rate Act in 1739 the Justices of the Peace possessed powers of local taxation, and in the decades after 1750 the Quarter Sessions were increasingly concerned with the construction and improvement of roads, bridges, prisons and other public works.

The extent to which the greater landowners continued to dominate the political life of the country in the middle and later decades of the eighteenth century is a matter for debate among historians. What is unquestionably true is that the nature of their relations with the local gentry and the mercantile and professional classes underwent a profound change. Increasingly, they sought to play down differences of status and hierarchy between them, emphasizing instead a collection of shared cultural values often referred to as 'politeness': easy and affable behaviour; a knowledge of 'taste' or current fashions; and acquisition of a particular set of social skills (including, above all, an ability to hold cordial conversation avoiding at all times 'enthusiasm', or religious or ideological ardour).[24] The new patterns of behaviour began to develop during the early eighteenth century, but 'polite society' really flowered in the decades after 1740.

'Polite society' embraced not only the great landowners and the local gentry but also the upper echelons of the middle class: the people who owned, and who ran, the nation. They were thought of as a group distinct from the 'common people', whose fortunes were, for the most part, in steady decline through the second half of the eighteenth century. In rural areas, in particular, new social gulfs were opening up between the local gentry and the local community of small farmers, cottagers, and labourers, as the consolidation of farms to form more economic units, the spread of enclosure, demographic increase and the consequent decline in wages all took their toll.

The development of garden design in the second half of the eighteenth century was, as we shall see, inextricably bound up with the emergence of 'polite society': with the way in which it was defined, and with its relations with the increasingly impoverished and alienated world around it. It was out of this particular constellation of social and economic forces that the landscape park was born.

THE ARCHITECTURAL CONTEXT

To a surprising extent the study of gardens has remained divorced from that of architecture. Such a division would have puzzled most eighteenth-century gentlemen who, under the influence of Italian Renaissance writers, were accustomed to think of the design of house and garden as a unity. A new mansion would be provided with a new garden, designed to complement its architecture and to show it off to best advantage. Building and landscaping schemes were often contemporary and coordinated, and the shape and size of the house would have an important influence on the layout of its surroundings. In addition, the internal plan of a mansion affected the way in which the grounds outside were seen, and therefore arranged. There were innumerable connections.

This traditional neglect of architecture is particularly surprising given that many of the great names who dominate garden history themselves practised as architects (in the sense, that is, that they designed plans and façades, rather than involved themselves in the more mundane matter of how the edifice should actually be made to stay up). William Kent, for example, only became actively involved in the design of gardens after a career as an architect; Lancelot 'Capability' Brown, whom we tend to think of as the most 'natural' of landscape designers, designed numerous country houses, as well as lodges, garden buildings and bridges. Repton likewise dabbled in architecture, and wrote copiously on the subject, most notably in his last published work, *Fragments on the Theory and Practice of Landscape Gardening*. As he succinctly put it in his Red Book for Panshangar in Hertfordshire: 'I am convinced that some knowledge of architecture is inseparable from the art I express.'[25] His comment is as relevant to the modern student of landscape as it is to its designers of the eighteenth or early nineteenth centuries. And we shall, in the following chapters, trace some of the ways in which the architecture of the house affected the design of the garden, how the design of the garden affected that of the house, and how both together were influenced by the wider social, economic and political forces of the time.

CHAPTER TWO

The Triumph of Geometry: *c.* 1680 to *c.* 1735

The eighteenth century is often described as a period in which the 'reign of nature' held sway in English gardens. Yet this, in many ways, is misleading. For most of the century the majority of English landowners were content to live with gardens of an essentially geometric character. At all social levels the dominance of a formal style remained unchallenged for the first three decades of the century: indeed, it is possible to argue that this period saw the finest flowering of the geometric tradition. During the following twenty years some landowners added more naturalistic, serpentine compartments to their gardens, but it was only in the period after 1750 that the geometric garden really began to go out of fashion. Even then its decline was painfully slow, and there were many country gentlemen in the 1770s who enjoyed, out of their front windows, a view over enclosed geometric grounds.

BEFORE THE CIVIL WAR

The eighteenth-century designers of formal gardens were heirs to a long tradition: but it was a tradition which had undergone many vicissitudes over the previous centuries.

Up until the Civil War the gardens of the gentry were, for the most part, comparatively small spaces which were clearly separated from the surrounding world by high hedges, fences or walls. Their design was dominated by geometry: by topiary – that is, by plants like box, privet and (later) yew cut into a variety of geometric shapes; and by horizontal patterns defined by bands of box, thrift, lavender or similar plants and infilled with flowers or coloured earths – gravel, brick dust, soot, etc. The latter designs, because of their complexity, were often referred to as *knots*: Cardinal Wolsey's garden at Hampton Court had 'knots so enknotted it cannot be expressed'.[1] Tudor and early Stuart gardens also contained various characteristic forms of 'hard landscaping'. There were garden buildings, many of which functioned as 'banqueting houses' in which a 'banquet', an elaborate and sometimes slightly quirky final course to a meal, would be eaten, usually in a room on the first floor. There were also terraces which ran around the sides of the main garden areas, and raised mounds or 'mounts'. All these features provided views out over the high walls of the garden and into the surrounding countryside, for even in the sixteenth and seventeenth centuries most gentlemen found pleasure in a prospect over the fields and woods of their demesne. Their main purpose, however, was to provide an elevated vantage point from which the geometric patterns below could be enjoyed. Such an aerial perspective was also available from the main rooms of the house. With the decline of the hall as the principal public room (and the growing tendency to reserve the parlour for the private use of the family), increasing social importance was attached to rooms at first-floor level: to the great chamber above the parlour, and to that new invention of the sixteenth century, the long gallery. The spatial organization of the house might thus have some effect on the layout of the garden, but the design of the two was rarely considered as one, or developed as a single coherent scheme. To judge from surviving maps and plans, the garden courts were usually ranged in a rather haphazard fashion around the walls of the mansion.[2] They thus mirrored its architecture, for while there was an increasing tendency in this period for gentry houses to exhibit external symmetry, their internal arrangement normally remained irregular.

There were, however, a small number of more sophisticated gardens which, while just as formal and geometric as those described, were more carefully integrated both with the houses they served and with the surrounding landscape.[3] Their design was influenced by Italian Renaissance writers such as Leon Battista Alberti, or by their owner's direct experience of Italian gardens: for even in the sixteenth and seventeenth centuries some aristocrats and gentlemen were making what was later to be known as the 'Grand Tour'. Here they saw gardens more complex and varied than those of their homeland. Constructed, in many cases, on rising ground, they often included open terraces, which provided unrestricted views out across the owner's domain. They contained cascades, fountains and grottos – all welcome features in a warm climate – and often functioned as open-air museums, containing a plethora of statues and sculptures looted from local classical ruins. If a temple or similar structure could be adapted *in situ* as an interesting feature, then so much the better. A main axis of symmetry, shared by both house and garden, was frequently extended as a walk or vista for some distance out across the surrounding landscape. The garden areas arranged either side of this would become more and more irregular with increasing distance from the house, often terminating in areas of woodland threaded with serpentine paths. It was this element of variety that English visitors seem to have found particularly appealing.

Italian influence on garden design began to be felt in England during the late sixteenth century, but only really among the Court aristocracy. Initially, various Italianate features were simply added to existing gardens (as at Kenilworth in the 1570s, where the grounds were supplied with a grotto, statuary and a terrace). But the construction of great 'prodigy houses' by members of the Elizabethan and Jacobean Court – Renaissance palaces such as Wollaton Hall (Notts), Holdenby House (Northants), or Longleat (Wilts)– provided the opportunity for more thoroughgoing imitation. House and garden were

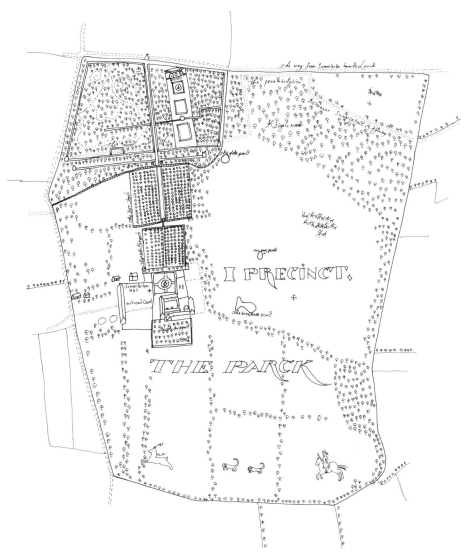

8. *Somerleyton, Suffolk. A fine estate map of 1653 shows the magnificent Renaissance gardens laid out around Somerleyton Hall. Note the single main axis of symmetry and the way that the gardens ranged either side of this become progressively less regular with increasing distance from the house. The whole* ensemble *is set within an extensive deer park.*

increasingly designed as one; terraces, sculpture, grottos, balustrading proliferated. Moreover, as the aesthetic possibilities of the surrounding landscape began to be appreciated, its structure and layout came to be manipulated accordingly. At Chipping Camden (Glos) the pattern of roads within the adjacent town was reorganized to provide an imposing new entrance to the hall[4]. At Holdenby (Northants), part of the village was removed to make way for terraces and parterres. Rebuilt on a neat plan around a green, it could be viewed from the garden through an arcade.[5] Such radical interventions in the wider landscape were not new – the surroundings of some late medieval castles seem to have been landscaped to provide a suitably pleasing setting, as at Bodiam (Sussex) or Kenilworth (Warwickshire).[6] What was novel was the extent to which the layout of outer landscape, garden, and the architecture of the house were now being considered together.

Great Italianate gardens such as those at Chipping Camden and Holdenby were expressions of wealth, but also of knowledge. Now that political power was no longer negotiated by armed force, status was no longer measured by the size of a man's retinue or the apparent strength of his home, but instead through his familiarity with the culture of Renaissance Italy and classical Rome. These were the social skills necessary for success at Court, now the fount of all authority.

But there was another equally potent symbol of status in the early modern landscape. This was the deer park: a specialized enclosure surrounded by a wall, fence, ditch, bank, hedge, or some combination of these. The hunting and consumption of deer had been activities reserved for the élite since the earliest times, but parks were probably introduced by the Normans, together with their principal occupants, the fallow deer. Domesday Book records thirty-five parks. Their number increased inexorably in the buoyant economic conditions of the twelfth and thirteenth centuries, and by 1300 there were probably more than three thousand in England.[7] Some were attached to great residences but most lay in remote locations, far from the home of the owner. They therefore contained a lodge which could provide accommodation on hunting trips as well as serve as a home for the keeper, the official responsible for the maintenance of the park and its herds.

Parks were used for hunting but their principal function was the production of venison, the food of the élite *par excellence*: eaten on special occasions, given as a mark of particular favour. Parks also fulfilled other functions, however. They provided grazing for pigs, cattle and horses and produced timber and fuel, in the form of faggots from pollards and coppices.[8] They were, in essence, private places where the various products and facilities provided by the now dwindling wastes could be shepherded, for the benefit of their owners. They were little slices of nature, privatized.

Medieval parks were largely composed of 'wood pastures', that is, areas in which animals grazed beneath closely spaced timber-producing trees and pollards. Many also contained stands of coppiced woodland surrounded by banks and fences to exclude the deer during the early stages of the coppice rotation. Parks were expensive both to create and to maintain. In particular, the perimeter pale had to be constantly repaired, not only to keep deer in but also to keep

9. Hatfield Forest, Essex. The mixture of old pollarded trees and open grassland provides a good impression of the kind of wood-pasture landscape which characterized early deer parks.

poachers out. The threat here came not so much from starving peasants as from political rivals, for 'park-breaking', hunting openly in an enemy's park, was the supreme affront.

In the later Middle Ages the number of parks in England declined. As the economy slumped and real wages rose in the decades following the Black Death, parks simply became too expensive for most members of the gentry. The climatic deterioration which accompanied these economic changes may also have played a part. Fallow deer, a Mediterranean species, have little subcutaneous fat and an inadequate coat to withstand what became a series of unusually bitter British winters. The epidemics that decimated herds of cattle and flocks of sheep in the fourteenth century may well have taken their toll on deer, too.[9] Restocking parks would have heaped an additional expense on already stretched manorial incomes.

The number of deer parks continued to decline into the sixteenth century, but then began to rise again. They did not, however, recover to anything approaching medieval levels and, although there were some members of the local gentry who possessed a park, they were now far more of an aristocratic privilege than in earlier centuries. Moreover, from the later Middle Ages the appearance, location and significance of parks were changing. No longer were they simply deer farms and hunting reserves, located in distant places. Increasingly, they were being established immediately adjacent to the gentleman's residence and considered a fitting – indeed, an essential – adjunct to a great house.[10] At the same time, the density of trees within them was being reduced and wide areas of pasture were becoming more prominent, allowing owners and guests to enjoy extensive prospects, and thus to appreciate the full size of the park (and thus the extent of conspicuous waste involved in its creation). The wild irregularity of the park provided a pleasing contrast to the geometric order of the gardens around the house; but the main reasons for the park's new role must be sought in important social changes. As the landed wealth of traditional feudal families was increasingly challenged by those who had made their fortunes in administration, trade, and the law, possession of land – and the candid, wasteful display of that possession – became an increasingly important marker of status, and thus something to be made clearly visible at the heart of the owner's domain. Changing attitudes to nature may also have played their part. Now that so much of the country was enclosed, tamed and farmed there was something particularly distinctive and appealing about a wild and uncultivated prospect. By the second half of the seventeenth century the ease and effectiveness with which a park could be created was a vital factor in deciding where a gentleman might build his home. In 1670 John Evelyn could describe how he helped choose the site for a friend's new house at Burrough Green (Cambs): 'a spot of rising ground, adorned with venerable woods, a dry and sweete prospect East and West and fit for a parke'.[11]

The Tudors and early Stuarts thus bequeathed a number of important concepts to the Georgian age. The idea of the Italian Renaissance garden with its ruins and statues, its groves and its prospects, and above all its variety constituted a seed which, in time, was to flower in a number of ways. So, too, as we shall see, did the notion of the ornamental park – a wide, romantic, sylvan landscape unsullied by signs of agriculture – as the proper setting for a gentleman's house.

THE LATE SEVENTEENTH CENTURY

However, to some extent this dual legacy – the Italianate and the indigenous – was temporarily obscured in the late seventeenth century by fashions coming into England from Holland and France. During the Civil War many English landowners had been exiled abroad and returned with new ideas. Charles II had himself spent much of his time in France: and a different range of Continental influences arrived in 1688 with the accession to the English throne of William of Orange, already *Statdholder* (ruler) of the United Provinces of the Netherlands.[12]

During the seventeenth century France and the Low Countries had both been strongly influenced by Italian concepts of garden design, but had developed these in different ways. In the Low Countries gardens usually consisted of a number of distinct compartments, arranged with rigid symmetry around a central axis, with their perimeters defined by hedges and lines of trees. The outer boundary of the garden was similarly defined, and frequently marked by a canal or moat as well.

Cascades and terraces were of limited importance in these designs, but immaculate topiary and parterres, and the display of rare and exotic flowers, were extremely popular. Their most characteristic feature was the *cutwork parterre* in which the pattern was made by shaped flower beds, cut into turf, planted with gaily coloured flowers.[13]

Even the greatest Dutch gardens were comparatively limited in scale. They seldom had deer parks or forests attached, and did not spill out across the adjoining landscape to any extent. In all this, they differed markedly from many in France. Here, under the influence of designers like André Le Nôtre and André Mollet, some extremely large gardens were laid out during the seventeenth century, of which Le Nôtre's creations at Versailles and the Tuileries are today perhaps the best known.[14] The classic French garden had a hierarchy of elements derived ultimately from the structure of Italian gardens. *Parterres de broderie* (swirling arabesques of box, infilled with coloured earths or bedding plants) were laid out near the house; *parterres de gazon* (plain turf lawns) often fringed with topiary were placed further away; and last of all came *bosquets*, or ornamental woods. As in many Italian gardens, these features were arranged either side of a strongly defined central axis, which was often continued as an avenue as far as the eye could see, out into parkland and forest. Such gardens – certainly the largest ones – were not, however, laid out with an eye to strict symmetry, with component rigidly reflecting component in the great mirror of the central axis. Their scale was so great that such stiff regularity was unnecessary: the eye could simply not take it in. Instead, Le Nôtre advocated a looser concept of 'balance', in which different forms and structures either side of the axis were of generally comparable form, but not necessarily identical. Subsidiary axes, running obliquely or at right angles off the main one, proliferated in both garden and park.

These differing national styles were related to the social and environmental characteristics of the nations concerned. Holland was a young Protestant republic dominated by a wealthy gentry and a merchant bourgeoisie, densely populated and lacking the land necessary for extensive parks and chases. Much of the terrain was level, especially the polderlands, which were also windswept and dissected by drainage canals; hence the lack of terraces and cascades and the importance of high sheltering hedges, moats and canals. Far-flung trading connections were the prime source of this nation's wealth and this, together with a long tradition of innovative agricultural practices to feed its teeming population, ensured a strong interest in the cultivation of rare and exotic plants. France, in contrast, was a centralized absolutist monarchy, dominated by an immensely powerful Court aristocracy. Its garden styles were forged by men with money and – in a relatively underpopulated country – land to spare. Versailles symbolized the wealth and power of the Sun King, Louis XIV; lesser gardens such as those at Vaux-le-Vicomte, that of his courtiers and ministers.

Such national styles, once forged, could be exported beyond the countries whose distinctive characteristics had given them birth. Thus when Nicolaas Bidloo, a Dutch doctor, went to live in Moscow in 1702 he laid out a typical Dutch garden, with canals and compartments defined by high hedges, around his home.[15] But in the course of the seventeenth century, at the highest social levels, the two styles become ever more confused, especially in Holland. Here the growing power of the *Stadtholders* was reflected in the increasing magnificence of their gardens, and by the adoption of such quintessentially French features as the *parterre de broderie*. Perhaps the finest example of such a hybrid Franco-Dutch garden was that created at Het Loo by William, Prince of Orange a few years before he became king of England. We should not, then, expect to find clear or pure examples of French or Dutch gardening in England, and contemporary illustrations – such as those published by Johannes Kip and Leonard Knyff in their *Britannia Illustrata* of 1707 – confirm that by the early eighteenth century the gardens of the greatest landowners usually contained features in a mixture of foreign styles (Figure 10).[16] The proliferation of topiary on the Dutch model was especially noticeable – Stephen Switzer later described gardens 'stuffed too thick with Box, a Fashion brought over out of *Holland* by the *Dutch* Gardeners'.[17] Dutch in influence too were the numerous canals and highly compartmentalized layout: the gardens, that is, generally consisted of a number of conjoined enclosures. French influence is perhaps clearest at the wealthiest sites, in the sporadic use of *parterres de broderie*, as at Hampton Court, or complex water parterres and *jets d'eau*, as at Boughton House (Northants). The clearest signs of Continental influence, however, can be seen not so much in the adoption of particular features as in new attitudes to overall structure. By the 1690s Renaissance ideas were making a wider impact, outside the narrow confines of the leading Court families. The garden courts were now arranged with more care around the houses of most great landowners, often symmetrically around one or two axes which were also shared by the house itself. A main axis was often extended, in the French manner, through house and garden and then as an avenue far into the surrounding countryside.

Indeed, the proliferation of avenues was perhaps the most distinctive feature of the period. Some had been planted even in the sixteenth century but they only became common after the Restoration. By 1700 they were ubiquitous. Most avenues were planted with lime, later described by Switzer as 'the only Furniture of all our Country Seats' (some fine examples still survive, as at Cornbury (Oxon) or Rougham (Norfolk), planted in 1664 and *c.* 1693 respectively), although sweet chestnut was also frequently used.[18] Open ironwork grills and gates, set in the perimeter walls of the garden, allowed extended vistas down their length. Contemporary illustrations show that some aristocratic mansions were surrounded by a dense mesh of radiating and converging avenues, planted out across the surrounding parkland. But the central avenue, focused on the main façade of the house and continuing the main axis of symmetry of the gardens, was usually the longest and always the widest. As Langley was later to put it, 'let the Length of Avenues fall as it will, you must always observe, that the grand Walk be never narrower than the front of the building.'[19]

At least among the top ten or fifteen families in each county, the design of mansion house, garden and estate garden was now being more carefully integrated. But this belated triumph of Renaissance ideas was only possible because of new developments in country house architecture. At the highest social levels, the Civil War marked a watershed. The lead set by the great Elizabethan and Jacobean prodigy houses was now everywhere followed – indeed, surpassed.

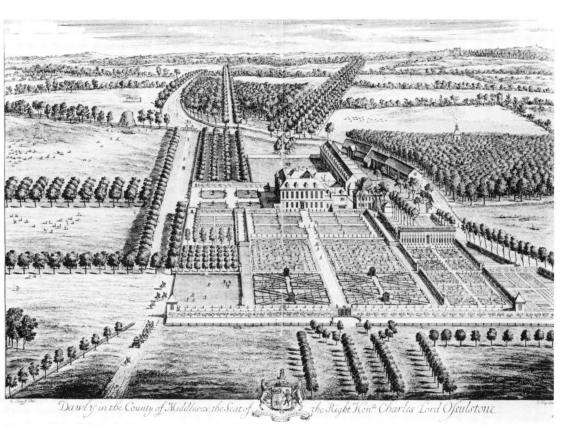

10. This illustration of Dawley in Middlesex, from Kip and Knyff's Britannia Illustrata *of 1707, shows the kind of mixed French / Dutch style of geometric gardening current at élite sites in the first decades of the eighteenth century.*

Exiled English gentlemen had seen Continental houses, and liked what they saw. Classical forms, more accurate and distinctive than those of the Elizabethan and Jacobean manor house, were adopted for window openings, doorways and much else. And no more would great houses be built to the old asymmetrical medieval plan, with a hall and cross-passage, one room deep and ranged around three or four sides of a courtyard. All new houses of any importance were now compact double- or triple-pile structures, symmetrical both in internal layout and external elevation. By the end of the century it had become usual to emphasize their central bays by a pediment or by a slight projection, an external expression of the hierarchy of rooms inside, for the two most important and public rooms of the house were now located centrally, one behind the other: the hall, and the great chamber, now renamed the saloon under French influence. Suites of rooms were arranged either side of these, which were occupied by individuals (the owner, members of his family, or visitors) and were arranged as *enfilades*: that is, in a linear sequence, each successive room more private and exclusive than that before it. The final room in the sequence could be penetrated only by social equals or superiors.[20] Towards the end of the century some great landowners and designers took emulation of Continental models even further, building country houses (as at Chatsworth or Blenheim) in the elaborate and florid classicism of the baroque.

The development of internally symmetrical houses naturally encouraged the adoption of overall symmetry in the layout of their surroundings. It also, naturally enough, encouraged the idea of giving house and gardens a single shared axis, which could then be extended into the surrounding estate land. It is, perhaps, worth noting that the illustrations in Kip and Knyff's *Britannia Illustrata* – like almost all others made of country house landscapes at this time – are drawn from an impossible aerial vantage point. For it was only from such an elevated perspective that the full extent of the design, the unity of house, garden and wider estate land, and thus the wealth and power of the owner, could be fully expressed.

Many of the landscapes illustrated by Kip and Knyff were created by the proprietors of the Brompton Park nursery in Kensington. This was established in 1681 by a group of prominent gardeners, and run after 1688 by George London and Henry Wise. Wise himself became Royal Gardener, and London advised on many of the greatest gardens.[21] Indeed, Stephen Switzer was later to comment that he 'Actually saw and gave Directions, once or twice a Year, in most of the Noblemens and Gentlemens Gardens in *England*'.[22] The gardens associated with the Brompton Park partners – Castle Howard, Longleat, Chatsworth – epitomize the mixed Franco-Dutch style dominant in late seventeenth- and early eighteenth-century England. Yet we should be a little cautious, perhaps, of blithely interpreting all aspects of garden design in this period as the result of this or that foreign influence. Some features usually explained as foreign imports probably owed a lot to indigenous tradition. Canals, for example, may have developed in part out of earlier moats, and the two were certainly confused in English minds. Roger North, writing in 1713, described moats as 'a Delicacy the greatest Epicures in Gardening court, and we hear of it by the name of Canal'.[23] And we need to pay some attention to the indigenous social and economic reasons for the adoption (or non-adoption) of particular foreign fashions. Thus, in particular, the popularity of avenues in this period was not simply a manifestation of French cultural influence. It was also one facet of a more general passion for tree-planting which was sweeping England at this time, as landowners followed the advice of John Evelyn's famous work *Sylva* and established woods and plantations widely on their estates.[24] The general decline of woodland which had continued more or less inexorably in England since the early Middle Ages had intensified during the Civil War, when much timber had been felled on the estates of defeated Royalists. With the Restoration of 1660 'Planting began again to raise its dejected head'.[25] Evelyn and others argued that the practice was a patriotic duty because it provided the Royal Navy with much-needed oak, but landowners had other less altruistic motives. As a medium- to long-term investment forestry made good economic sense now that dynastic continuity seemed more assured and the upheavals of the Civil War were over. Planting continued apace and contemporary maps and plans show that many aristocratic residences were bordered by extensive areas of semi-ornamental woodland.

The planting of an avenue, however, had a particular symbolic significance. It demonstrated the planter's ownership of all the ground over which it passed, and emphasized its status as *enclosed* land: for, as we have seen, it was impossible to establish trees in open fields or on commons, as the local inhabitants would simply remove them for firewood or allow their animals to graze over them. The long lines of trees, extending out like a web through the surrounding countryside, were thus a potent expression of ownership and control (Figure 11).

Yet we must not assume that the kinds of grandiose layout depicted in *Britannia Illustrata* – the vast gardens, the complex networks of avenues – were typical of the landscapes laid out around the homes of English landowners. The majority of the local gentry were content with smaller plots in which the more extravagant fashions for topiary and box-work were adopted only sparingly. Plain grass walks and gravel paths, fringed by herbaceous borders, were the order of the day, sometimes with the addition of a separate enclosure for flowers. Moreover, their courts and gardens were not usually laid out in a neat and symmetrical

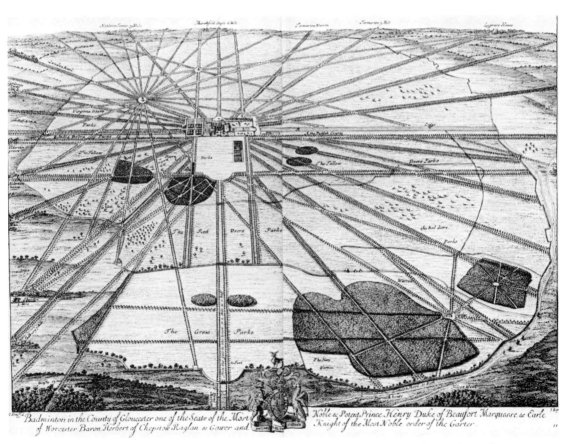

11. *The geometry of power. Badminton, Avon, the seat of the Duke of Beaufort, as depicted in Kip and Knyff's* Britannia Illustrata *of 1707.*

12. Cassiobury Park, Hertfordshire: the lime avenue, probably planted around 1710. Lime was the most popular tree for avenues in the seventeenth and early eighteenth centuries.

manner, sharing a common axis with the house: the local gentry continued to resist the influence of the Renaissance. Above all, in place of the complex avenues, stretching out across parkland, most local squires had only one, focused on the main façade, which ran out across the adjacent farmland: for relatively few members of this social group possessed the luxury of a deer park.

A 'COMELIE SUFFICIENCY'

There were, nevertheless, many features shared by the gardens of all large landowners, by those of the local squire and great magnate alike. The most obvious is that they were, with few exceptions, contained within walled enclosures. It is worth pausing for a moment to consider why this should have been so, given that in the next century educated opinion was to revile the practice.

To some extent the popularity of walled gardens may have been related to the architecture of the houses they complemented. While new compact and symmetrical houses might, from the 1660s, be erected by the principal county families, most members of the gentry continued to live in houses of 'single pile' construction (that is, only one room deep). For reasons of practical convenience, such structures were ranged around three or four sides of a central courtyard, an arrangement which naturally encouraged the idea that adjoining areas of the residential complex – service yards and gardens – should likewise take the form of enclosed compartments. Walls and gates were elaborately embellished to mirror the architecture of the house itself, emphasizing their role as outdoor rooms. But walls served other functions. The highly structured and artificial patterns in the gardens they surrounded made the best visual sense when clearly segregated from the less ordered environments around them. To the modern observer these gardens appear as places where nature has been ordered, tamed, even tortured – quintessentially 'unnatural'. Whether contemporaries would have seen them quite like this is less clear. Their more educated owners would perhaps have explained them in Neoplatonic terms, as expressions of the perfect forms underlying the imperfect shapes of the material world.[26] They were thus 'natural', not according to the later eighteenth-century meaning of the word, but in the sense that they manifested the 'ideal form of things', an appealing idea in an untidy world. Thus, for example, topiary could be seen as a practice designed to bring out the true 'natural' form of the plant, the shape (a cone, globe or whatever) to which its essential form appeared to approximate.

Most members of the gentry, however, were more interested in plants than philosophy, and it was probably the horticultural benefits of walled enclosures which were most valued. The collection and cultivation of numerous different varieties of fruit trees and, to a lesser extent, other types of plant was something of an obsession among the gentry. At East Turnbull (Berks), for example, the new garden and orchard created in 1696 contained 450 fruit trees: in all, more than ninety different varieties of apples, pears, peaches, nectarines, apricots and quinces were represented.[27] This was not unusual; and whether it was flowers, fruit, vegetables, or herbs that were being grown, all would have benefited from the microclimate established by high sheltering walls.

Although Sir Thomas Hanmer's *Garden Book* of 1659 recommended that the kitchen garden should be located away from the house, this was seldom the case in the seventeenth century, even on the greatest estates.[28] Lesser men did not have the option. Roger North, writing at the end of the seventeenth century, described how he

> ever had a dislike for evesdropping, or spouting the water from the roof about an house; for it . . . hinders planting of fruits, sweets, or sallads, neer the walls.[29]

Indeed, many gentlemen's gardens (as in medieval times) contained a mixture of what we would today consider aesthetic and utilitarian planting. Certainly, the distinction was not entirely clear cut. Lawson in 1617 argued that gardens should be compartmentalized, with the 'Garden for Flowers' distinct from the kitchen garden, so that the appreciation of flowers was not ruined by the smell of onions. He stressed, however, that he did not envisage a 'Perfect . . . distinction, that the Garden for flowers should, or can be without herbs good for the kitchen, or the kitchen garden want flowers'.[30] Moreover, the very fact that he urged some degree of separation implies that many contemporary gardens were more promiscuously arranged. As late as 1691 no less a personage than the Marquess of Worcester had a kitchen garden at Beaufort House in Chelsea which contained beds of anemones and tulips.[31] The collections of fruit trees which were such a feature of seventeenth-century gardens were, it should be noted, planted against the walls of pleasure grounds and kitchen grounds alike. As so much else in the gentleman's garden, they were at once ornamental and utilitarian.

Most gentry houses were surrounded by other enclosures which provided the resources necessary to sustain the household: gardens, stable yards, orchards, nut grounds, all separated from each other by walls, hedges, or fences (Figure 13).[32] Farmyards and barns usually lay close by, for most members of the gentry were, from the start of the sixteenth century, actively involved in the cultivation of their home farms. This was partly for economic reasons – rising agricultural prices in the period before 1640 made this a sensible move – but it was also because of the impact of the Renaissance, and the dissemination of classical texts (by Columella, Virgil, Cato and Xenophon) which demonstrated that involvement in the minutiae of estate administration and husbandry had been an acceptable activity for the Greek and Roman gentlemen on whom Tudor and Stuart landowners increasingly modelled themselves.[33]

The presence of food-producing facilities in the immediate vicinity of the house was symbolic as well as functional. They expressed the owner's active involvement in the husbandry of his estate, and they proclaimed his 'comelie sufficiency': they announced loudly that he ate more food, rarer food, and more varied food than his neighbours. Not surprisingly, many of these facilities seem to have developed an aesthetic appeal of their own. Dovecotes, in particular, were often located in prominent positions, elaborately built and carefully designed. They had a particular significance because they were by law a prerogative of the manorial gentry: 'the right onely & badge of a lordship or signorye'.[34] This monopoly was a direct consequence of the fact that pigeons fed indiscriminately

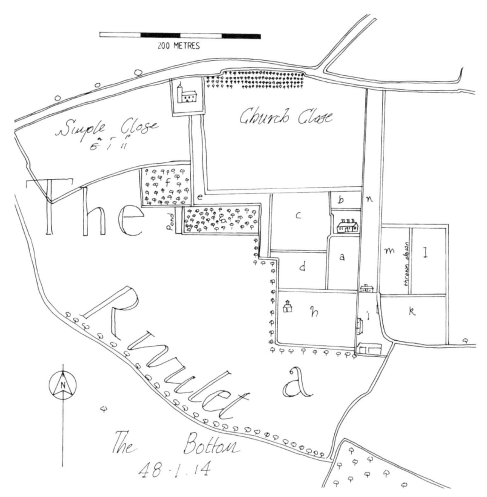

200 METRES

Simple Close

Church Close

The Rivulet

The Bottom

48·1·14

13. *A jumble of enclosures around Besthorpe Hall, Norfolk, shown on a map of 1748. The map has a key which includes: (a) The Court Yard; (b) The Back Yard; (c) The Great Garden; (d) The Kitchen Garden; (e) The Church Walk; (h) the Dove House Yard; (l) and (m) the Nurseries; and (n) The Walk.*

on the local grain crops, and thus represented a neat way of converting your neighbours' investment and labour into your own reserves of meat protein. Dovecotes provided other benefits: 'Dovesdunge is an excellent compost & Mucke for enriching of Grounds', as many noted, and they were thus often erected close to gardens.[35]

Fish ponds had a similar appeal. Larger ponds (often referred to as 'great waters') were frequent features of deer parks, but smaller 'stew ponds', used for holding fish prior to consumption, were often located in the garden in order to guard against theft, and because 'your Journey to them is Short and easy, and your Eye will be often upon them, which will conduce to their being well kept, and they will be an Ornament to the Walks'.[36] Most ornamental canals and basins in gardens were, in fact, used in this way. Fish and pigeons both formed an important part of the system of reciprocal gift exchange which helped bind local society together, and to structure it. As Roger North said of fish, 'You may oblige your Friends and neighbours, by making Presents of them, which, from the Countryman to the King, is well taken.'[37]

Work and recreation were inextricably mixed and muddled in the courts around a gentleman's house. Farm, fruit trees and fish ponds were a source of pleasure as well as profit. North, for example, emphasized not only the economic but also the recreational importance of fish ponds:

> Young People love Angling extremely: then there is a Boat, which gives Pleasure enough in Summer, frequent fishing with Nets, the very making of Nets, seeing the Waters, much Discussion of them, and the Fish, especially upon your great Sweeps, and the strange Surprises that will happen in Numbers and Bigness. . . .[38]

And, indeed, the courts arranged around a gentleman's house also had to cater for a range of purely recreational activities, most notably the game of bowls. Already by 1541 this was so popular that the government, alarmed by the betting it attracted and the neglect of archery it supposedly encouraged, made it illegal to play the game anywhere – except in private gardens. By the time of the Civil War there were few gentry gardens which did not include a bowling green. The mixture of features – aesthetic, recreational, and productive – in the vicinity of gentlemen's houses is often evident from letters and diaries. The head gardener at Croft Hall (Yorks) was forced to nail up the door leading from the ornamental garden to the bowling green, because visitors to the house were in the habit of helping themselves to the gooseberries growing in the borders around the latter (to no avail: visitors continued to pilfer the fruit, according to the gardener, 'tho he looked very narrowly to 'em').[39]

The enclosed geometric gardens which the eighteenth century swept away cannot, therefore, be understood in isolation from the architecture of the houses they accompanied, from the layout of the other enclosures around the house, or from the kind of lifestyle which all together expressed. Moreover, the fact that great landowners and local gentry led rather different lives probably explains why Renaissance ideas of garden design diffused so slowly down the social scale. Both the ethic of domestic production, and the organization of the residential complex which this engendered, were to some extent shared by all landowners. But for the local gentleman residing in his 'country' questions of convenience and domestic economy tended to take precedence over fashion. As the needs and fortunes of such families changed, so the arrangement of structures around the walls of their homes continued to alter and develop. Piecemeal change produced the chaotic arrangement of enclosures which swarmed somewhat uneasily around the walls of many residences. The grounds of aristocrats and courtiers, in contrast, were more likely to be redesigned at a

*14. Upper Broomhall Farm, Kempsey, Worcestershire. This detail from an estate map of
c. 1725 shows the kind of geometric garden popular among the middle classes and local gentry
during the first four decades of the eighteenth century.*

stroke, and along lines dictated by national or international fashion rather than
domestic convenience. This distinction was to become, if anything, more
marked in the early decades of the eighteenth century.

THE EARLY EIGHTEENTH CENTURY:
THE LATE GEOMETRIC GARDEN

The geometric tradition of garden design was neither dead nor dying in the early
eighteenth century. Among the local gentry gardens with topiary and box-work
continued to be popular into the 1730s and beyond. But at the level of the élite –
of the greater landowners – formal gardens continued to develop, in striking ways,
as we can see if we compare the illustrations of seats presented in *Britannia
Illustrata* of 1707 with the plans of gardens included in Colen Campbell's
Vitruvius Britannicus of 1725.[40] In some ways the latter are simpler – they are less
cluttered with fussy detail – yet in others, and especially in their layout, they
appear more complex. Their design was dominated by plain grass 'plats' and
gravel paths: complex box-work had now declined in popularity and topiary was
simplified and relegated to the edges of lawns and paths. Yet at the same time
these gardens have a much greater proportion of their area occupied by
ornamental woodland – by groves and wildernesses – and these were dissected by

very complicated networks of paths and clearings. Perhaps their most novel feature, however, was that they were no longer divided into separate walled enclosures, and in many places even the perimeter wall was replaced by a ha-ha – essentially a ditch hiding a wall or other barrier.

This new form of 'late geometric' garden developed gradually – and only really at the highest social levels – from the 1690s. The simplification of parterres seems to have begun around the turn of the century. Stephen Switzer was later to describe how in 1703 Queen Anne ordered the destruction of the complex box-work at Kensington Palace and, a little later, at Hampton Court, 'the Gardens laid into that plain but noble manner they now appear in'.[41] By 1727 Sir John Clerk of Penicuik, touring through England, noted the progress of the new taste. At Wricklemarsh House near Greenwich he described how

> The gardens are very rural & of a new taste consisting only of a few gravel walks with large Squares and Steps of Green turf there are no evergreen trees or shrubs. There is a large circular pond on the front of the house. . . .[42]

Elsewhere he noted how 'The present method of Gardening is a little alter'd vise into great pieces of open Green plots.'

To some extent these changes simply represented a reworking of the existing repertoire of design elements, rather than the invention of something radically new. Plain grass lawns and gravel paths had long been important in English gardens, and wildernesses had existed in many gardens since the sixteenth century. What was important were the changes both in the relative importance of such elements within élite grounds, and in their location. Wildernesses had originally been located in peripheral positions, often flanking the furthest end of the main axial walk. From the 1680s and '90s, however, they began to occupy a greater and greater proportion of the garden and, while they were still usually ranged either side of the main vista, they were often brought close to the mansion. Their layout varied from place to place (and from period to period) but a common pattern was neatly summarized by Thomas Hamilton, looking back from the mid-1730s:

> There was a Center, Straight Walks from it, Ending on as good Views as could be had. There were also Serpentine Walks that run through the whole hedged, as the Straight Walks were, and the Angles with Different Shades mixt.[43]

Planting details also varied, although the wilderness established at Raynham (Norfolk) around 1700 was fairly typical. This, according to a contract, was to have hedges

> Planted with hornbeams of two sizes ye Smaller Size of about 2 foot high and Better and ye Larger Size of 4 foot high and Better: the Quarters to be planted with ye sevll. Varietys of Flowering Trees Undermentioned ye walkes to be laid all with Sand and ye Center places to be planted with Spruce and Silver Firs.[44]

Hornbeam was a particular favourite for hedges because of its rapid growth and tolerance of shade, although yew, elm and even oak were also used. At Raynham the 'Flowering Trees' to be used in the central sections included lime, horse chestnut, wild service, laburnum, guelder rose, lilac, bladder sena, wild olive, 'stript' (i.e. variegated) sycamore, beech and birch, mixed with a range of evergreen trees – 'Silver Firs, Spruce Firs, Scotch Firs, Pine'. Other writers refer to the use of honeysuckle, sweet briar, jasmine, and roses to provide colour and fragrance.[45] The prominence of conifers at Raynham was typical: Stephen Switzer in 1718 described how the planting of such exotics 'has been followed in all our modern wildernesses'. But there was much variation. The trees present in the wilderness at Stow Bardolph (Norfolk) in 1712 included pears, apples and cherries, as well as various kinds of 'fir'.[46] At Wrest (Beds) in 1691 the wilderness had sections dominated by different species: the accounts refer to the 'Ewe [yew] Wilderness' and the 'Blackthorne Wilderness'.[47]

The handful of wildernesses that still survive give rather a poor impression of their original appearance. The finer details of the planting, the flowering plants and the conifers, have long gone, leaving only the forest trees. Nevertheless, such survivals do provide some impression of what these places must have been like. That at St Pauls Walden Bury (Herts) was probably created around 1730, when Edward Gilbert built a new mansion there (Figure 15).[48] It occupied the majority of the garden and still runs almost to the rear door of the house. Its straight paths or *allées* were originally hedged with hornbeam but these were replaced in the 1930s with beech. One focuses on the parish church, just outside the garden; another on an elaborate garden building, the octagonal Organ House, built in 1735.

The wilderness here was a large one made (at least in part) by cutting rides through an existing wood. This was a common practice, and one of the earliest examples is Moseley Wood, Cookridge Hall, near Leeds (Yorks), laid out in 1696. It covers an area of more than 50 hectares and was widely admired: one visitor described it as a 'most surprising labyrinth which at once delighteth and amuseth the spectator with the windings and variously intermixed walks'. These met at no less than 65 intersections, providing 306 different views – variety indeed.[49] At Bramham Park in the same county an even more elaborate arrangement was created around 1710 which featured three large woods, dissected by straight *allées*, some of which were continued from wood to wood as avenues through the intervening parkland. From the 1720s a number of temples were constructed within the woods, forming the terminations to the principal vistas.[50] Another surviving example is the 30-hectare Spring Wood in Hackwood Park (Hants). This has eight avenues radiating from a central *rond point* and again contained a number of classical buildings, designed by James Gibbs, including a pavilion in the form of a Greek cross and a Doric rotunda (illustrated in his *Book of Architecture* of 1728).[51]

During the 1720s and '30s classical temples such as these became indispensable features of the larger wildernesses, and began to appear in other parts of the garden. At Holkham (Norfolk) in the late 1720s a geometric wilderness was planted in the customary position either side of the main axial approach to the

15. *The gardens at St Pauls Walden Bury, Hertfordshire. Created in c. 1735, these are perhaps the finest woodland gardens from the eighteenth century surviving in England.*

hall but, unusually, on the summit of a hill some 500 metres to the south of the main façade. Its intricate network of *allées* was focused on two classical structures, an obelisk and a temple. Both were apparently designed by William Kent and still survive in good condition.

Classical sculptures, which had been a feature of earlier gardens, also seem to have become increasingly prominent. Writers gave detailed advice on which gods and goddesses were suitable for which areas: Jupiter or Mars for 'the largest Open Centres and Lawns of a grand Design', Neptune for basins and canals, and fauns and sylvans for the depths of wildernesses.[52] In the garden at Marston in Somerset in 1733

The Goddess of Spring & her Follower the Deity of Summer, stand smiling at the beautiful Prospect in the distant Vale, while Bacchus in another Cabinet of Wood presents you with the product of the Autumn, to dissipate Melancholy. . . .[53]

16. *The gardens at Studley Royal, North Yorkshire: the Temple of Piety of c. 1730. Classical temples such as this were an increasingly popular feature of the geometric gardens of the 1720s and '30s.*

This, then, was the 'simple yet still formal style' (as Horace Walpole was later to describe it)[54] which gradually developed in the first third of the eighteenth century. It was the style in which men such as Joseph Carpenter, Wise's successor as Royal Gardener, and Charles Bridgeman, successor to Carpenter, altered the grounds of England's élite. It was crisp and clean, simple in detail if often complex in plan, redolent with classical allusions. Yet it was not entirely novel, and it is really only with the dubious benefits of hindsight that it can be perceived as a stage in the development towards the naturalistic landscape parks of 'Capability' Brown. In reality, it was the product of the interplay of a number of influences, social, cultural and economic.

EXPLAINING THE LATE GEOMETRIC GARDEN

To explain the late Geometric garden, we must begin with the progresssive simplification of parterres and topiary, with the removal of clutter and detail and the gradual dominance of plain grass lawns or *plats*. One factor in this was apparently the inherent instability of late seventeenth–century designs: that is, excessive displays of topiary were removed because the plants had simply grown too big. In 1721 John Clerk noted a number of gardens which had been ruined by outgrown topiary, and described how their replacement by plain lawns

> Came naturally to be the consequence of the evergreen trees and shrubs which were formerly planted in so great numbers that now they grow up and choak the aire.[55]

Another factor may have been rising maintenance costs at a time of improving wages, coupled with the increasing size of gardens. Following the accession of George I in 1714 the royal Court ceased to be the principal arbiter of taste in garden design, and the pace was set by the great magnates and politicians of the age. In the competitive climate of the early eighteenth century gardens, like houses, played an important part in the game of politics. Gardens which were already large became larger or, as Switzer put it in 1718,

> Gardens have gradually, insensibly, and at last even necessarily swell'd to a greater Extent than the Owner at first designed them, so great indeed as to sink under their own Weight, and to be a Burden too heavy for the greatest Estates.[56]

Gardens had to be big to impress the owner's clients and his local 'interest': and contemporary accounts attest their success in achieving this, for visitors frequently mention the size of a garden as if it were a reliable index of the importance of its owner, and only rarely seem to describe its beauty or intricacy. A visitor to Blenheim Palace (Oxon) in 1712 thus reported with approval:

> The Gardens of 80 acres, the middle gravel walk from ye house to ye End of ye Garden is 2220 feet long; ye many hedges in ye Gardens are said to be in Content near 20 measured miles.[57]

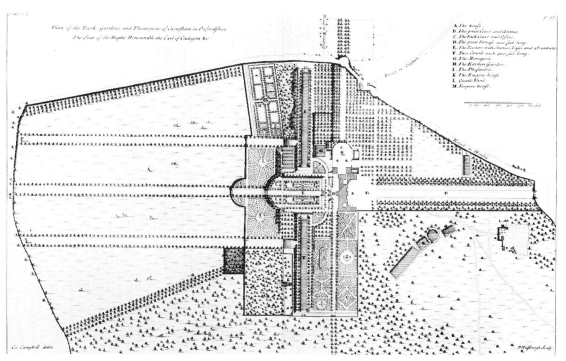

17. *Caversham, Berkshire: Stephen Switzer's design of 1718, illustrated in Colen Campbell's* Vitruvius Britannicus *of 1725.*

Yet we must not push this argument too far. The clean lines of such gardens demanded much maintenance. Turf 'plats' had to be kept smooth with scythe and roller; hedges had to be endlessly clipped. At Canons Park (Middx) in 1721 the great grass parterres were scythed two or three times a week and weeded every day.[58] Moreover, whatever they cost to maintain, such gardens certainly cost a great deal to create in the first place, not least because this generally involved substantial feats of earth movement. At Caversham (Berks), for example, the contract drawn up between Stephen Switzer and the Earl of Cadogan in 1718 describes in meticulous detail the multifarious alterations which were to be made to the natural contours (Figure 17).[59] Switzer was to level extensive areas for parterres, raise numerous terraces, dig canals, excavate fishponds and make a new kitchen garden and orchard, the surfaces of which were to be raised between one and two feet 'with Dung and mold'. In other ways, too, no expense was spared: the trees for the new wilderness, for example, were all to be at least 10 feet in height. The earl supplied many of the plants and ornaments but Switzer and his team were nevertheless to be paid the immense sum of £1,392 4s 9d.

More important than factors of cost in the progressive simplification of grounds was probably the challenge posed by the organization of visual space in such extensive layouts, coupled with the development of new, compact and symmetrical house plans. Together these invited the creation of designs based not on geometric clutter, on fuss and detail, on a profusion of separate walled courts but on broad clean vistas and block planting. In the seventeenth century, landowners had found walls objects of beauty, especially if expensively constructed with large quantities of stone or brick. But the development of compact houses in a classical style seems to have undermined such enthusiasm. In 1727 Sir John Clerk noted of the gardens at Wimpole (Cambs): 'very neat but too many walls'. Clean and compact, new houses like this did not invite a profusion of courts in the way that older residences, ranged around three or four sides of a courtyard, seem to have done. And a simpler though still geometric landscape set them off to good advantage: the clean lines of the late geometric garden emphasized perfectly their regular and slightly austere elevations. Of course, the new compact houses had initially been provided, somewhat incongruously, with a profusion of walled courts – as the illustrations in Kip and Knyff's *Britannia Illustrata* make clear. As we have seen, one of the main purposes of walls had always been to provide a sheltered microclimate. Their gradual fall from favour in the early eighteenth century marks something profound: an increasing acceptance on the part of the greater landowners of the importance of aesthetics and fashion over the requirements of horticulture.

Changing architectural fashions were important in other ways in the development of the late geometric garden. The rather loose classicism of the late seventeenth century began, in the 1710s, to be challenged by a more rigorous interpretation. The new style, called Palladianism, was fostered by leading members of the Whig élite following the accession of George I, and their own political triumph, in 1714. Its most important propagandists were Lord Burlington and his influential clique, who patronized designers and writers including Colen Campbell and, a little later, William Kent. Palladianism purported to be a more faithful interpretation of ancient architecture than the debased and eclectic baroque style favoured by the previous Tory administration, which Burlington's circle associated with the decadent absolutist monarchies of the Continent.[60] They told a story which went something like this. The ancients had discovered a set of correct, 'natural', perhaps God-given rules of architectural design. These included, in particular, adherence to a defined set of proportions, analogous to the notes in a musical scale. As Robert Morris put it in 1734,

> In musick are only seven distinct notes, in architecture likewise are only seven distinct proportions, which produce all the different buildings in the universe, viz. the cube; the cube and a half; the double cube; the duplicate [i.e. ratios] of 3:2:1; 4:3:2; 5:4:3; and of 6:4:3 produce all the harmonic proportions of rooms.[61]

The Greeks and Romans had also invented the system of orders – the Corinthian, the Doric, the Ionic and the Tuscan. These stylistic rules for the use and combination of columns and entablatures had to be rigorously followed in order to create the correct and most harmonious effect. This was something which the rather free, more dramatic architecture of the baroque had singularly failed to do, its practitioners combining the various forms somewhat indiscriminately. According to Palladian theory, all these ideas had been rediscovered in the sixteenth century by the Italian architect Andreas Palladio and taken up in England in the early seventeenth century by Inigo Jones. Since the Restoration, however, architectural truth had been neglected by a ruling clique happy to ape the styles of Continental despots.

The rise of Palladianism explains, in part, the proliferation of classical temples in the gardens of this period. Burlington himself built several in his garden at Chiswick, beside the Thames near London, and between 1727 and 1729 constructed a 'villa', closely based on a design by Palladio, as an adjunct to his house there.[62] This was, in effect, simply another and extremely large garden building rather than a dwelling, but country houses in this style, such as Mereworth (Kent) or Houghton (Norfolk), were already appearing.

The rising tide of Palladianism may have had another effect on garden design. The Palladian interest in mathematics, proportion and geometry was easily transferred from the buildings to the grounds in which they stood. Thus at Chiswick the forecourt to the west of the house had cedars planted on the 1:3:9:27 module recommended by Alberti in his *De Re Aedificatoria*, a book which had been translated into English by Burlington's client Giacomo Leoni in 1726.[63] In general, interest in garden geometry seems to have flourished in the 1720s. Batty Langley's *Practical Geometry* of 1729 offered much useful advice to the garden designer, and ought to be compulsory reading for all those who believe that the geometric garden was in sustained retreat in this period. Various designs for paths or ponds are described in terms like the following:

> Describe the double spiral line FG, HI, KL, MN; and on Ea, describe the semicircle or rather arch bc, and on the same center, the arch d, e, f. With the former opening ba, turn the compass from c to g, and on g, describe the arch ch. . .[64]

And so on (Figure 18). Provincial gardeners were busy at the same game. Peter Aram in West Yorkshire wrote his unpublished treatise on 'The Practical Making and Management of Gardens' shortly before 1730. It too is full of complex geometry. The 'Tetrahedronic Grove', for example, was based on a triangle in which

> Walks may be made which disposes the whole Figure into 4 Equilateral Triangles ye Centres of which are Statues within a circle.[65]

Some of this geometry was abstract but some was intended to foster visual illusion, to make gardens (in Switzer's words) 'that are but small . . . appear *as very large ones*'. Langley, for example, advocated the manipulation of perspective to make walks and avenues appear longer than they really were (by gradually narrowing their farthest end, a device employed by the designer Charles Bridgeman at a number of sites).[66]

The increasing simplicity of élite geometric gardens in the first third of the eighteenth century thus seems to have had a number of causes and, in spite of

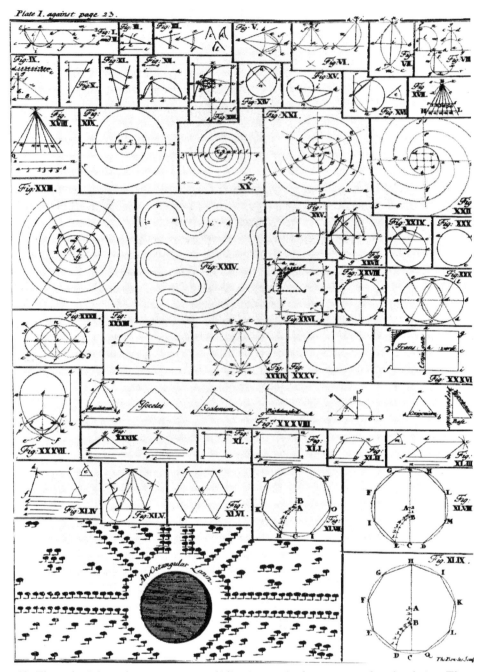

18. The early eighteenth century saw an abiding interest in the geometry of garden design. These ideas for generating patterns for paths and planting are from Batty Langley's Practical Geometry *of 1729.*

what is sometimes suggested, was not really a stage towards the naturalistic parkland of 'Capability' Brown. Nor indeed was it uniquely English. Parallel developments were occurring in France, where by 1700 elaborate parterres were beginning to give way to lawns. By 1722 A.J. Dezallier d'Argenville, in the second edition of his *La Théorie et la Pratique du Jardinage*, was able to argue that elaborate box-work and the like should be replaced by 'the noble simplicity of steps, banks, ramps of turf, natural arbours, and simple clipped hedges'. French ideas were widely disseminated in England in books such as Philip Miller's *Gardener's Dictionary* of 1731. They had an important and now rather neglected influence on two of the leading writers of the day: Stephen Switzer, whose *Ichnographia Rustica* was published in 1718; and Batty Langley, whose *New Principles of Gardening* appeared ten years later. In French as well as in English texts we learn of the increasing importance of wildernesses and groves, and of the complicated arrangements of paths and spaces within them. Groves, according to Miller, were 'the chief of a garden, being a great ornament to all the rest of its parts, so that there cannot be too many of them planted'. Following d'Argenville, Miller advised that they should be varied by 'compartments . . . verdant-halls with bowling greens, arbour-work, and fountains in the middle': they should be 'placed near the house . . . that you have no need to go far to find shade, and beside this, they communicate a coolness to apartments which is very agreeable in hot weather'.[67] The proliferation of groves and the increasing complexity of the paths within them offered more variety of experience: and Miller emphasized that gardens ought to be 'diversified' so that, for instance, the same works ought never to be repeated on two sides of a vista 'except in open places where the eye, by comparing them together, may judge of their conformity'.

To some extent, however, this emphasis on variety also represented a resurgence of older currents in English garden design, drawing directly on the inspiration of the Italian Renaissance garden. Just as an interest in Italian architecture revived in the 1710s and '20s, so too did an interest in Italian gardens: and the wildernesses threaded with paths and studded with temples and sculptures were clearly inspired, in part, by the varied grounds of Italian villas, which were being increasingly visited by English gentlemen in the first two decades of the eighteenth century, as the Grand Tour became an indispensable feature of upper-class life.

The development of this more diversified structure was reflected in a significant shift in the way gardens were drawn, painted, or engraved. They were now more likely to be illustrated from ground level, often in a series of views, rather than from the kind of impossible aerial vantage point favoured by artists in the previous century. Moreover, such illustrations (those by Pieter Rysbrack of Chiswick in *c.* 1730, for example, or those by Balthasar Nebot of Hartwell (Bucks) in 1738) generally show people wandering about, exploring. And, indeed, the hidden delights of grove and wilderness – the temples and sculpture 'lost' in the recesses of the trees – assume a rather different pattern of use than the wide parterres depicted on seventeenth-century illustrations, in which everything (and everybody) was visible at a glance. The structure of the design was increasingly geared to exploration, by individuals and small groups. As we shall see, the decades after 1735 saw this tendency extended and elaborated in significant ways.

Perhaps the most striking feature of the late geometric garden was not the increasing importance of wildernesses, nor the simplification of parterres, nor even the reduction in the number of walled courts. It was the disappearance of external walls, and their replacement by the ha-ha: something which appears to have occurred at the highest social levels during the late 1710s and early '20s. These early ha-has were not the discrete wall and ditch of the later eighteenth century, nor were they really designed (as later ones generally were) to create the illusion of open parkland sweeping up to the walls of the house. Instead, they were usually massive, often with a substantial terrace walk running along the inside and sometimes featuring prominent half-circular projections at intervals, reminiscent of the bastions in contemporary military fortifications, as at Houghton (Norfolk) or Bramham (Yorks).

The adoption of the ha-ha was, and is, often attributed to a desire to lay the garden open to the 'extensive Charms of Nature, and the voluminous Tracts of a pleasant Country'.[68] But in fact, at the kinds of aristocratic site where this development was most common in the 1720s and '30s, what was opened to view was not the agricultural countryside but the deer park. This continued to be the quintessential expression of wealth and status. Indeed, its importance seems to

19. Averham Park Lodge, Nottinghamshire. Built around 1725 by Lord Lexington as a second home, on a hill overlooking the main family residence at nearby Kelham. This is one of several examples of elaborate hunting lodges constructed in the years around 1700. They attest the continuing importance of deer and deer parks among the landed élite. Note the open fields, ploughed in ridges, in the foreground: similar ridges are preserved under the parkland grass in the distance. Painting by an unknown artist, c. 1730.

have been increasing in this period, and new parks were being created in some numbers in the decades after the Restoration. Venison continued to be a luxury reserved for the rich, given as a mark of respect and in return for favours: and its status was enhanced by the notorious Black Acts of 1723 which, among other things, made the sale of deer on the open market illegal (in the somewhat optimistic hope that this would deny poachers a market). All this naturally raised the esteem of the landscape with which deer were particularly associated, and in the early eighteenth century the greatest landowners almost invariably had a park beside their homes. Visitors were keen to estimate its size, and the number of deer it contained. The removal of perimeter walls was thus, above all, symptomatic of the continuing rise in the importance of the park. This was indeed a signpost to the path of future developments, to the growing importance of a naturalistic setting for the mansion. Yet in its immediate vicinity, the gardens themselves continued to exude the rigours of geometry.

CHAPTER THREE

The Challenge to Geometry

SHAFTESBURY, POPE AND SWITZER

The suggestion that the geometric garden was flourishing in the early eighteenth century might appear odd to some readers. Many will know a different story, still often presented in books on garden history: that this period saw mounting criticism of formal designs. Opposition first surfaced, it is said, in the writings of intellectuals such as the 3rd Earl of Shaftesbury, Alexander Pope and Joseph Addison; and was subsequently elaborated in texts by garden designers such as Stephen Switzer or Batty Langley. In his book 'The Moralists', published in 1709 but written as early as 1705, Shaftesbury expressed his preference for

> Things of a *natural* kind: where neither *Art*, nor the *Conceit* or *Caprice* of Man has spoil'd their genuine order. . . . Even the rude Rocks, the mossy *Caverns*, the irregular unwrought *Grottos* and broken *Falls* of waters, with all the horrid graces of the *Wilderness* itself, as representing NATURE more, will be the more engaging, and appear with a magnificence beyond the mockery of princely gardens.[1]

Addison, in a famous essay published in the *Spectator* in 1712, expressed slightly different sentiments, apparently displaying an enthusiasm for more muted pastoral scenes similar to those later created by 'Capability' Brown:

> Why may not a Whole Estate be thrown into a kind of garden by frequent plantations? . . . If the *natural* embroidery of the meadows were helped and improved by some small additions of Art . . . a man might make a pretty Landscape of his own possessions.[2]

In the same year Alexander Pope, writing in the *Guardian*, attacked complex topiary and the predictable regularity of gardens, and urged a return to the 'amiable simplicity of unadorned nature', a theme later developed in his 'Essay on Criticism' and, in 1731, in the 'Epistle to Burlington': 'In all, let Nature never be forgot. . . . Consult the Genius of the Place in all.'[3]

Stephen Switzer quoted both Pope and Addison with approval in the *Ichnographia Rustica* of 1718. His ideas seem to echo those of Addison, arguing for the throwing down of garden walls to allow in the 'extensive Charms of nature'. But he also advocated alterations to this wider prospect, considering the aesthetic possibilities of the whole estate in a form of 'Rural or Extensive Gardening'.[4] This Switzer consciously contrasted with the 'diminutive and wretched performances everywhere met with', dominated by 'a few clipp'd plants and hedges'.[5]

Yet when we turn from these writings to consider the actual layout of gardens in this period we immediately encounter a curious contradiction: for there is little evidence on the ground for the creation of more 'natural' scenes, as Brown and his contemporaries might have understood this fifty years later. At all social levels, square level lawns, straight walks flanked by topiary, wildernesses criss-crossed with *allées*, and avenues focused on the main façade of the house continued to be popular into the 1730s and '40s, and indeed beyond. The contrast between the notions apparently propagated by these famous texts, and the real practice of gardening, is epitomized in Addison's own garden at Bilton Hall (near Rugby) which was laid out 'in straight lines, with long thick hedges of yew', and organized around a single axis of symmetry defined by trees uniformly spaced in parallel lines.[6] Shaftesbury's garden at Wimbourne St Giles (Dorset) was equally geometric, with walks, canals and hedges in profusion.[7] In 1707 he gave his gardeners specific instructions to cut, shape and trim evergreen trees into various figures.[8] The great formal gardens designed by Stephen Switzer at Caversham (Berks), described in Chapter 2, were actually begun in 1718, the very year in which *Ichnographia Rustica* was published.

This last case offers one possible explanation for the conundrum, of course. Switzer was a practising nurseryman and whatever his own views, he could do no other than give his customers what they wanted. In other words, ideas about garden design developed by intellectuals and philosophers need have, at best, only a very tangential connection with the actual practice of garden design in the real world. Society at large may simply not have been ready for the kinds of change these people were advocating. But the gardens of Shaftesbury and Addison suggest a more intriguing possibility: that later historians have, to some extent, misinterpreted these famous texts in their eagerness to fit the whole of eighteenth-century garden history into a single-minded quest for 'nature', reading into these rather vague aspirations the seeds of a naturalistic gardening style which the authors themselves would, in reality, have neither recognized nor liked.

It is, perhaps, better to consider these texts in the context of previous and contemporary ideas and practice rather than as precursors of what was to come. Some modern scholars have already begun to do this. In particular, in an important article David Leatherbarrow explained the apparent contradiction between Shaftesbury's ideas and the layout of his garden by showing that the famous passage had been ripped out of its context in a complex piece of philosophical writing.[9] Shaftesbury's garden embodied the traditional Neoplatonic ideas about perfecting the true 'natural' form of a tree or a bush by sympathetic topiary. Such forms were correct for the garden. The uncultivated landscape is preferable to this order only as a locus for philosophical meditation and enquiry: as a place where the inquisitive mind might best penetrate beneath the surface reality to perceive the true order of nature. This did not mean that the garden itself should take on a rude, uncultivated form because its role was different: to express, as far as possible, these hidden forms of nature latent in the physical world.

There is little real evidence that any of the other writers usually quoted as advocates of an irregular, asymmetric or serpentine form of design were, in fact, anything of the kind. An alternative reading would be that all were simply promoting, and lauding the achievements of, the late geometric style: its diversity, its capacity to surprise, its extent. All, however, wanted to take current developments further, and in particular to adapt the emerging style for a wider clientele. This is the real significance of the writings of Pope, Addison and, in particular, of Stephen Switzer.

It is the latter's *Ichnographia Rustica* that provides the clearest statement of these ideas. Switzer has two main aims. The first is to disseminate accurate and relevant horticultural information in England: a pressing need, he argues, because of the increased importance of gardening in contemporary cultural life, and because 'so few Books have been originally publish'd in their own Native Language'.[10] Such native texts as had been produced – such as Evelyn's *Sylva* – were often too philosophical and élitist to be of much practical use: thus the section on soils in Evelyn's *Philosophical Discourse on Earth* was 'withal so nicely drawn, that t'would be hard for an honest plain Country Planter to extract Rules for the composing of Earths proper for his simple Purpose'.[11] Indeed, most of the first volume of the three-volume work is concerned with practical aspects of forestry, husbandry and horticulture. Switzer, following a tradition going back to the seventeenth century (and related in part to the example of classical authors such as Virgil and Columella) thus places gardening firmly within a wider context of husbandry and estate management. Such a link would have seemed an obvious one to the broad mass of the rural gentry.

Switzer's second aim is to forge a style of landscape design suited to this same group, one which would allow the creation of much larger landscape designs than were currently enjoyed by most of its members. Switzer was no enemy of the dominant European tradition in garden design: his main concern was that English gardens lagged behind those of the Continent. They were, in particular, less magnificent than those of the French which, under Louis XIV, had been 'brought to the most magnificent Height and Splendour imaginable'.[12] It is not 'nature', not curves and irregularity that interest Switzer, but 'magnificent gardens, Statues, Water-Works'.[13] These are needed as a matter of national pride, to 'complete the Grandeur of the *British* Nation'.

> 'Tis then we may hope to excel the so-much-boasted Gardens of *France*, and make that great nation give way to the superior Beauties of our gardens, as her late Prince has to the invincible Force of the British Arms.[14]

The gardens of the greatest landowners had, for the most part, adopted something of the grand sweeps of the Continental garden. But in the 1710s and '20s those of the gentry were still enclosed spaces, dominated by potted flowers, topiary, and other 'trifling decorations', which were fit only for 'little Town-

Gardens, and not for the expansive Tracts of the Country'.[15] If the French *grande manière* was to be more widely adopted in England, however, it had to be altered to suit the social environment. Le Nôtre, as it were, had to be made to speak English. If the gardens of the gentry were to be made larger then they needed to be both simpler, and more closely integrated with the wider working landscape. The local gentry simply could not afford to maintain large and complex gardens, or put extensive areas down to unproductive, purely aesthetic, uses. Moreover, such conspicuous waste would have conflicted with their interest in husbandry and estate administration, with their perennial interests in the details of domestic production. Switzer thus provided a form of large-scale geometric design suited to the needs and pockets of a broader constituency than the élite of Whig grandees, one that integrated the aesthetic with the Virgilian Georgic idyll, gardening with forestry and husbandry.

Switzer maintains a clear distinction between the 'inner garden' and the beautified estate land beyond. The former must consist not of 'Interlacings of Box-work, and such-like trifling Ornaments', but rather of plain grass parterres, and gravel walks 'in which we so much excel other countries', for this will 'very much reduce the Expense of Keeping as well as making'.[16] The main axes of this inner area should be extended out into the estate land as ruler-straight rides or avenues 'as far as Liberty of Planting will allow', so that the whole would 'appear as a part, and add to the Beauty and Magnificence of the Garden in the View, tho' not in the Expense of Keeping'.[17] The outer landscape should be extensively planted with woodland, intended to be both beautiful and profitable. Switzer's descriptions, and accompanying illustrations, make it clear that both inner and outer areas were to be designed in the simplified geometric style now fashionable in élite gardens.

In so far as it is possible to judge from their rather vague comments, this was probably the kind of gardening envisaged by Addison and Pope, rather than anything more serpentine and irregular. Thus in the 'Epistle to Burlington' of 1731 Pope advocates features already common in the gardens of the very rich – the removal of garden walls to open up vistas, extensive use of groves and woods. In addition, however, he advocates practices well suited to the needs of the local squire, urging for example the concealment of boundaries and the integration of elements of the wider estate landscape into the overall scheme of the garden, and criticizing expensive earth-moving and excavation which altered the natural topography of a place. The poem parodies 'Timon's Villa' and its garden, robustly and wittily attacked because of the 'vanity of expense' involved in their creation. Some writers have suggested that Pope had in mind here Robert Walpole's new house at Houghton. Although this is probably untrue, there is nevertheless an implied criticism of the great houses and gardens of the Whig grandees. It is dangerous to make too simple or direct a link between concepts of garden design and political and social ideas, but there is a clear connection here between the search for 'affordable magnificence' advocated by Switzer, and a broadly Tory ideology. Switzer's enthusiasm for the minutiae of husbandry and estate administration, his ambivalent attitude towards the French and their culture, would all have found favour among the local squires, hostile to the centralizing power of the Whig oligarchs, to their supine foreign policy, to the naked magnificence of their gardens. Pope and Addison were noted critics of the Walpole regime. Switzer had some association with leading Tories such as Viscount Bolingbroke and Lord Bathurst, whose gardens (at Dawley and Richings (Middx)) expressed many of the ideas advocated in the *Ichnographia Rustica*. The latter, for example, included a wilderness in which the quarters contained areas 'for sowing of Corn, Turnips etc and for feeding of Cattle'.[18]

Switzer, Pope and Addison were not therefore stylistic predecessors of 'Capability' Brown. And yet there is a thread of continuity here, for Switzer was responding to new possibilities, and to new social needs, which were later to be addressed by these designers. Firstly, the extension of the 'grand lines' of the garden as far as the eye could see assumes, of course, that the planter owned all the land within the prospect. Increasingly, with the demise of the small freeholder, the consolidation of rural estates, and the spread of enclosure this was indeed the case, for local squire as much as for great landowner. Switzer's style represented one way in which large aesthetic landscapes could be created at little cost, by integrating landscape design with estate management. Brown's, as we shall see, was another. Secondly, and more importantly, Switzer's style represented a quest for a mode of landscape design which could be shared by great and lesser landowners alike: one which would, in tune with current opposition ideology, help to heal the divisions in the body politic, to limit the power of faction. Switzer also posited a clear distinction between 'city' gardening – concentrating on detail, clutter, flowers and walls – and country gardening, involving 'Woods, Coppices, Groves, and the busie and laborious Employs of Agriculture, with which *Gardening* is unavoidably as well as pleasantly mix'd'. The ideal of a shared style of landscape design for rural landowners, consciously different from that practised by a bourgeoisie with less land to spare, was to be developed with greater success by Brown and his contemporaries. But, as we shall see, this later generation were to consciously abjure the kind of overtly productive landscape beloved of Switzer.

CHARLES BRIDGEMAN AND THE STARKNESS OF GEOMETRY

So far as the evidence goes, variations on the late geometric theme continued to dominate garden design until the years around 1730. Then, however, landscape design did indeed begin to move into a new phase. Two quite different kinds of challenge to geometry developed among the landed élite, both of which continued in parallel into the 1740s and '50s, often occurring together on the same sites.

The first 'challenge' represented, arguably, not a new fashion at all but simply an intensification of existing trends. The late geometric style was, as it were, taken to its logical conclusion. It was made ever simpler, ever more extensive and magnificent, until the greatest houses began to be set in landscapes of stark simplicity. As we might expect, the pace was set at the gardens of the greatest in the land, and in particular at the home of Robert Walpole, the Prime Minister.

Houghton (Norfolk) had long been the main residence of the Walpole family. It was an old house, and Walpole's new-found wealth and status demanded

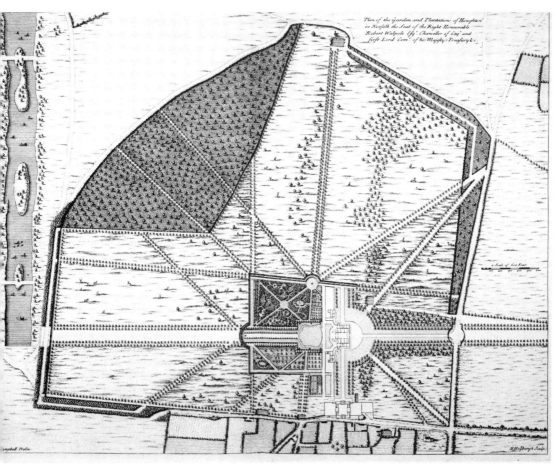

20. The late geometric garden: Houghton, Norfolk, in 1722, as illustrated in Colen Campbell's Vitruvius Britannicus of 1725.

something more fashionable. It seems that Sir Robert originally intended to alter the existing house, and then decided to rebuild it entirely on the same site, before finally deciding on a new position, a little to the east. During the 1710s, however, before this final decision had been made, an elaborate geometric garden had been laid out around the hall, and this was retained while the new house was being built (Figure 20). The latter was an impressive stone-built Palladian mansion, principally designed by James Gibbs and Colen Campbell, and it required a setting of comparable magnificence. Various plans were made to extend the park, and the geometric mesh of avenues within it. But when expansion eventually occurred in the late 1720s the park was also radically redesigned.[19] In 1728 Walpole described to a visitor 'His further design of planting and placing his woods for the avenues which will be very long and large upon three sides of the house.'[20]

Sir Thomas Robinson, visiting Houghton in 1731, described how Walpole and Charles Bridgeman showed him

> The large design which is the present undertaking: there are to be clumps and avenues to go quite round the Park pale, and to make straight and oblique lines of a mile or two in length, as the situation of the country admits of. This design will be about 12 miles in circumference.[21]

This 'design' was probably the basis for the plan published in 1735 in Isaac Ware's *Plans, Elevations and Sections . . . of Houghton in Norfolk* (Figure 21). Although the more grandiose of the features which it depicts (most notably, the vast

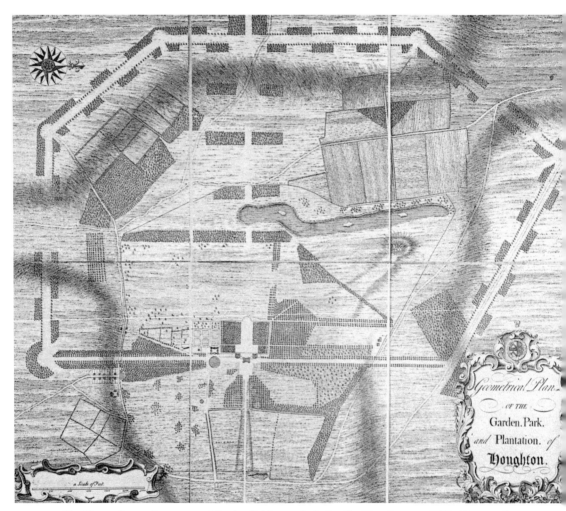

21. The starkness of geometry: Charles Bridgeman's design for Houghton, c. 1730, illustrated in Isaac Ware's Plans, Elevations and Sections . . . of Houghton in Norfolk *of 1735.*

perimeter ride flanked by block plantations) were never executed, most were, and form the basis for the present pattern of planting in Houghton park. Gone was the dense mesh of intersecting avenues: in its place was a starker, more monumental design. The eastern and western vistas from and towards the house were now more subtly implied by massed planting. To north and south of the house wide, double-planted avenues now framed its façades. A great deal of new planting had taken place between these new avenues, so that they ran in part through woodland rather than through open parkland. It was a design which, in its vastness and its simplicity, served to both complement the crisp Palladian lines of the hall, and proclaim the supreme power of its owner.

Many of Bridgeman's later works show this kind of stripped-down formality, and other prominent designers began to work in the same simple but sombre style. The later designs of Stephen Switzer, such as that prepared for Nostell Priory (Yorks) in *c.* 1735, display a similar sense of sober monumentality, although here combined with some more elaborate detail (Figure 22).[22] The landscape is still organized after *la grande manière* with (as at Houghton) great vistas framing the house. But these were now implied, fragmented, defined by blocks and clumps rather than crudely emphasized by regular lines of trees. The keynotes were expansion and simplification, the removal of fuss and clutter.

Wolterton Hall (Norfolk), the home of Walpole's brother Horatio, is another example. Here the great gardens laid out by Joseph Carpenter from *c.* 1724 beside another new Palladian house had hardly been completed before simplification began.[23] A letter written to Walpole by the architect Thomas Ripley in June 1735 discusses how the complex wilderness to the west of the house was to be thinned, and the trees transplanted 'in the walks to make the whole a grove', a necessary move because 'the walks is short and points to nothing'.[24] Partly under the influence of Bridgeman (who was a friend of the architect, and occasional visitor to Wolterton) the complex pattern of *allées* was replaced by a single vista focused on the house. This was to frame a view out into the surrounding landscape, and so the laurel hedge on the far, western side of the grove was to be removed and replaced with a ha-ha consisting of 'a wall of 4 feet high, set in a fosse'.[25] Simplification of wildernesses was a widespread feature of the 1730s and '40s, and involved not only a reduction in the number and complexity of paths, but also in many cases the removal of the underwood between and the hedges beside them. Thus Thomas Hamilton, writing about wildernesses in 1733, noted 'Now I hear they are Weary of the Hedges'.[26]

As hedges were removed from the perimeter of the wilderness quarters, greater attention seems to have been paid to the planting of flowering shrubs within them: thus began the evolution of wilderness into shrubbery.[27] A more general hostility to the excessive use of clipped hedges in gardens seems to have been gathering pace at this time. It was accompanied by a rejection of topiary. Switzer had attacked the practice as early as 1718, and in 1731 Pope criticized, in a footnote to his 'Epistle to Burlington', the

> Ill taste of those who are so fond of Ever-greens (particularly Yews, which are the most tonsile) as to destroy the nobler Forest-trees, to make way for such

22. Stripped-down formality: Stephen Switzer's design for Nostell Priory, Yorkshire, c. 1735.

little ornaments as Pyramids of dark-green continually repeated, not unlike a
Funeral procession.

By this stage, such ideas were becoming more widely accepted. Thus, for
example, we find Thomas Hamilton in 1735 insisting that the yew tree 'Arrives at
Great Beauty and Value . . . If not kept down by Formal Clipping'.[28] Hostility to
clipping led to a decline in the élite's enthusiasm for planting limes or sweet
chestnuts in walks and avenues (both, and in particular the first, responded well
to pleaching and topiary) and to the increasing popularity of oak and beech for
these purposes.

There were other important changes. As more and more attention was given to
altering the landscape at increasing distances from the house, so too there was a
tendency for features of the garden to migrate outwards, into the park. From the
early 1730s classical buildings began to be built away from the gardens,
terminating vistas in the open parkland. Highclere Park (Hants) is a good
example. Here a classical temple (now known somewhat incongruously as
'Jackdaws Castle') sits prominently across the lawns from the house, while
'Heaven's Gate', a triple-arched feature of brick, stood on Sidown Hill, closing
the vista in another direction. Jeremiah Milles described the former as 'newly
built' when he visited the house in 1739.[29] Some parks in the 1730s were
positively stuffed with classical structures. At Castle Hill near South Moulton in
Devon the main clumped avenue was terminated by a triumphal arch, while a
painting of 1741 shows obelisks, a pyramid, a rotunda, and no less than four
temples scattered around the grounds (Figure 23).[30]

These simple yet brooding landscapes were the apogee of the late geometric
tradition: quintessential expressions of the power of the great landowners. But
they also, to a greater degree perhaps than any designed landscapes before them,
exuded a distinct aura of exclusivity and social segregation. In the seventeenth
century parks had often been attached to the rear of a great mansion which, at its
front, bordered a public road and looked out on to the cottages and farms of the
estate tenants. Now, however, there was a growing tendency for parks to expand
in such a way that the mansion was entirely isolated within them. Thus at Nostell
Priory (Yorks) Sir Richard Wimm and Stephen Switzer intended diverting the
Doncaster road in order, as Switzer put it, to 'place ye House in ye Middle of ye
Park'.[31] If the park was so to be wrapped, like some excluding and exclusive
blanket, around the mansion house, then farms, cottages, sometimes whole
villages might have to be cleared out of the way. Settlements had occasionally
been moved to make way for parks in earlier centuries, but the 1720s and '30s saw
a marked increase in the phenomenon. At Houghton the village, which
archaeological evidence shows had been dwindling during the previous century or
so, was completely demolished to make way for Bridgeman's expansion of the
park.[32] A replacement was built – a neat street of plain semi-detached cottages –
on its fringes, leaving the parish church isolated within. The banishment of the
village beyond the pale was a vivid expression of the great landowners' growing
separation from the local community, just as the removal of the kitchen garden to
some more remote location – behind the stables, or to the other side of the park,

23. Castle Hill, South Moulton, Devon. The prospect from the hill above the house looking north, as painted by J. Langs in 1741. The park contains a plethora of ornamental buildings: temples, arches, pyramids, rotundas and obelisks.

something which again became increasingly common at élite sites from the late 1720s – represented their divorce from the humdrum details of agricultural and domestic production. So too did the removal of home farms, stackyards, pigeon houses and the rest.

These were crucial developments. Many earlier parks had offered a degree of isolation and segregation. But these functions now became paramount, as the élite increasingly distanced themselves from local communities and agrarian life. At this stage, however, the process was in its infancy, restricted to a few places, the homes of the super-rich. It was to develop apace, as we shall see, as landscape parks spread like a contagion through the English countryside in the years after 1760.

WILLIAM KENT AND THE LANDSCAPE GARDEN

Just as this monumental and simplified form of geometry was being widely adopted by leading members of society more radical alternatives to traditional styles began to appear. These seem to have originated with William Kent. Kent was an artist by profession – a set designer and landscape painter – who had spent ten years, between 1709 and 1719, travelling widely in Italy.[33] His enthusiasm for all things Italian placed him firmly in a long tradition of English dilettanti. It also (combined with his undeniable artistic genius) ensured a warm welcome among Burlington's Palladian circle on his return to England. At first he worked for prominent Whigs primarily as an interior designer. Increasingly, however, he turned his attention to architecture, to the design of both mansions and garden buildings. The early 1730s saw a further development in his career. In 1734 Sir Thomas Robinson wrote to his father-in-law, the Earl of Carlisle, in a now famous letter:

> There is a new taste in gardening just arisen, which has been practised with so great success at the Prince's garden in Town [i.e. Carlton House] that a general alteration of some of the most considerable gardens in the kingdom is begun, after Mr Kent's notion of gardening, viz., to lay them out, and work without either level or line. By this means I really think the 12 acres the Prince's garden consists of, is more diversified and of greater variety than anything of the compass I ever saw; and this method of gardening is the more agreeable, as when finished, it has the appearance of beautiful nature, and without being told, one would imagine art had no part in the finishing. . . . The celebrated gardens of Claremont, Chiswick, and Stow are full of labourers, to modernise the expensive works finished in them, even since everyone's memory.[34]

In the later 1730s and '40s a number of other famous gardens were laid out in this new irregular style. These included those at Hagley, Holkham, Painshill, Painswick, Wilton, and Wroxton. The crucial feature of them all was that they were not arranged on symmetrical or geometric lines. Instead they were organized around winding paths, and contained shrubs and trees (and sometimes flowers) massed in serpentine or irregular blocks, or scattered casually across grass lawns. They also made considerable use of framed views – either of distant features in the landscape, or of structures within the garden itself, especially classical temples and other kinds of garden building. These often constituted a three-dimensional version of the kinds of Italian landscape painted by artists such as Claude Lorrain or Poussin (eagerly collected by the rich at this time), not only in terms of their subject matter but also because they were arranged in such a way as to emphasize three distinct planes: a foreground, a middle ground, and a distant view. With the aid of inscriptions (often containing classical allusions) these composed scenes were supposed to inspire contemplation and evoke moods and sentiments. Arthur Young described his visit to Stowe (Bucks) in the 1760s entirely in terms of a series of set views, almost as if he was wandering through a picture gallery – which in a sense he was.[35] The precise route taken through the garden could therefore be important, and even when maps or plans seem to show a number of ways of negotiating a site, there was often one particular route which would make the garden's meaning most clear or show its scenes and features to best advantage. Thus a letter written to the owner in 1750 by John MacClary, head gardener at Rousham (Oxon), refers to the 'undulating walk' which is the 'way to view the garden'.[36] William Shenstone often showed the various views and features at his

24. William Kent: design for the South Lawn and the Temple on the Mount, Holkham, Norfolk, c. 1740. The drawing clearly indicates the radical difference between the new serpentine compartments in élite gardens of the 1730s and '40s, and the older geometric style of landscaping.

gardens at the Leasowes, created in 1745, in person. He grew angry with visitors if they proceeded the wrong way around the circuit.[37]

The Leasowes, however, was a slightly different (although closely related) kind of garden. It was a *ferme ornée*, an 'ornamented farm': a kind of ribbon-like garden, a strip of path bordered by shrubbery and copses (mainly consisting of fast-growing conifers) which wound around this small estate in the west Midlands. Openings in the foliage framed various views, each accompanied by inscriptions to inform the reader of their significance.[38] Often there was a seat provided, to aid comfortable contemplation. The Leasowes was not the first such garden: the idea had been tried out ten years earlier at Wooburn Farm (Surrey) (Figure 25). Here Philip Southcote had used the money acquired from his marriage to the 67-year-old Duchess of Cleveland to lay out a network of sand-covered paths running through the fields to various garden buildings, flanked by herbaceous borders containing golden rod, crown imperial, hollyhock, and lily, edged with pinks and backed by a variety of shrubs including sweet briar, syringa and lilac.[39]

New ideas for landscapes and gardens thus came thick and fast in the 1730s and '40s: the monumental simplicity of Bridgeman's designs, the serpentine picture-painting of William Kent. In part these developments were associated with further changes in country house architecture. Palladian houses were now

25. *Philip Southcote's* ferme ornée *at Wooburn, Surrey, as depicted in Luke Sullivan's print of 1769.*

becoming popular, and as they proliferated the prevailing late geometric style may have seemed still too fussy for the compact lines of an Italian villa. Under Bridgeman and others this style was thus further simplified, creating landscapes (like that at Houghton) which emphasized the plain grandeur of the new architecture. The rising tide of Palladianism was, however, part of a more general upsurge of interest in all things Italian, and this had a direct influence on, among others, the gardens of William Kent. The temples flanked by groups of pines, standing beside serpentine paths in irregularly planted groves, constituted a complex, dream-like image. They were a conflation of at least three things: happy memories of the Italian landscape as experienced on the Grand Tour; similar memories of the irregular grove areas of villa gardens; and the paintings of the Italian landscape (and the numerous published prints derived from these) by artists such as Poussin, Salvator Rosa, or Claude Lorrain (Figures 26 and 27).

POLITICAL GARDENING

To some extent such three-dimensional Italianate picture-painting had an ideological significance. In the 1710s and '20s Palladianism had been a distinctive

26 and 27. The paintings of Gaspar Poussin and Claude Lorrain were a major influence on the new serpentine style of gardens. Here, at Stourhead, Wiltshire, the arrangement of bridges and temples may echo the disposition of features in Lorrain's Coastal View of Delos with Aeneas.

badge of Whig ideology. Radical Whig theorists had insisted that the model for English society should be Republican Rome: and so the appropriate architectural style for the new élite was that of the Romans, although of necessity mediated through Renaissance Italy.[40] The garden buildings in the formal groves at Chiswick proclaimed a patriotic confidence in the new political establishment, in Britain's role as the new Rome. The gardens created by Kent and others in the middle and later 1730s were in one sense a development of the same theme. Yet by this time the political situation had changed. Walpole's administration had now been in power for twenty years, and English politics was less clearly organized around a simple Whig/Tory divide. Opposition to Walpole came from a broad base: from disaffected Whigs who considered the cause betrayed by the establishment grandees, as well as from Tories grown old in opposition. Various attempts were made, by Henry St John Viscount Bolingbroke and others, to weld the various strands together into a coherent opposition. Bolingbroke became friendly with Frederick, Prince of Wales, at a time when the latter was becoming increasingly estranged from his father George II: and the Prince's household and circle became a centre of opposition to the political establishment.[41] Frederick was an important figure, not so much for anything he ever did as for what he symbolized: a future alternative to George II (and, therefore, his Prime Minister Walpole).

The genesis of the new serpentine style was in part associated with this group. Most of the earliest landscape gardens – the term increasingly used for these pleasure grounds – were created by prominent opponents of the political establishment. That at Stowe – third in Robinson's list (Frederick's own, it should be noted, comes first) – illustrates most clearly the connections between politics and pleasure grounds.[42] Its history begins in 1715 when, following the accession of Queen Anne, Richard Temple (later the 1st Viscount Cobham) was dismissed from his post as an army commander because of his Whig beliefs. Like many in a similar situation before and after him he turned his attentions to building. He called in Sir John Vanbrugh to rebuild the house, and also to design classical buildings for the gardens. Bridgeman was commissioned to design the gardens, the construction of which continued throughout the 1720s. After Vanbrugh's death further garden buildings were designed by the architect James Gibbs, and the grounds were gradually extended. Cobham meanwhile had resumed his career in the army. In 1733, however, he resigned his commission during the political crisis over Walpole's excise bill, and joined the ranks of the opposition.

It was at this point that Kent arrived at Stowe and, in association with Cobham, began to lay out the eastern area of the gardens as a distinctive compartment which became known as the 'Elysian Fields'. He created the 'River Styx' – in reality a narrow lake – and planted up the area around with irregular groups of trees. In conjunction with Gibbs, and under the direction of Cobham, he designed a number of new buildings. The Temple of Ancient Virtue, a circular Ionic temple built on the western bank of the 'river', contained statues of Socrates, Homer, Lycurgus and Epaminondas (respectively the greatest philosopher, poet, lawmaker and general of antiquity). Near it, and in implied contrast, stood the Temple of Modern Virtue, a ruined structure containing a headless figure which was generally taken to represent Walpole. The meaning of these two structures was made clearer by the presence of another building on the far side of the river, the Temple of British Worthies. This was not really a temple at all but a semi-circular arrangement of niches containing a variety of busts. Some were figures who were generally considered important by all Whigs, part of a widely shared mythology of the seventeenth-century revolution: John Hampden, Locke, Bacon, Newton, Milton, and William III. Others, however, were more idiosyncratic choices, representing in various ways extreme Whig opposition to Walpole. These formed what might seem (to us) an odd collection: King Alfred, Sir Thomas Gresham, Sir John Bernard, Sir Francis Drake, Sir Walter Raleigh, Inigo Jones, Alexander Pope, and Edward, the Black Prince.[43]

The Temple of Friendship was built at the southern end of the Elysian Fields. This contained busts of Frederick, Prince of Wales and other members of the opposition. Even the Gothic Temple designed by Gibbs – an unusual building, crenellated, triangular in plan, in a rather odd mixed-up Tudor/gothic style – had a political significance. Cobham referred to it as the Temple of Liberty: it represented the ancient principles of the English constitution, and Old English liberty, evoking the Baron's Wars, Magna Carta, and King Alfred (in popular political mythology, the founder of a system of civil liberties lost at the Norman Conquest). The architectural style of the building was also a reference to the supposed democratic principles of the 'gothic' – i.e. Germanic barbarian – tribes, in contrast to the effete decadence and tyranny of Roman society. Over the door Cobham placed the motto: 'I thank the Gods that I am not a Roman.'

Similar political symbolism was manifested, although with less complexity, at Chiswick. Burlington was sympathetic to the opposition and Kent carried out significant modifications here in the mid-1730s. He constructed an imposing exedra containing statues: Caesar and Pompey, despots responsible for the decline of the Roman Republic, were confronted by Cicero, its defender, in another critique of the Walpole hegemony.[44]

It was not just disaffected Whigs who could play this kind of game. Older-style Tories also laid out politically symbolic gardens. Allen, 1st Earl Bathurst, a close friend of Pope, created a massive geometric landscape in Cirencester Park (Glos) from 1715.[45] He had time on his hands, his public career having been ended by the triumph of the Whigs and the accession of the Hanoverians. In 1741 he erected a statue of Queen Anne (last of the reigning Stuarts) on a tall column, directly in line between his home and the parish church: thus, it is said, symbolizing his support both for the Stuarts, and for the closer relationship between Church and State which had existed under them. Somewhat confusingly, he also erected, in 1721,'Alfred's Castle', perhaps the earliest of all gothic garden buildings. Clearly, Alfred was a symbol acceptable to traditional Tories as well as to the new, wider opposition: he stood for Britain's ancient constitution, for the legitimacy of royal succession, and he represented a time before political faction.

Many other early landscape gardens were associated with the opposition group and, in particular, with the household of Frederick, Prince of Wales: Painshill (Surrey), created from c. 1738 by Charles Hamilton; Wroxton Abbey (Oxon), laid out by the Earl of Guildford, Lord of the Prince's Bedchamber, between c. 1735 and *c.* 1751; or Hagley (Worcs), made in the early 1740s by Charles Lyttleton, the prince's secretary and Cobham's nephew.[46] Political iconography in these gardens was less striking than at Stowe, but present to some extent. All contained gothic buildings (a ruined castle at Hagley, a gothic dovecote at Wroxton, a pavilion at Painshill). Wroxton and Painshill also included Chinese structures, and Painshill had a 'Turkish tent'. It is possible that the former, at least, had some kind of ideological significance as a reference to the supposed virtues of the Chinese political system (it could be safely invested with any number of virtues, being so far away). Indeed, the very irregularity of these gardens was often said to be inspired by Chinese styles of landscape design, although very little was really known about oriental gardens at this time.[47]

Yet we must be careful not to exaggerate the importance of politics, and especially of one political clique, in the development of the landscape garden in the 1730s and '40s. Symbolic gardens were no monopoly of the opposition. Kent himself was commissioned by Queen Caroline to design the Hermitage and Merlin's Cave in Richmond Gardens. The former contained busts of Newton, Boyle, Locke and others which proclaimed the Queen's ideas about science and 'natural' religion.[48] It was not the only garden building constructed in the mid-eighteenth century to convey an overt religious message. Although in the popular mind the eighteenth century often seems a rationalist, irreverent age, in reality nonconformity, deism, and the eruption of Methodism were all matters of keen interest to the nobility and gentry.[49] At Denbies near Dorking (Surrey) Jonathan Tyers (proprietor of the Vauxhall Pleasure Gardens in London) began laying out an elaborate garden in 1734. Partly, perhaps, because he only really used it when Vauxhall was closed on a Sunday, the mood was religious, indeed melancholy. The main feature was a wood dissected with the customary *allées*, one of which was terminated with male and female skulls accompanied by appropriately sombre verses. Other ornaments included a temple containing a clock which struck at every minute,

> One stroke succeeding another just as the sound of the former is dying away; incessantly admonishing us that Time is fleeting, and even the least portion of it is to be employed in reflections on Eternity.[50]

These imaginative gardens were not, therefore, simple expressions of a particular political creed or necessarily of any political creed at all. What they really represented was a new attitude to the relationship between ideas and philosophies on the one hand, and landscape on the other. No longer did gardens merely serve to express simple messages about the owner's membership of the ruling social group by, for example, demonstrating a knowledge of classical civilization. Gardens could now be used as media to vent all sorts of highly personalized views of the world, political or otherwise.

CULTIVATING THE INDIVIDUAL

This new role for the garden, no longer merely an attribute of rank but now an expression of the owner's personal ethos, was symptomatic of a significant shift, at least among the upper and middle classes, in attitudes towards the individual. Following the ideological and political upheavals of the seventeenth century, new ideas had emerged concerning the nature of individuals and their relationship both with society as a whole and the groups within it. The free actions of autonomous individuals were increasingly prioritized, challenging older ideas of paternalism, social solidarity, and the 'moral economy'.[51] By the middle decades of the eighteenth century, as a more capitalist society developed apace, this trend had developed further, bringing a new stress on emotional relationships and experiences, and on the gratification of individual needs through the consumption or acquisition of fashionable products: the 'Consumer Revolution' was under way.

The role of the individual and the nature of personal identity were important matters of intellectual enquiry, and there was particular concern about the relationship between private self interest and the wider good of society, and about that between a person's public persona and his or her private personality. Rampant individualism was widely seen by members of the élite as a threat to the stability of the social system, and it has been suggested that the *public* presentation of *private* concerns and fantasies in these landscape gardens may have been one way of diffusing this danger. Certainly, gardens were a natural arena for the expression of the new individualistic ethos.[52] They were extensive areas entirely under the control of wealthy individuals who often – and especially if excluded from political life – had time on their hands. But statements about politics or philosophy, or indeed about anything else, are somewhat pointless if there is no one there to see them. The key to understanding gardens such as Stowe or Hagley is that they were experienced not just by the owner, his friends, and local political clients, but by a far wider range of people drawn from the upper and middle classes.

Tourism, and in particular country house visiting, was already an established part of upper-class life in the seventeenth century.[53] Tourists such as Celia Fiennes had visited, however, on an informal basis. The usual procedure was to send a servant to enquire whether it was convenient to view the property. If the answer was yes the visitor would then be shown round by one of the principal servants. In the course of the eighteenth century the scale of visiting increased relentlessly, and as a result visits became more organized, some especially popular attractions being supplied with inns (sometimes paid for by the landowner himself). Indeed, by the 1750s country house visitors were so numerous that they could form the subject of polite mirth, as in a poem dedicated by one Mr Graves of Claverton to William Shenstone:

> In the vacant season of the year
> Some Templar gay begins his wild career;
> From seat to seat o'er pompous seat he flies,
> Views all with equal wonder and surprise,
> Till, sick of domes, arcades, and temples grown,
> He hies fatigued, not satisfied, to town.[54]

Shenstone would have known all about this. His gardens at the Leasowes were opened to the public almost as soon as they were completed, and were perennially popular.

The importance of individual expression in the landscape garden was not solely confined to the role of the owner. The individuality of the visitor was also being cultivated and emphasized. Although there were some places, such as Stowe or the Leasowes, where guide books were available which explained the meaning or significance of scenes or buildings, in most cases visitors were left free to interpret what they saw on their own terms. Walking the circuit through the exotic, eclectic ensemble at Painshill, or picking their way through the erudite allusions at Stowe or Stourhead, the sequence of inscriptions, seats and buildings stimulated imaginative excursions through time and space. The experience and imagination of the individual mind was thus cultivated, and celebrated.[55]

And yet at the same time, as numerous contemporary illustrations make clear, visitors enjoyed such essentially individual stimulation in the company of others (Figure 28). The experience of the visit was as much about being a member of a particular kind of social group as it was about being an individual. Indeed, the very nature of the demands made upon visitors helped define such an entity. Not everyone in society could understand, or was supposed to understand, the thirty-five quotations from classical authors, inscribed on seats, urns and obelisks, at the Leasowes. Nor could everyone know what was signified, what you were supposed to consider or imagine, when confronted with a hermit or a Turkish tent. The correct response required not just a conventional classical education, but also 'taste', knowledge of current fads, fashions and norms. Taste was what defined

28. *The gardens at Chiswick, c. 1738. This drawing by Jacques Rigaud typically shows large numbers of visitors enjoying the various views and buildings.*

'polite society', and it was this emerging group that formed the audience for the famous landscape gardens which loom so large in books on garden history.

The intellectual demands made on visitors to these gardens should not be exaggerated. Art historians sometimes overemphasize the philosophical character of these places. Some owners, rejoicing in their wealth and in the land at their disposal, were simply having fun. At Seaton Delavel (Co. Durham), for example, one visitor in 1752 noted that the gardens contained 'Some sheep . . . plac'd up and down, which would deceive almost anybody till very near them'. [56] Another, at Worksop (Notts), described

> a very large and fine piece of Water flanked on each side with a fictitious Battery, above this on a rising piece of ground is a Building to represent a Castle with 2 great Guns on a rampart . . . this Water is made more beautiful by a number of small vessels being stationed upon it.[57]

Similar forts and 'fictitious batteries' were constructed elsewhere in England, into the 1760s: like that designed by Thomas Wright on Codger Crag, Rothley (Northumb) in 1769, which still survives.[58] And at the same time we must be careful not to overemphasize the intellectual preoccupations (or abilities) of visitors. The famous Chatsworth willow fountain, which showered unsuspecting visitors with water, was perennially popular ('a merry conceit', thought one visitor in 1742).[59] Serious collections of art, in contrast, were often given short shift: one tourist in 1752 dismissed the sculpture collection in the gardens at Castle Howard (Yorks) as 'an abundance of trifling ornaments'.[60] Nor were the philosophical messages at places such as Stowe necessarily understood, or even of interest, to visitors. Seeley's guide book to the gardens at Stowe – and the guide by George Bickman which was put on sale to rival it in 1750 – may have needed to go into so much detail to explain the various classical allusions because many members of polite society could understand them only with great effort, if at all. Some visitors simply went for thrills, for entertainment, for a laugh: and some famous gardens clearly went some way towards pandering to this. Thus as at Hawkstone (in Shropshire) the attractions included an attendant dressed as a druid, and a hermit who, as visitors approached, would come out of his cave waving – instead of arms – two bloody stumps, and crying 'Memento mori'.[61] The line between complex intellectual game, emotional stimulation, and cheap thrills is not always an easy one to draw in the English landscape garden. Some members of polite society entertained themselves in more basic ways. Philip Southcote was obliged to close his famous gardens at Wooburn Farm after 'savages, who came as connoisseurs, scribbled a thousand brutalities in the buildings'.[62]

THE SURVIVAL OF GEOMETRY

Stowe, Rousham and the rest loom large in most books on garden history, and rightly so, for they were artistic works of the highest order. But we should not imagine for one minute that they were representative of the gardens of England's landowners. Nor should we necessarily assume that the landed classes universally began to reject geometry in favour of flowing, serpentine irregularity in their gardens during the 1730s and '40s. Nothing could be further from the truth.

In the first place, it is important to emphasize the rather structured and artificial nature of the landscape gardens of this period. These designs were not flowing, casual and irregular in the way that the parks of Brown were later to be. Features that seemed new and 'naturalistic' in the 1730s and '40s already seemed stiff and unnatural thirty or forty years later. François de La Rochefoucauld visited Holkham (Norfolk) in 1784 and described how 'In front of the house, someone has planted trees in clumps of varying size but similar shape, giving an unfortunate, slightly shocking, sense of regularity.'[63] He was referring, in fact, to William Kent's clumps on the north lawn, planted in 1753. When we read in descriptions of the 1740s and '50s that this or that garden appeared 'natural' we need to be very cautious about what is meant: not least because the word 'nature' retained some of its old Neoplatonic meaning well into the eighteenth century. One tourist, visiting Studley Royal in 1752, reported that 'Nature has done everything of herself', but went on to discuss how there was an

> abundance of cuts thro the Trees as you pass along, for views to Buildings . . . the canals are form'd into a kind of Parteries. The Trees round it are cutt into regular arches, which . . . has an extream pretty effect not much unlike some parts of the Gardens at Versaille and Marly.[64]

A much more important point, however, is that most of the famous landscape gardens were slotted into, or around, more conventional geometric grounds, and it was these which continued to function as the main setting for the house. Thus at Painshill in 1744, when much of the basic structure of the gardens had been established, John Rocque's map shows that the formal gardens below Hamilton's mansion – which included a series of terraces leading down to what was probably a banqueting house – still survived.[65] As late as 1770 George Mason described how 'you are conducted to a view of the lake through specimens of French and Italian gardening'.[66] At Stowe, Kent's Elysian Fields formed but one compartment within Bridgeman's great geometric landscape, which for a long time survived unmodified.[67] Arthur Young, writing in the 1760s after its older formal framework had been simplified and made more serpentine and irregular, described how the gardens had been

> sketched at first in the old stile of broad straight gravel walks and avenues of trees; with regular waters; but many of these circumstances are much changed, and the grounds modernised as much as they would permit.[68]

Such fashionable modifications had not occurred everywhere by this time. When Sir John Parnell visited Stourhead in 1768 he was charmed by the stately avenue leading to the house. 'Here . . . is a specimen of the old fashioned straight lined gardens, so much decried in the present age. How comes it here in a new improvement admired for elegant taste?'

The answer, perhaps, is that when originally laid out these early landscape gardens were not necessarily thought of as *alternatives* to geometric ones, but as something to be combined with them as an integral part of a single scheme. The predictability and order of the geometric structures acted as a contrast to the more serpentine lines and evocative scenes. To some extent the two kinds of garden fulfilled different, complementary functions. The geometric structures were focused on the great house and a suitable complement to its pomp and formality. The landscape gardens, in contrast, were often quite separate and visually divorced from the mansion. At Hawkstone, Painswick, Stourhead, Rousham, and Claremont the house was scarcely visible from the landscape gardens, and this was also the case at famous *fermes ornées* such as the Leasowes.[69] Indeed, in a few cases the landscaped grounds were completely detached from the mansion, as at Studley Royal, where they lay more than a kilometre away. It is noteworthy that Young's only criticisms of the gardens at Stowe concerned the way in which they related to the house. Thus the view from the Temple of Friendship, he thought, would be improved 'when the wood is enough grown to hide the house'; while to his description of the prospect from the Gothic Temple he added the note: 'Query, should the spires &c of the house be seen here?'[70] All this should not surprise us. The landscape garden was a place where moods could be stimulated and ideas expressed, where you could in effect wander through a series of three-dimensional paintings. It needed to be a fairly separate space. Moreover, the most famous and most visited gardens perhaps needed to be distanced from the house for another reason: to ensure the owner's privacy, to avoid the intrusion and inconvenience of tourists.

Even in the 1750s serpentine and naturalistic features were not simply regarded as distinct alternatives to geometric ones. Indeed, professional designers had no problems working in both idioms. Henry Ellison, a Norfolk designer, proudly boasted in an advertisement in the *Norwich Mercury* in January 1752 that he undertook

> All Sorts of Gardening Works, Wood-Works, Forest Planting, and Planting in all branches whatsoever, in altering old Gardens, as well as making new ones . . . viz. Parterres, Kitchen-Gardens, Fruit and Flower-Gardens, Planting of Grandlines, Avenues, Vista's, Serpentine Walks, Groves, Woods, Labyrinths, Porticoe's, Arbours, Salons, Cabinets, Amphitheatrios, Platoons, Wildernesses; and upon proper Situation Water-Works: viz. Aqueducts, Grotto's, Cascades, Canals, Fountains, Basons, Serpentine Rivers and Reservoirs, or any sort of Works that adorn and beautify magnificent Gardens . . .

But there is a third important reason why we should not exaggerate the extent to which geometry and formality were in full retreat in the 1740s and '50s, and this is perhaps the most important reason of all. Even among the landed élite, the new landscape gardens remained rare. That is why Arthur Young, writing at the end of the 1760s, could suggest that

> the ornamental grounds at *Stow* are more peculiar than the house. They were for many years the admiration of all that viewed them, not only for their real

beauty, but for the scarcity of other improvements of the same kind in the kingdom.[71]

In the 1740s and '50s, so far as the evidence goes, many élite gardens became less enclosed, more open to the surrounding landscape. Serpentine shrubberies and pleasure grounds, less elaborate than those in gardens like Stowe and Painshill, were added to formal gardens, and were often given some appropriate embellishment – a small wooden temple, a Chinese bridge. But otherwise, geometry continued to reign supreme. Thus when in 1743 Sir Nicholas Carver considered making alterations to the gardens at Beddington (Berks) the main question was 'how to preserve the Simetry and take away some part of the Expense'.[72] A plan of a garden at Kendals, a small estate in Aldenham (Herts) shows a layout typical of a fashionable gentleman's residence in *c.* 1750 (Figure 29).[73] In front of the house was a walled rectangular flower garden divided symmetrically into four equal plots. Beyond this the main axis was extended as a broad walk through a large wood which – to judge from the ground flora, and the massive, outgrown stools of hornbeam and sweet chestnut which still survive there – was an ancient coppice wood. This was threaded with serpentine paths, meeting at clearings.

    In some of the greatest gardens in the land the new fashion for the serpentine was largely ignored. Cliveden (Bucks) for example, the home of the Earls of Orkney, retained a rigidly geometric layout into the 1760s. Here the owners had lavished large sums of money on the grounds in the 1720s and '30s and were thus, one presumes, reluctant to indulge in substantial alterations just as the planting was coming to maturity. Yet well into the 1750s designs of an essentially geometric nature were not only being maintained, but also newly commissioned. Raynham (Norfolk) was the seat of the wealthy Townshend family. Their grounds had been deformalized with peculiar thoroughness, probably with the aid of William Kent, as early as 1735. Yet a planting plan drawn up more than twenty years later, in 1758, would if executed have filled the park with a complex pattern of geometric woodland blocks, framing rigid vistas, very much on the lines of Bridgeman's later works.[74] That such a plan could even be considered as late as this at a residence of Raynham's social standing seems extraordinary. But should we be surprised? Well into the 1750s, when Brown began to lay out his landscape parks, formal gardens could still be championed by the educated and the articulate. Sir John Dalrymple's *Essay on Landscape Gardening*, written shortly before 1760, lauded the new natural style but could still recommend, for areas of flat featureless terrain in particular,

> *Bosquets*, statues, vases, trees cut into arches, *jets d'eau*, cascades forced up and made to tumble down an hundred steps, regular basins, . . . long vistas, star plantation . . . All the magnificence of VERSAILLES, without its conceits. . . .[75]

He also praised avenues and even mounts. Above all, the fact that Brown was able to destroy so many walled formal gardens in the 1760s and '70s should alert us to the fact that many still remained to be destroyed, even at the exalted social levels at which he generally worked.

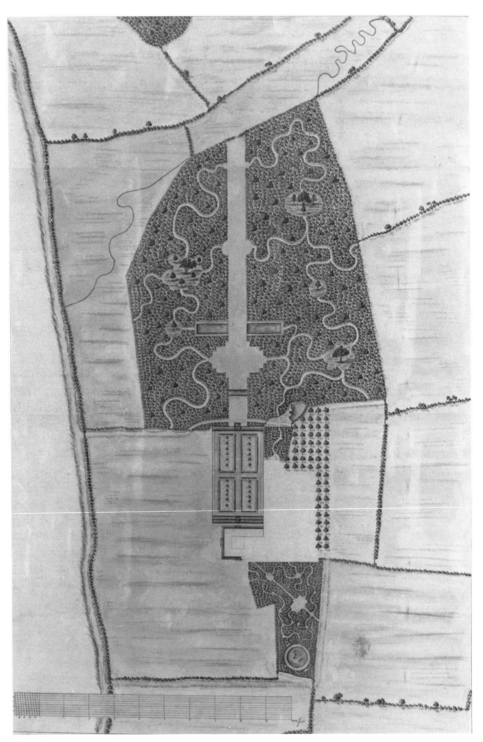

29. *The survival of geometry: an uncompleted plan of, or perhaps a design for, the gardens at Kendals Hall, Aldenham, Hertfordshire, c. 1750.*

In short, the kinds of garden most closely studied by garden historians were by no means typical of the 1730s and '40s. But then, why should they have been? Famous gardens such as Stowe or Hawkstone were, in a sense, the eighteenth-century equivalents of theme parks. Visitors did not automatically attempt to emulate what they had seen in them on their return home: in modern terms, this would be like getting ideas for garden design from a visit to Alton Towers.

If geometry remained popular at the highest social levels then we should not be surprised to discover an even deeper attachment to the old styles among provincial squires. The great and fashionable might embrace the simplified geometry of Bridgeman, but lesser landowners in the remoter parts of England continued to maintain or even create much more archaic gardens well beyond 1750. Maps and plans show that irregular collections of walled courts still clustered around many rural manor houses, with geometric wildernesses beyond. If these were unfashionable relics of a bygone age, they were nevertheless maintained with some enthusiasm, to judge from contemporary letters, diaries and gardening texts. Henry Stevenson's *The Gentleman Gardener's Recreation*, first published in 1716, was thoroughly revised and reprinted for the eleventh time in 1764, with no hint that the form or structure of gardens had changed in the meantime: wildernesses, gravel walks, 'Dutch Box Edgings to Borders', and 'Grass-plats' are all there.[76]

In fact, geometric arrangements probably only really began to go out of fashion among the gentry during the late 1750s. Repton, writing in 1806, recalled a childhood experience: his father, noting the new vogue for implying vistas with block planting rather than defining them rigidly with closely spaced lines of trees, had observed 'that, perhaps, this will lead to the abolishing of avenues'. Repton added: 'I believe few were planted after that date.' This conversation had, he recalled, taken place when he was 'about ten years old', that is, around 1762.[77]

Some readers may have noted the omission of one oft-repeated piece of evidence that would argue a contrary case: that the new serpentine landscape gardens were popular enough, by the 1750s, to be ridiculed. The critical text here is an article in *The World* for 1752 in which Francis Coventry parodied 'Squire Mushroom', who made a villa out of a farmhouse and laid out two acres of gardens with 'A yellow serpentine river, stagnating through a beautiful valley, which extends near twenty yards in length.'[78] The river was crossed by a bridge 'partly in the chinese manner', leading to a grove containing a hermitage and a temple. Yet we must not take this passage at face value. Like all quotations it needs to be placed in its context. Firstly, the article makes it clear that the garden included a range of more formal features: the grove contained a 'labyrinth of horn-beam hedges', and a circular parterre with flower borders. More importantly, Coventry emphasizes that 'whimsical variations of GARDENING' such as Mushroom's were essentially a phenomenon of the 'counties adjacent to London'. The article needs to be read as a piece of social satire rather than an objective description of current developments in garden design. Coventry, a spokesman for the traditional landed élite, is using the character of Mushroom to parody a wider group of nouveaux-riches merchants and financiers living in the immediate vicinity of the metropolis. 'It is not necessary to relate . . . by what

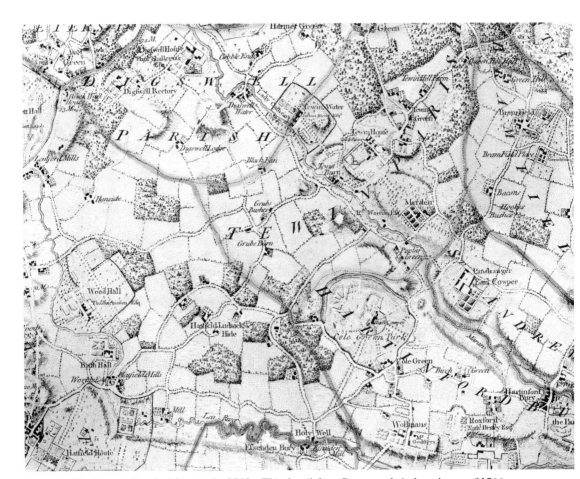

30. *Central Hertfordshire in the 1760s. This detail from Drury and Andrews' map of 1766 shows the wide variety of geometric styles current in the middle decades of the eighteenth century.*

steps he rose from primeaval meanness and obscurity to his present station in life', noted Coventry. 'Let it be sufficient to say, that at the age of forty he found himself in possession of a considerable fortune.' Yet Mushroom had not really joined the ranks of the established élite because he had only purchased a small estate. He was laying out a garden which was ridiculous partly because he had only a limited understanding of landscape design, but mainly on account of its diminutive size. The passage is thus a typical expression of establishment concern that traditional social hierarchies were being eroded by the development of an increasingly commercial society. Designed, ornamental landscapes – most visible of all artefacts – were vital in the negotiation of status in eighteenth-century England. The problem with the new landscape gardens – or so Coventry appears to be saying – was that they could be aped by anyone with some money but little land and less taste. Indeed, the first description of the new style that we have –

Robinson's letter of 1734, quoted above – emphasizes the new style's ability to make small pleasure grounds appear larger than they really were. Problems of social definition were to become increasingly acute in the decades after 1750, with important consequences for the development of landscape design.

THE RISE OF THE PARK

So far we have been discussing gardens: what is perhaps more interesting are the changes which were occurring in the design of parks in the middle decades of the century. Pleasure ground and park continued to be distinct entities – the former maintained by gardeners, the latter by livestock – but the widespread adoption of the ha-ha was bringing them into increasing visual integration, and this ensured the continued migration of aesthetic features out from the former to the latter. Classical (or occasionally gothic) buildings were constructed at the end of vistas, and large lakes began to appear. The fashion for the latter embellishment began in the 1720s, with the construction of areas of water which, while not as serpentine as those later created by Brown and his contemporaries, were nevertheless less rigidly geometric than earlier canals – a consequence, in part, of their size. Under the influence of Kent lakes grew more curvilinear through the 1730s and '40s, although still stiff enough by later standards. It was Kent, too, who popularized 'serpentine rivers', winding if artificial-looking watercourses which were sometimes contained within the garden, but which sometimes (as at Holkham in Norfolk) ran out into the park to discharge into the lake, or connected two areas of water within the park.

The growing emphasis on the park naturally ensured that more attention was paid to the planting within it. The 1740s and '50s saw, for the most part, a continuation of the kinds of planting which we have already seen in the 1730s at Nostell and Houghton: geometric vistas framed by blocks of woodland, and avenues consisting of clumps rather than individual trees (although avenues of conventional form were everywhere maintained, and some new ones planted, in this period). Clumps were also used to frame views and architectural features, to give depth and interest to a prospect.

Prospects were also often improved by the alteration of contours, and this period saw some phenomenal feats of earth-moving. At Houghton, for example, in the mid-1740s several thousand cubic metres of earth and subsoil were excavated to open up a vista to the east of the hall, an enterprise poorly documented in the estate accounts but briefly mentioned in an undated memorandum: 'item the matter of moving the hill to be decided.'

Yet the most fundamental development in this period was the way in which the concept of the *park* was gradually ceasing to have any necessary association with *deer*. True, in earlier centuries there had been some minor members of the local gentry who had used the term rather loosely, almost pompously, to dignify some well-timbered piece of pasture beside their manor house. But during the 1730s and '40s major landowners began to follow suit, laying out large parks but making no provision for deer-proof fencing. The reason was simple: the more money and effort that was invested in the design and ornamentation of these landscapes, the less keen landowners were to keep deer within them, for they stripped the bark from young trees and did great damage to clumps and plantations. It is hard to overemphasize the importance of these deer-less *transitional parks*, to coin a phrase. The park's significance as an essentially aesthetic landscape had now overtaken its importance as a place where deer were kept. This was a crucial change, pregnant with possibilities for the future.

CHAPTER FOUR

The Age of Brown

THE LANDSCAPE PARK

In the years around 1750 great aristocrats and local squires alike thus possessed grounds which were still, in essence, arranged along geometric lines. Three or four decades on, however, and everything had changed. Almost all members of the landed classes – anybody, one might say, who was anybody – now had their home set within a *landscape park*, an open landscape of grass and irregularly scattered trees (Figures 31 and 32). Geometric planting was banished and the house set free of enclosed gardens, so that open turf appeared to flow up to its very walls.

Landscape parks varied considerably in appearance but a number of features were standard, indeed essential. Linear planting, such as avenues or geometric vistas, was shunned. All blocks of woodland – an important feature of these designs – had curvilinear, serpentine outlines. Two forms of planting were particularly distinctive and popular. One, the most common, was the placing of thin strips of woodland, generally referred to as 'belts', on the periphery of the park. Sometimes these ran all the way around the boundary, so that the park was effectively sealed off from the surrounding landscape. The other – rather less ubiquitous – was the placing of small ovoid groups of trees – clumps – casually across the interior. Serpentine carriage drives ran through the park, some forming approaches to the mansion, others (especially in the larger parks) providing entertaining excursions. These often meandered around the edge of the park, in and out of the belt, giving a series of views of the house and its landscape. Many parks, and the majority of the larger ones, had a lake. Ideally this was positioned in the middle distance when viewed from the windows of the house. It was invariably of irregular or serpentine form.

Everything in these landscapes was intended, so it was said, to appear 'natural'. We should not, however, assume from this that the park was necessarily unstructured or undesigned. Contemporary texts such as Thomas Whately's *Observations on Modern Gardening* (1770) reveal the care and subtlety with which such landscapes could be laid out, paying careful attention to the effects of colour, perspective, light and shade. The visual effects of different shapes and sizes of tree or tree groups, of different configurations of natural landforms, were all carefully considered, at least by the better designers. Buildings could also be used to lend variety to a scene or to focus a vista. These were generally of the kinds we

31. Typical parkland landscape at Blickling, Norfolk. The lake was created in c. *1764.*

have already encountered in the gardens and parks of earlier decades: rustic 'root houses', classical temples, occasionally gothic ruins. Some parks contained large numbers of them, but on the whole they were now employed more sparingly than in the gardens of Kent and his ilk: more often designed, perhaps, than built. So far as the evidence goes they became progressively less important with every passing decade.[1] They might still be used to invoke moods and emotions – Lybbe Powys in 1766 described the 'Gothic root-house' at Taplow (Bucks) in which 'the upper part of the windows being painted glass gives a pleasing gloom',[2] but sentiments were now principally to be stimulated by the shape of the natural land forms and the disposition of planting. Elaborate iconographic schemes were likewise less fashionable, although the park itself could be interpreted in terms of Whig political theory. It symbolized the synthesis of art and nature, just as the British constitution represented a happy medium between despotic monarchy and the rule of the mob.

The landscape park was a distinctive and striking environment, and it will absorb our attention for much of what follows. For in spite of its essential visual simplicity it was a highly complex landscape, and we must work hard to tease out its various meanings, uses and functions.

32. Typical parkland landscape at Ickworth, Suffolk, with oaks scattered casually across the parkland turf.

BROWN AND HIS 'IMITATORS'

'Capability' Brown is undoubtedly the most famous English landscape designer, and large numbers of his creations still survive, albeit in varying states of decay.[3] Yet much about his art remains enigmatic. This is largely because, unlike his successor Humphry Repton, he did not commit his ideas to paper. There is but one exception to this, a letter written in 1770 to the Revd Thomas Dyer, the relevant passage of which reads:

> In France they do not exactly comprehend our ideas on Gardening and Place-making which when rightly understood will supply all the elegance and all the comforts which mankind wants in the Country and (I will add) if right, be exactly fit for the owner, the Poet and the Painter. To produce these effects there wants a good plan, good execution, a perfect knowledge of the country and the objects in it, whether natural or artificial, and infinite delicacy in the planting &c. So much Beauty depending on the size of the trees and the colour of their leaves to produce the effect of light and shade so very essential to the perfecting of a good plan: as also the hideing what is disagreeable and shewing what is beautyful.[4]

We have one other insight, perhaps more illuminating. Mrs Hannah More recorded a conversation which she had with the famous man one day in 1782. In this, he 'compared his art to literary composition'.

'Now *there*', said he, pointing his finger, 'I make a comma, and there', pointing to another spot, 'where a more decided turn is proper, I make a colon: at another part, where an interruption is desirable to break the view, a parenthesis; now a full stop, and then I begin another subject.'[5]

The choice of analogy is interesting: it is one which would have appealed to an educated person. Yet Brown's own origins were quite humble. Born in 1716 in Kirkhale in Northumberland, he was the fifth of six children of a yeoman farmer.[6] Some commentators, embarrassed by such lowly origins, have suggested that Brown was in fact the illegitimate son of a local landowner: but there is of course no evidence for this. In 1732, at the age of sixteen, Brown left school and took a job as gardener at nearby Kirkhale Hall, seat of Sir William Lorraine. His experiences here no doubt provided him with a thorough practical training, especially as Sir William was, at this time, involved in large-scale land improvement and planting schemes on his estate (between 1694 and 1738 he planted no less than 24,000 forest trees, and more than 488,000 hedgerow plants).[7] But there is no evidence that Brown was involved in directing operations, still less in designing landscapes, at this time. It was not until later, after he moved to the south of England in 1739, that Brown began to give rein to his own outstanding gifts in these areas.

He first went to Kiddington (Oxon), but soon proceeded to Stowe, where Kent was busy laying out the Elysian Fields. Brown's involvement in the detailed execution of this design must have been a major influence on the development of his own 'capabilities'. By 1741 he had been appointed head gardener there, responsible for a staff of some forty men.

His career really began, however, in 1751. Having carried out a few commissions for friends of his employer Lord Cobham, Brown moved to London and set up as an independent designer. His practice grew quickly. By the end of the decade he had worked on perhaps twenty landed estates, and in 1764 he was appointed Royal Gardener at Hampton Court, a prestigious but not onerous post. By 1767 the author of the anonymous poem 'The Rise and Present Progress of the Present Taste in Planting Parks, Pleasure Grounds Etc' clearly assumed that his educated readers would know the identity of one referred to only as 'immortal Brown'.[8] He had arrived.

By the time of his death in 1783 Brown had worked on some hundred and seventy major commissions. Moreover, his activities were by this time not restricted to the design of landscapes. Like Kent before him and Repton after, he 'fancied himself as an architect', designing not only garden buildings but also country houses such as Croome Court, Newnham Paddox, Fisherwick, Claremont, and Cadland.[9] But it was not all plain sailing to the winds of fashion. Brown's smooth, pastoral style began to be criticized even in his own lifetime. The architect William Chambers in 1772 castigated 'gardens which differ little from common fields', and after his death the prophets of the picturesque – Uvedale Price and Richard Payne Knight – were to mount a sustained and at times savage attack on Brown and his work.[10] Indeed, throughout the following centuries many prominent writers echoed their complaints, from John Claudius Loudon in 1804 ('Wherever his levelling hand has appeared, adieu to every natural beauty') to the damning comments of Gertrude Jekyll in 1937:

> As he knew practically nothing of his subject . . . he adopted a set formula . . . it is difficult to understand how anyone of intelligence could have believed that this sort of empty formality was worthy to be described as landscape gardening.[11]

But tastes are ever changing, and a reaction to all this set in during the twentieth century, especially with the writings of Christopher Hussey and Dorothy Stroud. By the 1950s Hussey was able to describe Brown as 'the most celebrated English landscape architect of the eighteenth century', and subsequent writers on garden history have tended to follow suit.[12] Thus it was that Brown was returned to the prominence which he had enjoyed in his own lifetime: or perhaps, to a yet more exalted station. For the concentration on Brown as a pioneering artistic genius has perhaps led to some misunderstanding of his true place in history.

Whether or not Brown was really a great artist is, like all such judgements, beyond the reach of rational argument. Opinions will always vary from individual to individual and from generation to generation. What is undeniable is that he was a phenomenally successful *businessman*. At the height of his career in the 1760s and early '70s the turnover of his practice regularly exceeded £15,000 per annum and in one astonishing year, £34,000.[13] These are sums that can only be converted to modern values by the addition of several zeros. Precisely what his own personal profit was from all this remains unclear, but it must have been substantial. By 1767 he was the owner of an estate of over 1,000 hectares at Fenstanton (Hunts): like all successful businessmen of the eighteenth century, he had joined the landowning class.

Much about the way Brown's business was organized, however, remains obscure. His account with the bankers, Drummonds, shows that he made regular payments to a large number of individuals, some of whom are known from other sources as artists or technicians in a variety of fields: master plasterers, surveyors, draughtsmen, nurserymen. This, together with the size of his annual turnover, and the sheer scale and number of his commissions (especially in the period between 1770 and 1780), suggests that Brown was, in effect, running a complex business, in which he provided the central idea and others, experts in their own particular fields, carried out the detailed design work and saw to the finer points of earth movement, dam construction and tree planting.[14] The key to Brown's success lay, in part, in his ability as a 'front man', communicating easily with members of the country's élite. In 1777 Lord Chatham told Lady Stanhope that she could not 'take any other advice so intelligent or more honest' than that of Brown, a man who 'sits down at the tables of all the House of Lords'.[15] This,

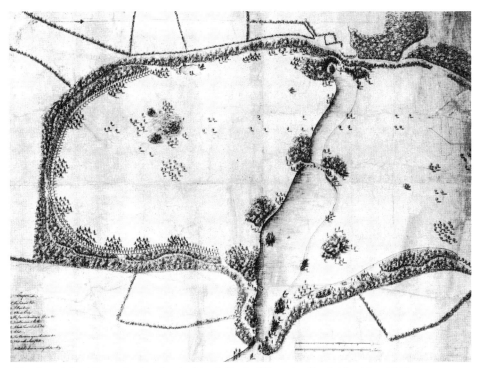

33. 'Capability' Brown's plan for the North Park, Wimpole, Cambridgeshire, 1767.

perhaps, is the real Brown: personable genius, director of a vast landscape architecture practice, successful businessman.

    While some of the earlier names in the roll-call of garden history – London and Wise, for example, or Stephen Switzer – had run wide-ranging businesses, theirs had never been on quite this scale. The sophistication of Brown's organization was, of course, one symptom of the 'consumer revolution' of mid-eighteenth-century England: a manifestation of the increasing specialization of the service economy. Another was the rapid proliferation of other designers and design teams. For although Brown's practice was unquestionably the largest in the country, it accounted for only a small fraction of the grounds being 'improved' in the new style. By the time of Brown's death in 1783 there must have been, at a conservative estimate, around four thousand landscape parks in the country: even Brown and his busy team can hardly have been responsible for more than 5 per cent of these. A host of other designers was at work, and while none operated quite on the scale of Brown several ran fairly impressive practices: men such as Richard Woods, Nathaniel Richmond, William Emes, Francis Richardson, or Adam Mickle. Earlier writers tended to dismiss such people as 'shadowy practitioners', mere imitators of Brown, who slavishly 'carried on his principles in various parts of the country'.[16] Thanks, however, to a new generation of scholars – including in particular David Brown, Fiona Cowell, Keith Goodway and David Jacques – it is now becoming clear that the situation was rather more complicated.[17] To some extent Brown's prominence in the annals of garden history may be due to the success of his business and the status and importance of his clients, rather than to any necessary superiority of ability – or even originality.

Certainly, although in financial terms these other designers may not have been in the same league as Brown, many were nevertheless gifted artists. William Emes, for example, a younger contemporary of Brown, was a designer of some importance and sensitivity. He worked on a number of prestigious commissions, especially in the Midlands, including Sandon (Staffs), Tixall (Staffs), and Hawkstone Park (Shropshire). Emes had a particular reputation for creating lakes and cascades. Nathaniel Richmond was also patronized by prominent members of society, and worked on the grounds of a number of important residences, including Saltram House (Devon) (for John Parker, with whom he appears to have fallen out). Richmond's ability was recognized by Humphry Repton, writing in 1788 a few years after the former's death and at the start of his own career. The circular letter he sent out to friends and prospective clients suggested that the profession of landscape gardener had been neglected 'since the loss of Brown and Richmond', adding that 'the works of Kent, Brown and Richmond have been the places of my worship'.[18] In the Red Book for Lamer (Herts, 1792) Repton described himself 'rather called in to compleat the plan suggested by the late Mr Richmond, than to take up the whole from the beginning', adding that he considered 'the late Mr Richmond as the only person since the immortal Brown whose ideas were at all correct' on the subject of landscape gardening.

Repton (as far as I am aware) makes no reference to Richard Woods, but the latter, too, clearly had a formidable reputation in the 1760s and '70s, and was considered by some of the greatest in the land as a perfectly respectable alternative to Brown. Lord Melbourne, for example, employed him to transform the grounds around his new mansion (designed by James Paine) at Brocket Hall (Herts), even though the main function of this residence was to entertain notables from the nearby metropolis and thus further Melbourne's political career.[19] Of course, we should not imply that all these practitioners had identical styles, although they did have much in common. There were particular differences, subtleties of emphasis. Thus, over the long space of his career, Brown gradually dropped the more architectural features from his parks and pleasure grounds, but these continued to figure large in Woods' designs to the end of his career. Woods continued, for example, to use Kent's device of a grotto to disguise the end of an artificial river.

Just as Brown had learnt part at least of his trade from working with Kent, some of these designers – such as Richmond, or Adam Mickle – originally worked as members of Brown's team before setting up in business on their own. Once established, however, their practices seem to have been more geographically circumscribed than that of Brown, whose commissions were spread fairly evenly across the country. Richmond seems to have carried out most of his work in Hertfordshire, Buckinghamshire and the adjacent counties, while Francis Richardson's activities were largely restricted to Yorkshire and Northumberland. Others changed the focus of their operations over the course of their careers. Thus Richard Woods' first commissions, between 1758 and 1761, were in

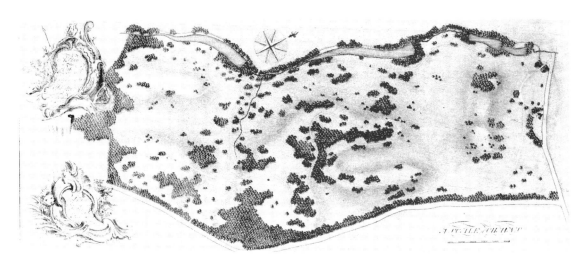

34. William Emes' design for the park at Oakedge, Staffordshire, 1776, features irregular naturalistic planting and serpentine carriage drives.

Berkshire and Buckinghamshire; in the early 1760s most were in Yorkshire or Northumberland, while from 1765 to 1792 well over half were in Essex or the adjacent counties, and of the remainder all except seven were in the south-east of England.[20]

As well as these important designers a host of other practitioners sprang up in the major provincial towns, advertising their services in the expanding local press. A little later, Repton was to be scathing about the competence of such men. But while there were unquestionably many who produced what seems, at least from the perspective of the present, to be derivative rubbish, others produced fine, striking designs. Many had, indeed, originally worked with Richmond, or Woods, or Emes: a fact they usually capitalized on in their advertisements. Thus *The Times* of June 1794 carried a notice that

> C. Sandys (late foreman to Mr Emes) respectfully offers his services to the Nobility and Gentry to lay out Pleasure Grounds. . . . No. 5 Buxton Place Lambeth.

But many landscape parks were not designed by professional designers at all, but by the estate gardener, the land agent, the owner, or some combination of these. The essential simplicity of Brown's style made it easy to copy, at least after a fashion. Members of the gentry continued to visit great houses and their grounds in the second half of the century even more assiduously than they had done in the first. By the 1770s some of the more popular destinations had fixed open days, and in the following decade some began to issue admission tickets.[21] Many landowners built inns near their residences to house genteel visitors, as at Castle Howard, where it was reported in 1768 that 'the entrance to the park is thro a magnificent Gateway on each side of which is a stone Building made use of as an Inn'.[22] At many of these places, it was the gardens as much as or even more than the mansion house that visitors flocked to see, and they would often be provided with transportation, in the form of a small chaise or sedan chair, in order to be shown the various sites and vistas. Returning home, they were keen to emulate what they had seen. This, together with the availability of professional designers in most of the major provincial towns, ensured that the designs of Brown and the others diffused swiftly down the social scale.

But not that swiftly. We should not assume that all members of the landed gentry eagerly accepted the new naturalistic style in the decades after 1750, or were happy to look out of their front windows across a boundless sea of turf. Map evidence, in particular, suggests that many were reluctant to demolish the walled courts around the house, even when they already possessed a park of some kind beyond them. Beeston St Lawrence (Norfolk), for example, had a park as early as 1756, but the walled gardens were still maintained all around the hall as late as 1776. When they were finally removed in that year Richard Hulton, brother-in-law of the owner, Jacob Preston, lamented to his sister how

> Mr Preston had one of the Gentleman Improvers here to modernise his grounds and is busy levelling his lawns, removing gardens, walls and trees and laying down a new kitchen garden more remote from the house. How it would grieve you if you were here . . . but so it must be, our ideas are more extensive than those of our ancestors. They were cribbed up in small apartments, and sat in little cane chairs admiring the pretty gardens edged with box and yew trees. We now indulge in elbow chairs, in apartments 20' by 30' by 15' high, and must extend our view over improved grounds as far as the eye can see without any disagreeable object intervening.[23]

Even among the larger landowners change was often slow. In 1769 Lybbe Powys described the 'Fine gloomy garden quite in the old style' beside the Waller family's residence of Hall Barn (Bucks), while a little later she visited Shotover (Oxon), with its 'Very fine gardens . . . straight avenues terminated by obelisks, temples porticoes &c: it has an air of grandeur.'[24] Nevertheless, by the time of Brown's death in 1783, resistance was fading. Not only the tide of fashion, but the increasing wealth available to make 'improvements', ensured that by the end of the century all residences of any consequence were surrounded by a landscape park, and appeared to stand in an open sea of grass.

THE GENIUS OF THE PLACE

Landscape parks thus became the *sine qua non* of true gentility, and by the end of the century their distribution was almost a map of polite society. In some areas there were many, in some few, a complicated pattern born of the interplay of a number of social and economic factors. There were, for example, some districts characterized by large numbers of small and medium-sized parks. These were, in particular, a feature of the hinterlands of the larger towns and cities – the county towns, the regional capitals such as Bristol, York, or Norwich, and the metropolis itself. The close packing of parks in such localities can be explained in at least two ways. Some surrounded the homes of established landed families who, all things being equal, preferred to dwell on that portion of their estates nearest a major population centre, for the eminently sensible reason that towns offered opportunities for the kinds of entertainment – assemblies, theatres, above all shopping – without which, in the minds of most members of polite society, life was unbearable. Living *within* a town, however, was equally anathema to these people. The growth of urban centres through the previous century, the spread of industrialization, all ensured that towns were increasingly seen as unwholesome places. From the late seventeenth century onwards, the joys of country living had been lauded by poets and essayists. The concentration of landscape parks in the vicinity of major urban centres reveals clearly that, like today's yuppies, the gentry chose (if the disposition of their estates allowed it) to have the best of both worlds.

Some of these parks, however, were the property of merchants, financiers or industrialists who, having made a significant fortune, were able to acquire enough land on the edge of town to build a neat villa in a small park, even if they did not aspire to a small landed estate in the fullest sense. Thus located, they could enjoy both the benefits of rural life and keep a keen eye on their business concerns.

It was not only the presence of a large urban centre that could produce clusters of parks. Areas of particular natural beauty, especially those within easy reach of the metropolis, also acted as magnets for the rich. Repton thought that the number of parks in the valley of the River Lea in Hertfordshire, between Hertford and Welwyn, would continue to grow until 'united woods and lawns will by extending thro' the whole valley enrich the general face of the country'.[25]

In marked contrast to such areas were those in which there were fewer parks, but these mainly large ones. Such districts were briefly discussed in Chapter 1: areas of light and often comparatively less fertile soils dominated by arable farming regimes, areas which, through the sixteenth and seventeenth centuries, had become increasingly dominated by very large landed estates. The heathlands of west Norfolk or east Suffolk, the wolds of Yorkshire or Lincolnshire, parts of Nottinghamshire, much of the downland of southern England, were all examples of such areas.

Thirdly, we should note those places in which parks of any kind were comparatively thin on the ground. These were mainly areas which were both remote from the main urban centres, and dominated by pastoral farming. In such areas there were often large numbers of small freeholders and while large estates had, by the eighteenth century, often bought up much of the land, there were few resident landowners of any consequence and thus few parks. The claylands of East Anglia, the Kent and Sussex Weald, parts of the West Country and much of the Highland zone of England fall into this category.

There were regional variations in the appearance, as well as in the distribution, of parks. The ideal landscape park contained, in the middle ground, a substantial area of water, preferably a serpentine lake. But environmental circumstances ensured that in some regions this ideal was systematically thwarted. In the Chilterns, for example, a large number of parks had been created by the end of the eighteenth century but only a few of these – West Wycombe, Latimer, Luton Hoo – had lakes. These were all located in the lower stretches of the principal river valleys. In their higher reaches, and on the level plateaux between them, it was impossible to create lakes because there were no surface watercourses, the rainwater disappearing almost immediately into the porous chalk. Thus it was that even extensive parks like those at Tring, or Beechwood, or Watlington, were devoid of ornamental water.[26]

Such variations were, however, relatively minor. As contemporary critics pointed out, the landscape park was in many ways a stereotyped product, its essential features the same from Northumberland to Surrey. In theory, art should be used to bring out and enhance the natural character of a place – a notion not entirely dissimilar to older Neoplatonic concepts of gardening in which topiary, say, had been employed to bring out the natural form of a tree or shrub. Yet the creation of a park was as often as not as much a negation of local character as an act of homage to the genius of the place: not least because 'nature' often required quite drastic improvement. One visitor to Welbeck Abbey (Notts) in 1768 candidly described how the park 'in some parts is much beholden to art for its beauty, in others it remains in the state that Nature has placed it, very dreary and disagreeable'.[27] Above all, the landscape park's quiet pastoral scenery was an alien imposition on the more rugged terrain of northern and western England. Smoothness of contours was everything, and at Alnwick (Northumberland) the slope below the castle was cleared of rocks and boulders and turfed by Brown in 1760.[28]

More important, perhaps, than any regional variations in the appearance and structure of parks were those relating to the status and wealth of their owners. The greatest landowners were more likely to employ sophisticated designers such as Brown or Richmond or Woods. At this level the casual, almost careless appearance of the landscape belied the meticulous care bestowed on every detail: as at Blenheim Palace (Oxon) where, travelling along Brown's drives at carriage height, 'a series of carefully composed views unfolds one after the other'.[29] The parks of the great landowners were also generally larger than those of the local gentry, sometimes extending over a thousand hectares or more, and were more likely to violate the 'genius of the place' through extensive schemes of earth-movement to open up views and vistas. The smaller parks of the parish gentry were less 'designed', less sophisticated. Yet once again the extent of variation should not be exaggerated. True, there was a lower level where not only cartographers, but society generally, were clearly uncertain about bestowing the epithet 'park' on a gentleman's grounds, preferring instead the term 'lawn' or 'paddock'. But above a certain size – probably around 25 hectares, if designed with care – an area of grass and trees would make a respectable park, and show the world that the owner was unquestionably a member of the landowning élite.

GARDENS AND PLEASURE GROUNDS

Historians always tend to seize on what is new in any period. An overemphasis on novelty, one could almost say, is an occupational hazard. What was new in the

35. Trentham Hall, Staffordshire, as illustrated in William Watts' The Seats of the Nobility and Gentry *(1779). The house looks out on to open parkland, apparently set free of all gardens.*

eighteenth century was the open parkland setting for the gentleman's mansion: and as a result, the fate of gardens and pleasure grounds in the period after 1760 has often been misunderstood. Contrary to what is still sometimes suggested, these did not disappear from the country estate – an assertion that may surprise some readers. From the early nineteenth century onwards, we have become accustomed to hear how Brown and his 'imitators' systematically destroyed all gardens in the vicinity of the house. Repton, for example, described in 1816 how 'The Pleasures of a Garden have of late been very much neglected', because of

> The prevailing custom of placing a House in the middle of a Park, detached from all objects, whether of convenience or magnificence, and thus making a country residence as solitary and unconnected as the Prison on Dartmoor.[30]

And it is true that late eighteenth-century illustrations of fashionable country houses invariably show them surrounded by the sweeping parkland, adrift in an endless sea of turf. Every house illustrated in Watts' *The Seats of the Nobility and Gentry* of 1779, for example, is set in the familiar, simple landscape of trees and grass, without a trace of parterres, shrubberies, flower-beds, or terraces (Figure 35).[31] Yet it is also clear that letters, diaries, and published texts produced in this period make frequent references to flowers, gardens, and pleasure grounds. This is another of those curious conundrums of garden history, but one with a simple solution. Pleasure grounds did indeed continue to be created and maintained at most country houses in this period, but they were now usually hidden away from the main façade of the house, placed to the sides or rear. This was a logical development, perhaps, of the marginal position which serpentine pleasure grounds had often occupied within the formal structure of many mid-century gardens although, as we shall see, there are other (and more interesting) explanations for this arrangement.

Such pleasure grounds continued to develop essentially along the lines established during the 1740s and '50s. Geometric layouts were occasionally employed, as at Wormsley (Bucks), designed by Woods in 1779, where the pleasure grounds were arranged in regular circles and elipses.[32] More usually they featured curvilinear, relatively narrow gravel paths, which ran through areas of grass and shrubbery planted with varying densities of trees. These usually

36. *Woodside, Old Windsor, Berkshire. This watercolour by Thomas Robins, c. 1755, gives a good impression of the elaborate pleasure grounds of the middle and later decades of the eighteenth century.*

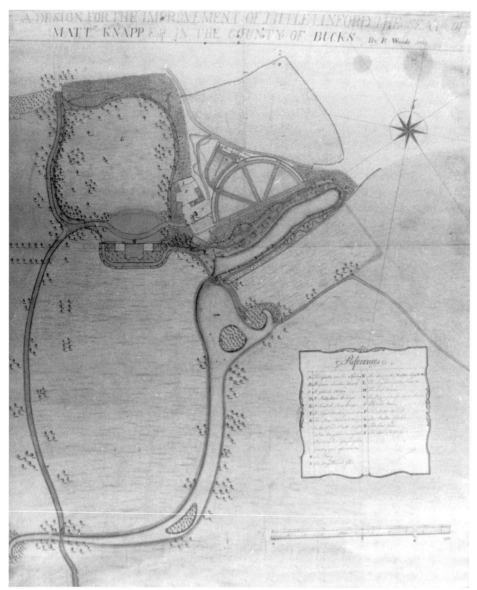

37. Linford, Buckinghamshire: Richard Woods' design of 1762. The house faces across parkland, but to the east there is an elaborate garden, laid out around a narrow lake.

provided a circuit walk, mirroring the circuit drive within the park. At Wimpole, following the demolition of the walled courts in 1752, the grounds consisted of 'a large green lawn . . . bounded by Clumps of Trees and flowering shrubs, a broad serpentine walk through them'.[33] Many pleasure grounds, like those of the previous period, were positively crammed with garden buildings and other features. Thus at Nuneham Courtenay (Oxon) the elaborate flower gardens laid out by William Mason had 'bowers, statues, inscriptions, busts, temples'.[34] The design drawn up by Richard Woods for Linford House (Bucks) in 1762 included, to the east of the mansion and away from the main front, a large pleasure ground arranged around a long, slightly serpentine lake (Figure 37). This consisted of an area of mown grass, bordered by dense shrubberies, and scattered with smaller 'islands' of shrubs. Typically, a varied collection of seats and garden buildings was strung along the circuit path: the 'Grotto over the spring', the gothic alcove, the Palladian bridge, the 'rustick stone bridge', etc.[35]

Such gardens were not simply commissioned by particularly conservative clients who could not accept the bold simplicity of Brown's sweeping lines. Brown himself generally laid out pleasure grounds of this kind. It was walled, geometric gardens in front of the main façade of the house which he systematically destroyed, not gardens *per se*. Thus, for example, his design for Petworth (Sussex) in 1751 featured an elaborate pleasure ground which contained two impressive garden buildings inherited from the earlier gardens: a classical rotunda and a Doric temple. A wide variety of flowering shrubs and flowers was planted, including butcher's broom, spiraea, lilac, and acacia. There were gardens for aloes, and for bay trees, plantations of evergreens and a cypress walk.[36] In 1763 Horace Walpole criticized Brown's work at Longleat (Wilts), noting that 'there is a new garden making, and a gate built, designed by Mr Brown, too small, and in a false taste'.[37] But the clearest indication of Brown's continued involvement in gardens comes from the pen of his bitterest opponent, Uvedale Price, writing a decade or so after Brown's death:

> In my idea, Mr Brown has been most successful in what may properly be called the garden, though not in that part of it which is nearest the house. The old improvers went abruptly from the formal garden to the grounds, or park; but the modern pleasure garden with its shrubs and exotics would form a very just and easy gradation from architectural ornaments, to the natural woods, thickets and pastures.[38]

The shrubberies in late eighteenth-century gardens often included, on their periphery, lower-growing herbaceous plants: and élite pleasure grounds often contained displays of flowers, sometimes in island beds or in specialized gardens. Plans or illustrations of these are known from Hartwell (Bucks, 1799), Nuneham Courtenay (Oxon, 1777), and elsewhere. The sophistication of gardens and pleasure grounds at the highest social levels in this period is reflected in the numbers of staff required for their maintenance. At Luton Hoo (Beds) in 1783 twelve men were employed 'exclusive of two head gardeners that is one for the grounds and shrubberies and one for the kitchen garden and pinery'.[39] In 1786, according to Thomas Jefferson, fifty people were employed in the pleasure grounds at Blenheim.[40] Staff were required not only to maintain the grounds, but also to look after the animals in the menageries which became an increasingly popular feature of gardens from the 1760s.

The residences of the local gentry featured smaller and simpler versions of this kind of thing. In 1784 the French tourist François de La Rochefoucauld described how

> Near the house, usually immediately round it, is what the English call the garden. It is a small pleasure ground, extremely well tended, with little well-rolled gravel paths; the grass is cut every week and the trees, which are of rare kinds, grow there naturally, though every care is taken to prevent moss and ivy growing upon them. In a thousand other ways, too, which one does not notice, care is taken to make these gardens attractive. Flowers are planted in them . . .[41]

The less fashionable members of the gentry had rather different arrangements: as we have seen, they often retained their walled gardens into the 1770s or even the 1780s. No less an authority than Horace Walpole suggested that

> Whenever a family can purloin a warm and even an old-fashioned garden from the landscape designed for them by the undertaker of fashion, without interfering with the picture, they will find satisfactions on those days that they do not invite strangers to come and see their improvements.[42]

'Without interfering with the picture' – that is a crucial phrase. If walled gardens lay away from the main façade, owners were more likely to retain them: and if so, might continue to enjoy old-fashioned geometric arrangements of flowers there (Figure 38). Other factors that encouraged the retention of such archaic arrangements included the age of the owner, for the elderly were less likely to indulge in 'modern' improvements. Even when the rising tide of fashion dictated the removal of walled gardens, some of their recreational and ornamental roles migrated to the kitchen garden, still walled but now usually hidden away behind the stable block or – more rarely – in the distant recesses of the park. Repton praised the kitchen garden's recreational role:

> There are many days in winter when a warm, dry, but secluded walk, under the shelter of a north or east wall, would be preferred to the most beautiful but exposed landscape; and in the early spring . . . some early flowers and vegetables may cheer the sight.[43]

Walled gardens were thus swept away from the vicinity of the mansion but gardens of some kind were retained. True, travellers' descriptions occasionally imply that country house gardens were of limited extent. One in 1777 criticized the surroundings of Newby Hall (Yorks) on the grounds that it required 'softening about the house and is too deficient in every thing in the Garden stile'.[44] But the very fact that such comments could be made indicates, clearly enough, what visitors *expected* to see at a fashionable residence.

38. Gawthorpe Hall, Lancashire, c. 1780. Where enclosed gardens such as these survived into the later eighteenth century, the planting within them could remain extremely formal.

THE LANDSCAPE OF THE PARK

The pleasure grounds of the 1760s and '70s developed directly from the serpentine compartments in the gardens of earlier decades. The landscape park, in contrast, had a very different pedigree. Contemporaries claimed that it was a 'natural' landscape, and many modern commentators have followed them. Yet what does 'natural' mean in the context of the eighteenth-century English landscape? There were no really natural landscapes left in the country by this date, if by the term we mean environments which had not been extensively modified by human intervention. There were only landscapes which seemed more 'natural' than others in the sense that traces of human activity within them were less obvious: non-arable landscapes, especially those without walls or hedges, such as forests, woods, heaths, upland moors and mountains (the latter increasingly admired by visitors and tourists from the middle years of the century). Yet these look nothing like the landscape park. It was a particular kind of nature which was presented, re-presented, here, as Horace Walpole pointed out as early as the 1760s. He traced the origins of the landscape style back to the ancient deer parks of England, which he described as 'contracted forests, and extended gardens', adding that it was

> Extraordinary that having so long ago stumbled on the principle of modern gardening, we should have persisted in retaining its reverse, symmetrical and unnatural gardening.[45]

This observation should come as no surprise, for we have already tracked the slow evolution of the deer park as an aesthetic landscape; the increasing integration of the design of parkland and garden; and the gradual separation of the idea of the 'park' from any necessary association with deer. In one sense, the stripping away of geometric clutter from the immediate vicinity of the house was simply the culmination of a long-drawn-out development, the final triumph of the park over the garden as the prime setting for the country house.

Not only did the style of the landscape park owe much to the decorative wood-pasture landscape of the post-medieval deer park. Many of the most famous landscape parks were, in fact, mere modifications of existing deer parks. This was particularly true of Brown's own designs: and hardly surprising, given the nature of his clientele, members of the country's élite and thus precisely the kinds of people who would have owned a park. The majority of 'Brown's' parks, in fact, had already been in existence for centuries. At places such as Longleat (Wilts) or Burghley (Northants) – both deer parks created in Elizabethan times – the removal of formal gardens from around the house simply allowed the parkland turf to sweep uninterrupted to its walls.[46] Brown's contribution here – or at such famous sites as Petworth (Sussex), Nuneham (Oxon), or Moccas (Heref.) – was principally one of subtraction, the removal of formal elements. True, he did add new plantations, especially belts and clumps; and frequently a lake in the middle distance (although, in many cases, this was through the conversion of existing formal canals and basins).

The majority of eighteenth-century parks – those designed by Brown's 'imitators' – were entirely new creations. Yet their sweeping irregularity – the turf, scattered trees and larger stands of woodland – clearly drew heavily on the scenery of the traditional park. So too, perhaps, did the idea of the lake, lying naturalistically in the middle distance: for many traditional deer parks, as we have seen, contained 'great waters', large fish ponds created – like the serpentine lakes of the landscape park – by erecting an earthen dam across the valley of a stream or river. Indeed, those who constructed such features in the 1750s and '60s sometimes confused the two. The elegant lake designed by Nathaniel Richmond for the park at Shardelowes (Bucks) was, significantly, described by the contractor as 'the Great Pond'.[47]

Careful examination of eighteenth-century parks reveals how painstakingly their makers utilized existing trees in order to create, from the start, an appearance of antiquity. Some large trees would be retained when avenues were felled, to add to the sylvan nature of the scene. More importantly, when an area was enclosed to make a park the hedgerows within it were invariably levelled and their accompanying ditches filled, but a proportion – often a very high proportion

39. A line of ancient pollarded oaks in North Elmham Park, Norfolk. The creators of eighteenth-century parks generally retained many of the trees which had been growing in the fields and hedges of the earlier agricultural landscape.

– of the hedgerow trees were allowed to remain. Eighteenth- and nineteenth-century maps of parkland often show large numbers of trees growing in rough lines which can frequently be correlated with the pattern of hedges shown on earlier maps. With the passing of time and the loss of timber, such alignments have generally become less noticeable in the landscape, but even so many parks still contain trees that were already old when the former were first created. These trees are often massive pollards, dating in some instances back to late medieval times (Figure 39). Sometimes slight banks, representing the levelled remains of the hedges in which they once stood, can be seen beside them. Existing woods and copses would also be incorporated into the new landscape. Indeed, the disposition of woods often had a determining influence on the boundaries of a park: belts were often formed by joining together a number of small woods and copses – the joining of 'willing woods', as Pope might have put it.[48]

The extent to which all this was possible, however, depended on the nature of the local landscape. In areas which had been long enclosed the 'genius of the place' smiled upon the park-maker. Here there were old trees and woods in abundance, just waiting to be used in the new landscape. In such areas eighteenth-century parks often preserve large chunks of the earlier working countryside. Thus at Sotterley (Suffolk) the massive pollards from the earlier hedgerows, left to create stands of open woodland in the park, give a clear indication of the phenomenal numbers of hedgerow trees which once existed in this landscape. Wood Hall (Herts), with its ancient hornbeam pollards, is another good example.

It was in the long since enclosed 'ancient countrysides' of the south and east of England, and the west, that ample opportunities for this kind of park-making were available to almost all land owners, from local squire to great aristocrat. In the Midlands, and in parts of the south and north-east of England, the situation was rather different. Traditionally these had been hedgeless 'champion' areas, open-field countrysides, and while the heartlands of the great estates had usually been enclosed long before, the lands of lesser landowners had often been but recently consolidated. Here there was often little in the way of pre-existing timber, and there was a strong temptation to rely on fast-growing softwoods to provide the basic structure of the park. Repton hated parks of this type, partly because of the often comparatively lowly social status of their owners, and referred disparagingly to 'bald naked' parks, 'belted and clumped with spruce firs, and larches, and Lombardy poplars'.[49] Such tacky landscapes were, to judge from surviving descriptions and illustrations, exceptions. Conifers were more widely planted in landscape parks than we sometimes suppose: the park at Woburn Abbey (Beds) was said to be full of 'oak and Fur' in 1768.[50] Most, however, were dominated by hardwood planting and thus continued the tradition of the decorative, one might almost say 'tidied up', parkland which had evolved in the sixteenth and seventeenth centuries. But we cannot necessarily derive all aspects of the landscape park from the traditional landscape of the deer park, and in particular we need to consider the origins of the two most characteristic and distinctive forms of parkland planting – the clump and the belt.

The origin of clumps – small, densely planted groups of trees, of oval or circular plan – has been the subject of some debate, and the inspiration for them may have come from a number of sources. In a recent article Asger Ørum-Larsen suggested that the clump may have been inspired by a medieval coppicing system frequently encountered in medieval and post-medieval Scandinavia: the so-called meadow copse (*loveng*).[51] These were small copses of ash, elm and other trees scattered irregularly about the meadows which were used to produce not only wood but also leafy hay for animal feed. The analogy is intriguing but there does not, at present, appear to be much evidence for this form of woodland management in England. What this country did possess in large numbers, however, at least in old enclosed areas, were small copses and 'grovets' – tiny woods in the corners of fields and around field ponds. Some at least of the clumps in eighteenth-century parks originated as these, and to some extent the idea for creating new ones may have done so too.

Traditionally, the origins of the clump have been traced to earlier phases of garden design, and in particular to the work of Brown's predecessor William Kent.[52] He used clumps both in the garden areas close to the house and also out in the wider landscape, usually as a device to frame some architectural feature, a classical temple or a lodge masquerading as a triumphal arch. Kent's clumps were thus an aspect of the classical picture-painting which formed so important a strand in the garden designs of the 1730s and '40s, and their inspiration can be found in the paintings of Italian landscapes by Claude, Poussin and the rest. Here

40. Clumps and perimeter belt in Wimpole Park, Cambridgeshire.

we can see small groups of trees shading romantic crumbling ruins just as Kent's clumps at Euston (Suffolk) or Holkham (Norfolk) flanked the correct Palladian structures which formed focal points in these great landscapes. Examination of the remains of Kent's clumps at Holkham shows that they were planted with beech, just like many of Brown's. We need, however, to be a little cautious here. The drawing which Kent prepared for the site shows the clumps containing a substantial, in many a dominant, conifer element: and this is apparently confirmed by the estate accounts which, for the years in which they were planted, record the purchase of quantities of cedar, silver fir, larch and pine (Figure 41).[53] Kent's picture was intended to show the mature appearance of the planting: the conifers were more than nurses but an intended part of the final effect, which clearly mirrored the appearance of the features in the paintings of artists like Claude. Their subsequent character is the result of the comparatively short lifespan of the conifer component. There is, therefore, something of a difference between the broadleaf clumps of Brown and his contemporaries, and the garden-like plantings of Kent aimed at producing a romantic echo of the Italian landscape.

Although Kent is often credited as the 'inventor' of the parkland clump, there is abundant evidence to suggest that it has a longer pedigree. Clumps, it is true, do not seem to have been a feature of medieval deer parks. But the more ornamental parks of the post-medieval periods sometimes contained small, tightly planted groups of trees very similar to Brown's clumps, as can be seen from some

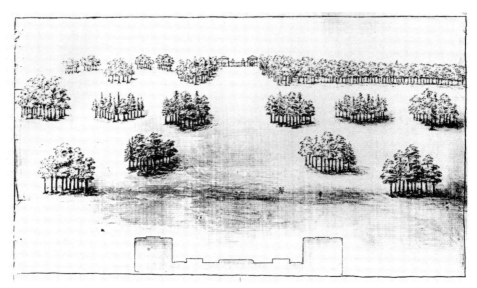

41. William Kent's design for the North Lawn, Holkham, Norfolk, c. 1745. Note the prominent conifer element in the clumps.

of the illustrations in Kip and Knyff's *Britannia Illustrata* of 1707.[54] Circular or ovoid clumps feature in a number of maps and designs in the early part of the eighteenth century, such as Stephen Switzer's design for Nostell Priory (Yorks). Philip Miller, writing in 1731 (before any of Kent's clumps were planted) noted that oak trees were 'very proper for a Wilderness in large gardens, or to plant in Clumps in parks'.[55] Kent may have been an influence in the development of Brown's clumps, but he was perhaps less important than has sometimes been suggested.

The origins of perimeter belts are, if anything, even more problematic, although it is clear that these too existed long before the advent of Brown. Like clumps, they may have owed something to traditional features of the working countryside. John Phibbs has pointed out the similarities between parkland belts and the strips of woodland which ran round the edges of many fields in the early-enclosed counties of Hertfordshire, Buckinghamshire and Kent, strips which often – like many of Brown's belts – had a path or drive meandering through them.[56] Whatever the truth of this suggestion, Brown was not the first to plant strips of woodland on the boundaries of parks. Some deer parks had them by the end of the seventeenth century – that at Wimpole (Cambs), for example, was in place by the 1690s.[57] By the mid-1720s Robert Walpole's park at Houghton had a belt which, like some of those later created by Brown, had a drive running down its centre.[58]

Yet to search for the precise origins of such features as belts or clumps – to seek their models in earlier phases of garden design, in the everyday 'natural' landscape, or in this or that school of painting – is to miss the point. The important question is why these features were now combined in this distinctive way, and why the resulting assemblage came to be considered the only correct setting for a gentleman's house. And this question can only be answered by examining the landscape park in its wider context; that of the rapidly changing society of England in the second half of the eighteenth century.

CHAPTER FIVE

Property and Prospect

THE LANDSCAPE OF EXCLUSION

Most modern historians agree that the late eighteenth century was a period in which the social map was being redrawn: one in which there was a fundamental realignment of divisions within society, and especially within rural society.[1] As we have seen, the early eighteenth century had witnessed a prolonged agricultural depression which, combined with high levels of direct taxation, had ensured a general decline in the fortunes and ultimately the numbers of small landowners, particularly freehold farmers. This was now followed by a period of economic expansion, rising agricultural prices and rising rents which greatly benefited the local gentry. What was good for the landowner and large farmer was less good for the rural poor, however. Poverty and unemployment increased inexorably after 1750, as population growth began to outstrip the number of jobs available in villages, as the value of real wages fell, and as inflation set in with a vengeance. The situation in rural communities deteriorated still further in the last decades of the century when Napoleon's blockade caused food prices to go through the roof.

Throughout the second half of the century landlords were keen to cash in on the opportunities offered by demographic recovery and economic expansion, and seem in general to have managed their estates with a greater eye to efficiency and profits than before. They were eager, above all, to amalgamate smaller family farms into larger, more productive units. In a multitude of ways the old rural order was changing. Frances Brooke no doubt exaggerated the situation in the following passage from her novel of 1761, *History of Lady Julia Mandeville*. But it is, nevertheless, a clear statement of how many contemporaries perceived change in the countryside:

It is with infinite pain I see Lord T— pursuing a plan, which has drawn on him the curse of thousands, and made his estate a scene of desolation; his farms are in the hands of a few men, to whom the sons of the old tenants are either forced to be servants, or to leave the country to get their bread elsewhere. The village, large, and once populous, is reduced to about eight families; a dreary silence reigns on their deserted fields . . .[2]

It is against this background of a growing gulf between rich and poor, between squire and community, that we first need to examine the landscape of the park. For what the creations of Brown and his 'imitators' offered, above all, was privacy

42. Old beech trees, Longleat, Wiltshire, probably planted during Brown's 'improvements'.

and seclusion. This much is immediately apparent from even a cursory examination of their spatial structure. The park was arranged in such a way that the kinds of views out into the surrounding countryside which had been a feature of many mid-century landscape gardens – a distant glimpse of a farm or a group of cottages – were now usually excluded. This, of course, was the main purpose of the perimeter belt which was the most characteristic form of parkland planting. The park was enclosed, segregating, secluding. More so, indeed, than it often appears on plan, for given the size of these landscapes the natural swell of landforms was often enough to obscure any views of the outside world. Belts were essential only where the lie of the land opened up distant prospects. The lodges constructed at the entrances to the park, features which became increasingly common from the 1770s, served a more direct function in the private landscape, monitoring access to it yet at the same time proclaiming the presence of a wealthy family and its establishment.[3]

The mansion thus lay in the midst of an insulating sea of turf, hidden from view by the encircling belts. And once established as a sign and symbol of exclusivity, the patterns of social contact which the park engendered could only serve to perpetuate the emerging divisions in rural society. But it was not just the crowded cottages of the impoverished *rural* poor and the fields of their labour from which the gentry increasingly wished to retreat. In the north of England, and in the Midlands, the quickening pace of economic change was beginning to leave ugly scars. The attitude of the landowners to industrial development was ambiguous: they might distrust the social changes it brought, the perceived threat to the established social order, but there was money to be made from exploiting, in particular, the mineral resources of an estate. Sir Thomas Wentworth of Bretton Hall (Yorks) wrote in 1782 how

> The lead trade and price have advanced which adds to one's spirits as I can now have more workmen to entertain me here pulling down the walls and trees of the courts and below the Terras and laying all open to the . . . Park.[4]

Industrialization might fund the development of gardens and parks but few wanted to view its consequences: spoil heaps, smoke belching from chimneys, or the mean dwellings of an emerging industrial working class. At Horsford Hall in Yorkshire the grounds to the north of the mansion rose sharply to the colliery on Hunger Hills: from the 1780s extensive tree-planting was carried out here, so that the presence of industry would not impinge on the scene.[5] At Parlington Hall in the same county the house and its park lay sandwiched between the town of Aberford and the Great North Road to the north-east, and a large colliery to the south-west. The coal pits and their accompanying engines were screened by a thick plantation, while the coal road running thence to the Great North Road was sunk in a cutting as it ran close to the house, between park and garden, forming in effect a gigantic ha-ha across which the main drive to the hall was carried on a substantial bridge.[6]

Some eighteenth-century writers on garden design criticized the park as a stereotyped landscape – an artificial construction imposed on the local countryside with (in spite of the contemporary rhetoric about consulting the 'genius of the place') scant regard for the character of the local topography. Mrs

Lybbe Powys described in 1776 how 'The rage for laying out grounds makes every nobleman and gentleman a copier of their neighbour, till every fine place throughout England is comparatively, at least, alike.'[7] Yet there is an important sense in which this mass-produced quality was part of the park's success. Consider for a moment the experience of a gentleman and his family visiting neighbours. They leave their house and step into one of the new, well-sprung coaches standing on the forecourt. They drive through, and then out of the park. They follow lanes and then turnpike roads – another crucial improvement, the very veins and arteries of 'polite society'. They pass through the intervening countryside but without stopping, observing the scenery at a distance, through the windows of their comfortable conveyance. Arriving at their destination they pass through the lodge gates and the belt and enter a landscape similar – in some cases almost identical – to the one they have just left. They move from one safe, artificial, insulating pastoral scene to another.

The quest for privacy could, on occasions, have a dramatic impact on the ancient pattern of rural settlement. Goldsmith's poem *The Deserted Village*, describing a mythical village destroyed to make way for a park, is a sentimental yet not entirely unreasonable representation of the process:

> Have we not seen, at pleasure's lordly call
> The smiling, long-frequented village fall?
> Beheld the duteous son, the sire decay'd
> The modest matron, and the blushing maid
> Forc'd from their homes, a melancholy train
> To traverse climes beyond the western main.[8]

This image, of an organic rural community uprooted and destroyed to make way for the empty idleness of the landscape park, is a powerful one, but both contemporaries and modern writers have probably exaggerated the extent of the phenomenon in the second half of the eighteenth century. Many parks do contain isolated churches or the earthwork traces of vanished settlements, but these had often already declined before the park itself was created. Parishes which had dwindled, for whatever reason, in the late and post-medieval periods were more likely to fall into the hands of a single owner, who would thus gain a park, in the eighteenth century. From the late sixteenth century, moreover, many landowners deliberately reduced the size of settlements, and those villages which were unquestionably cleared to make way for parks had usually already experienced a substantial measure of contraction. Under the terms of the Elizabethan Poor Law, the principal proprietors and tenants in a parish were responsible for paying the poor rate. In 'closed parishes', as they came to be known, a sole owner often worked to reduce the number of dwellings, in order to limit the number of people who might, through age or ill health or illegitimacy, become claimants for poor relief.[9]

Nevertheless, emparking did have an important impact on settlement, especially in areas characterized by nucleated villages, such as Northamptonshire. Here no less than eight villages were entirely destroyed and a further twenty-five had their plans significantly altered by emparking in the period from 1720 to

1850. In areas of more dispersed settlement manorial residences often lay isolated from, or on the edge of, the main concentration of dwellings in a parish, and the effect of park-making on the village nucleus was therefore less pronounced. Nevertheless, individual farms or small groups of cottages were often removed, to make way for the broad sweeps of the parkland turf.

What received less contemporary attention was the impact of park-making on the local road network. Public rights of way – roads, tracks or footpaths – were frequently, indeed almost invariably, terminated or diverted when parks were laid out. In the early and middle decades of the century, this had been a costly and rather complex process. The landowner had either to get an Act of Parliament to close or divert the road in question – a legislative sledgehammer to crack a rather local nut – or else use the archaic legal procedure known as the *Inquisition ad Quod Damnum*. This involved the issuing of a writ in the Court of Chancery in London which empowered the sheriff of the county to convene a meeting of all the freeholders in the hundred in which the proposed alteration lay. They would then assent to or dissent from the proposed move. The process was time-consuming, cumbersome and expensive. Partly because of the growth of turnpike trusts in the second half of the century, and partly because of the expansion in the number of landscape parks, a law was passed in 1773 which made road closures and diversions much easier. All that was now required was the agreement of two county magistrates, men from the same social group as the park-maker and, as often as not, his neighbours or friends. Road closure orders make amusing reading, for they always maintain the polite fiction that the proposed change is for the good of the general public. A road so effected is always described as superfluous to local requirements, as an unnecessary burden on the parish, or as inconvenient in some way. The replacement, of course, is always of better quality, and more direct. Seldom is the real reason for the change expressly stated.

There is little evidence that road closures met with active opposition. The opinions of tenants and labourers could safely be ignored, and gentlemen generally acquiesced in their neighbour's road closures, at least if the correct legal procedures had been followed. In effect, both Road Closure Orders and the earlier writs of *Ad Quod Damnum* were instruments of legitimation, intended to avoid opposition by subjecting such changes to the scrutiny of those who mattered in local society – the neighbouring gentry or their representatives, the county magistrates.

It could be argued that roads were closed simply for aesthetic reasons: because carts and other traffic would interrupt the view, spoil the prospect. Even if this was true, it would itself mark a significant shift in aesthetic priorities, for in the 1730s and '40s distant views of busy roads had often been included in the prospect from house or gardens, as at Rousham, where a glimpse of the traffic on the neighbouring highway was, according to the gardener, one of the most pleasing features of the garden.[10] But it was not just roads that were moved or terminated. Public footpaths were also systematically re-routed. It was the public who used these routes who were the real problem, as Repton made clear in the Red Book for Tewin Water (Herts):

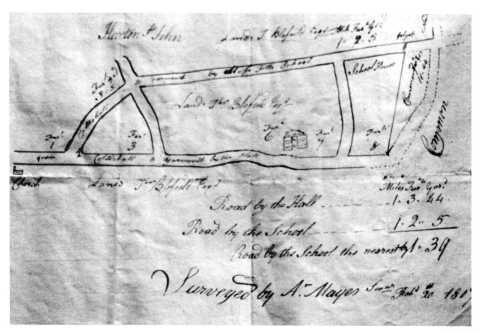

43. A road closure order for Hoveton, Norfolk, 1807. Such orders were usually accompanied by sketch maps like this. This one is typical: the road to be closed passes immediately in front of the mansion, too close for the new sensibilities of the landowners.

altho' the late possessor of Tewin Water might think a public road no less appropriate than cheerful immediately in front of the house; or a foot path . . . cutting up the lawn in another direction . . . passing close to the windows, leaving the house on a kind of peninsula surrounded by carts, waggons, gypsies, poachers, &c. &c. who feel they have a right of intrusion. Yet when the place with all its defects shall pass under the correcting hand of good taste, the view from the house will be changed with the views of its possessor.[11]

It is extremely difficult to estimate the number of roads and footpaths affected by emparking but the total must certainly have amounted to several thousand miles, particularly as the long and complex development and staged expansion of the larger landscape parks could (over a period of time) involve the closure of as many as five or ten separate rights of way. Although closed to the public, however, such roads did not always disappear entirely from the landscape. Running as they so often did past the front door of the mansion, they were often retained as one of the principal entrance drives, thus economizing on the cost of park-making. Where this did not happen, estate accounts suggest that great pains were taken to remove all trace of the feature by levelling and filling, and only occasionally does the line of a closed road survive as an obvious earthwork in the parkland turf. The remains of cleared villages – the sites of houses, the lines of property boundaries – were also subjected to peculiarly thorough (one almost wants to say ferocious)

44. Chippenham, Cambridgeshire. Late eighteenth-century lodge gates guard the northern approach to the park. The public road veers suddenly to the left here, indicating that it was diverted from its original course when the park was laid out.

levelling. It is as if every trace of the earlier community needed to be obliterated, expunged from memory.

The growing seclusion of the gentry did not go unnoticed. A local poet from Bedale in Yorkshire, for example, described the changes which had occurred in the parish during his own lifetime in the second half of the eighteenth century. The local squire had made significant alterations to his mansion house, The Rand. These completed, he had turned his attention to its immediate surroundings. Public roads and footpaths ran too close for the new sensibilities:

> And now them roads are done away,
> And one made in their room,
> Quite to the east, of wide display,
> Where you may go and come,
> Quite unobserved from the Rand,
> The trees do them seclude.
> If modern times, do call such grand
> Its from a gloomy mood.[12]

This, then, is the first and arguably the most important way in which we should read the park: as the landscape of polite exclusion. Walled gardens had, it is true, provided some degree of privacy. But the houses of neighbours, the cottagers with their pigs and their washing, had still been visible, if only from the upper-floor windows of the mansion. Now they were safely hidden behind the slowly maturing belts. Yet the park's ability to supply privacy may in part explain not only its popularity, but also certain aspects of its style. An insulating and segregating landscape had, by definition, to be an extensive one: and considering their size parks were a comparatively cheap form of ornamental landscape. They were certainly much cheaper to create and maintain than a geometric garden of equivalent size. We have already noted the extent to which the new landscapes perpetuated and utilized features of the old. When contemporary writers on landscape design urged owners to consult the 'genius of the place' – working with, rather than against, the character of the local topography, utilizing existing trees and woods – they were essentially advocating the creation of an ornamental landscape 'on the cheap'. Now it is true that some of the greatest landscape parks, especially those designed by Brown, featured substantial schemes of earth movement: the filling up of canals (as at Madingley (Cambs)), the raising of hillocks (as at Moor Park (Herts)) or the lowering of hills (as at Bowood (Wilts)).[13] But on the whole the new style involved – almost by definition – only rather minor alterations to the natural topography, and this had obvious implications for costs. The treatment of water is a case in point. The excavation of a geometric canal of any size could involve an expenditure of many hundreds of pounds. And as the scale of geometric gardens grew in the early years of the century, costs escalated accordingly. The semi-geometric lakes of the 1720s and '30s could be phenomenally expensive, imposed as they generally were upon the natural landforms. That created at Raynham (Norfolk) in 1720 covered only 3 hectares but cost no less than £1,690.[14] The serpentine lakes of the landscape park were, in comparison, much cheaper, at least if a stream and valley of suitable configuration were available, and the local subsoil impervious. Once the dam was constructed, nature did the rest. Other aspects of the landscape style were calculated to appeal to the cost-conscious squire. Bricks were expensive before the improvements in kiln technology of the nineteenth century. Large sums still had to be expended on the walls of the kitchen garden, but other walled courts could now be dispensed with. The pleasure grounds were usually separated from the park by a ha-ha: and if money was short this could always be constructed without a retaining wall of stone or brick, using instead a post-and-rail fence or even a hedge placed at the bottom of the ditch. Moreover, although some aristocratic parks were surrounded by perimeter walls dating from an early period (generally in areas where stone was freely available), these were not an essential feature of the landscape style and seem, on the whole, to be a phenomenon of the nineteenth rather than the eighteenth century. Of course, we should not take these arguments too far. The replacement of diverted roads, and the laying out of carriage drives, could be expensive; and although large numbers of existing trees might be retained from the existing landscape, large numbers of new ones needed to be planted, especially for the perimeter belts. Nevertheless, the point still holds. The landscape park represented a comparatively cheap way of creating landscapes which were both extensive and ornamental.

It is important to emphasize this comparative cheapness because many books on the history of garden design stress the opposite, pointing to the great sums expended on Brown's more costly creations: the £4,550 paid by the 3rd Earl Waldegrave for the alterations to the park and gardens at Navestock (Essex), the £5,000 spent at nearby Thorndon by Baron Petre, or the £21,000 stumped up for Langley (Bucks) and Blenheim (Oxon) by the Duke of Marlborough. These were indeed vast sums, although in relative terms perhaps not that great given that the owners in question were among the richest men in England and the payments spread over a number of years (ten at Navestock, six at Thorndon, and ten at Langley and Blenheim).[15] More usual was the £913 spent by Edmund Rolfe on

45. The landscape of exclusion. Doddington Park, Avon: the house isolated in its park as painted in 1796 by Charles Turner of Oxford.

creating his new park at Heacham (Norfolk) between 1768 and 1775, a figure which can be usefully compared with the £878 subsequently spent on the kitchen garden there and, a little later, the £4,128 expended on the new house. The park cost a great deal, but not an unreasonable amount. An analysis of Rolfe's accounts suggests that it never consumed more than 10 or 12 per cent of his annual average income, and this was probably typical.[16]

Parks were also comparatively cheap to maintain. Geometric gardens had long stretches of gravel paths, and extensive flower beds, which needed to be weeded, shrubs and hedges which had to be kept clipped. The landscape park, in contrast, had only the sweeping expanse of turf, which could be maintained at minimal cost. Payments might need to be made for flattening mole hills, or picking up boughs fallen from trees, but it was livestock rather than labourers who did most of the maintenance work: and from these a regular income could be derived. Moreover, as we shall see, the timber planted in and around the park was systematically exploited, a source of profit rather than (like the pleached trees of an earlier age) a constant drain on estate finances.

Yet while all this is true, we are still a long way from explaining the style of the park. Why did this *particular* form of landscape design develop, rather than some other? If an extensive but cheap way of laying out grounds was what society's élite required, then there were other ways in which this could have been achieved. Geometric blocks of trees, intersecting meshes of avenues, would not have been any more expensive to establish (or maintain) than designs based on irregular scatters and serpentine belts and clumps. Moreover, if the principal need was simply to enjoy an extensive private landscape, there is no obvious reason why this could not have included areas of garden (geometric or otherwise) prominently positioned in front of the principal façades of the house. Why, then, were the gentry so keen to marginalize and hide their gardens, to one side of the main façades of the house, while nevertheless in many cases continuing to spend substantial amounts of money on them? We have only told half the story: the real key to understanding the landscape of the park lies not so much in the growing gulf between rural landowners and their local communities as in the changing nature of social relationships *within* the propertied classes.

THE POLITE LANDSCAPE

Early eighteenth-century society had, like that of the previous century, been highly deferential and hierarchical. Great aristocrats and courtiers had been accorded a special status and dignity by the gentry as a whole, and relations between members of the two groups were hedged around with elaborate and often subtle rules of etiquette. Social gatherings involving the upper ranks of society were, in consequence, usually stiff and formal, almost ceremonial in nature, and guests tended to do one thing at a time, all together, in a group. During the course of the eighteenth century, however, all this gradually changed. The great landowners began to play down the extent of the division between themselves and the rest of propertied society. The upper strata of society began, as it were, to coalesce into a single group. New standards and rules of behaviour began to be

adopted, different social characteristics to be valued. Great landowners and local
gentry began to share a single lifestyle, began to mix and socialize in an easier, less
formal, more affable way. They began to behave as members of a single 'polite
society', to use the contemporary term.[17] In Girouard's words:

> The polite man was essentially social, and as such distinguished from arrogant
> lords, illiterate squires and fanatical puritans. . . . Not everyone could hope to
> be polite. Polite society formed a group within society as a whole. . . .
> Essentially it was made up of the people who owned and ran the country.[18]

The new, easier pattern of relationships originated in the first half of the
century, but it was only in the decades after 1740 that it really began to take hold.
Economic changes underlay or at least underpinned these important
developments: the recovery of the fortunes of the local gentry, and the general
expansion of the economy in the period after 1740. The development of polite
society was also closely connected with what some historians have dubbed the
'consumer revolution' in eighteenth-century England: the development of a
society in which 'more men and women than ever before in human history
enjoyed the experience of acquiring material possessions';[19] a society increasingly
dominated by short-term changes in fashions; and in which leisure was
increasingly commercialized. The new rules of social conduct were forged at the
emerging leisure centres for the rich: at Bath and other spa towns, at the
assemblies that were springing up in every provincial town. The 'polite' were thus
defined, to some extent, by their ability to consume, but also by their mobility.
Improvements in transport – better carriages, turnpike roads – allowed them to
move with relative ease from country house to country house, from spa to spa, to
race meetings and assemblies. Beyond the circuit of the carriage drive within the
park there was a wider circuit of social movement, increasingly separate from the
path trodden by the mass of society.[20]

These new patterns of social intercourse soon began to have an effect on the
design of country houses. During the early eighteenth century house plans had
continued to develop along the lines established in the previous century. The
largest houses generally had only two principal public rooms, the hall and the
saloon. Occupying the central area of the house, their prominence was proclaimed
externally by a central projection, portico or pediment. Other rooms on the
principal floor were arranged in suites, self-contained apartments often organized
as *enfilades*.[21] Such an arrangement was well suited to formalized social
encounters in which activities were regulated, in which nuances of precedent had
to be carefully calculated by the various social actors. But it was much less
suitable for the new forms of entertaining which were now emerging. These
demanded, in particular, that several different activities – card-playing,
conversation, dancing – should go on simultaneously under the same roof, the
guests drifting easily from one social space to the next. House plans based on
hierarchy and symmetry were thus gradually replaced by ones in which a number
of rooms – saloon, library, drawing-room, dining-room – were arranged in a
circuit, so that when the occasion required they could be thrown open for

informal entertaining. The new arrangements were pioneered as early as the 1740s at a few places, but they only came to be widely adopted from the mid-1750s, as gentlemen and provincial architects followed the lead set by Sir Robert Taylor's designs for villas such as Harleyford Manor (Bucks).[22] A decreasing emphasis on hierarchy and state in the design of houses was associated with the adoption of looser, less rigid forms of Palladian architecture. It was also reflected in the migration of the principal public rooms from their elevated, commanding position at first-floor level down to the ground floor. Here they were usually provided with direct access (increasingly via French windows) to the gardens.

These architectural changes inevitably had an impact on the design of the pleasure grounds outside the house. As internal symmetry and axial planning declined in importance, so too did their external expression, in the form of great avenues and vistas focused on the main façades. People began to enjoy the external view of the house from a number of slowly changing perspectives, rather than from a few fixed vantage points, at the ends of avenues and vistas. And as the main public rooms moved down to first-floor level, geometric planning of the gardens made less visual sense. Moreover, a more flowing, circular arrangement of the grounds was more appropriate to the needs of polite society. Just as, within the house, different social activities could take place in different rooms on the circuit, so too a walk along the serpentine paths of the pleasure grounds (or a more extended ride around the circuit drive) would be enlivened by taking tea in a temple, visiting a menagerie, or boating on the lake.[23] When Mrs Lybbe Powys visited Chesterfield she 'drank tea in one of the buildings', and 'the family being very musical and charming voices, the young ladies sang, while the gentlemen accompanied on their German flutes'.[24] In one sense the park was a private landscape, designed to exclude the poor. Yet at the same time it was a public one for the entertainment of the polite, and access to the largest parks was often open to all who appeared respectable. In 1760 Mrs Powys, wandering through the park at Edgecombe in Devon, came to a 'little temple', which had been

> Fixed upon by a large party of gentlemen and ladies, who came that day on a scheme of pleasure to Mount Edgecombe, as a place to enjoy in the most rural manner the cold collation they brought with them.[25]

But the development of polite society had a more basic and more profound effect on the evolution of garden design. To some extent the careless yet elegant irregularity of the landscape park can be read as a transformation, a mirror, of the new, easier pattern of social relationships. More importantly, the landscape park was a socially unifying style of landscape design, one which both local gentry and great landowners alike could share: as we have seen, vast sums *could* be expended on creating a park but a passable version was within reach of most gentlemen. In the decades after 1760 the old dichotomy between the gardens of the élite with their extensive displays of naked grandeur, and those of the local gentry with their enclosed, horticultural, domestic apsect, was steadily eroded. It belonged to a different age, in which the main division in society had been between the great aristocrats with their lifestyle based on London and the Royal Court, and the provincial landowners: between 'Court' and 'country'. The new shared style of the landscape park, in contrast, expressed new divisions, a new structural order: one based on social class.

It is within this specific social context that we need to understand the style of the 'natural' landscape park. For as we have seen, it was a particular kind of nature which was presented here, that of the deer park, a landscape of impeccable aristocratic pedigree and credentials. Stripped of avenues and other geometric intrusions, its rise to prominence over the long centuries was now complete. What better model could there be for a landscape symbolizing a new ruling group, a new social order?

Yet the real significance of the park was that it helped to define, at a critical time, important social divisions. 'Polite society' was a category distinct from the 'common people'. But contemporaries (and indeed, modern historians) were uncertain about where to draw the boundary between the two. England was a highly stratified society, with massive inequalities of wealth. But it had also long been a society in which there were innumerable gradations of status, each separated from the next by a comparatively small step, rather than by an unbridgeable gulf.[26] It was a social system which permitted a degree of upward mobility for the lucky, the capable, the unscrupulous. Status, in the sociologist's jargon, was not only ascribed: it could also be achieved. All this had, to varying extents, been true in the sixteenth and seventeenth centuries. But it was much more true in the eighteenth century, and especially after 1740, as the economy expanded and a new commercial, consuming society developed. For part and parcel of this development was the expansion of what we would now describe as a middle class: a wide, ill-defined group ranging from small farmers, shopkeepers, tradesmen and craftsmen through to clergymen, school teachers, doctors, other professionals and the minor gentry. Where, within this large and diverse continuum, would the line between the polite and the rest be drawn? And how?

The problem of who did and who did not belong to polite society was an acute one because the increasing pace of consumerism was progressively removing many of the traditional markers of status and distinction. Or so, at least, contemporaries believed. Writer after writer bemoaned the spread of London fashions and affectations out into the provinces, the downward diffusion of habits and artefacts and lifestyles which had once been the special mark of the gentleman. As Henry Fielding observed in 1750:

> While the nobleman will emulate the grandeur of a prince, and the gentleman will aspire to the proper status of a nobleman; the tradesman steps from behind his counter into the vacant place of the gentleman. Nor does the confusion end there: it reaches the very dregs of the people, who aspire still to a degree beyond that which belongs to them.[27]

These themes of competitive social emulation, and the erosion of traditional social distinctions, were endlessly repeated. One commentator complained in 1767 that

In England the several ranks of men slide into each other almost imperceptibly.
. . . Hence arises a strong emulation in all the several stations and conditions to
vie with each other; and the perpetual restless ambition in each of the inferior
ranks to raise themselves to the level of those immediately above them. In such
a state as this fashion must have uncontrolled sway. And a fashionable luxury
must spread through it like a contagion.[28]

Landscapes, as we have observed more than once in the course of this
investigation, were important markers of social status. The crucial feature of the
park in this context was not merely that it was a form of landscape which could be
shared by great landowners and lesser gentry. It was also one which was
completely unavailable to the broad mass of the middle class. Parks could only be
created by those who owned land in abundance. The upper echelons of this
middling social group – successful merchants, financiers, some professionals –
could aspire to a small property with a park on the fringes of town, but not the
rest. This was crucial. Only landowners had parks, and thus the adoption of the
park as the prime setting for the fashionable house clearly set the gentry, and the
upper bourgeoisie, apart from society as a whole. It was they who were
unquestionably the 'polite': traditional hierarchy was thus maintained in an
increasingly fluid world.

At the same time, by thus equating social status with the ownership of land, the
park served to perpetuate existing myths about the relative importance of landed
as against commercial wealth. Throughout the early and middle decades of the
century successive essayists and propagandists had represented land as a very
special source of wealth, and the landowner as a very special kind of person. His
role and character were repeatedly contrasted with those of the manufacturer,
merchant, or capitalist.[29] He was a wise figure who, by virtue of the fact that he
owned a portion of the nation, was thereby able to comprehend its true nature
and needs. While members of the capitalist class worked for their own self-
interest, and perceived only those aspects of an increasingly complex society
which had a direct bearing on their experience, the landowner's wealth was in the
nation and he therefore worked for the national good. Of course, to accept such a
myth involved considerable suspension of disbelief. Landowners were, as we have
seen, fully involved in the commercialization of agriculture, in the exploitation of
the mineral resources on their estates, and in the development of their urban
properties. But myths do not have to be true to be powerful. In a society ever
more dependent on commercial and industrial wealth, the ownership of land
remained an immensely powerful symbol of social status. And nothing
demonstrated land ownership so clearly, so visibly, as the landscape park.

Contemporaries were keenly aware of the importance of the park in this
respect; and of the extent to which, in certain circumstances, care had to be taken
to disguise deficiencies in ownership. William Marshall explained that parks
should be open to the surrounding world if all the land in view belonged to the
owner, in which case (as he candidly put it) the prospect would gratify his 'love of
possession'.[30] If, however, someone else's property entered the view from the
house, then it had to be obscured by thick belts or plantations; if it intruded closer

still then careful thought needed to be given to how the limited bounds of the estate could be obscured.

In the 1750s Coventry had ridiculed Squire Mushroom's attempts at creating a diminutive landscape garden. But ridiculous though the result may have seemed, the crucial fact was that Mushroom could make the attempt at all, on grounds extending over a mere 2 acres (*c.* 0.8 hectares). In contrast, Mushroom could not have even begun to lay out a landscape *park* on a plot of this size. However you chose to plant it, 2 acres of grass and trees was a *field*, not a *park*. The small spaces available to the middle classes thus demanded, by their very nature, different principles of design. This social group could do no other than lay out grounds with flowers, shrubs, hedges: and lay them out they certainly did. Indeed, the middle classes became increasingly keen on their gardens in this period, and the consumer revolution, the commercialization of leisure, had not passed gardening by. 'The seedsmen, nurserymen and bulb growers (with their printed, illustrated, fixed-price catalogues, their immense range of stock, all well advertised) successfully adapted the commercial techniques of other salesmen to the needs of bulbs and flowers and fruit.'[31] Seeds shops proliferated in the towns and cities, nurseries in their hinterland on an ever larger scale, something reflected in the massive increase in the number of florists societies, and their 'feasts', betwen 1740 and 1785.[32] The very scale and number of such enterprises makes it clear that their prime customers were the urban and rural bourgeoisie rather than the far smaller group of the landed rich.

As early as 1722 Thomas Fairchild had stressed that people whose business compelled them to reside in town ought to have a garden of some kind 'in order to increase their Quiet of Mind, to be fix'd in a right notion of Country Happiness, when their affairs will permit them to reach such pleasures'.[33] By the second half of the eighteenth century the garden had become the essential prerequisite of the middle-class home, to judge from the advertisements in the provincial papers. Almost every house of significance for sale or to let had a 'walled-in garden' and, as often or not, a summer-house. So expected was this that when in August 1788 a 'Genteel, large house' was advertised for sale in the *Norwich Mercury* the vendor was obliged to admit that it possessed 'every fashionable and domestic convenience – garden excepted'. 'Scarce a person from the peer to the cottager' one observer asserted in 1779, 'thinks himself happy without being possessed of a garden.'[34]

At this social level gardens continued to be highly structured, even geometric in their design throughout the eighteenth century (Figures 46 and 47). The garden of No. 4 The Circus, Bath was laid out shortly before 1760 and excavated in 1991. It was symmetrical in layout, with a gravel court into which oval and circular flower beds were set: paved paths and flower borders ran around the perimeter. This essentially formal structure was maintained, with only minor alterations, into the nineteenth century.[35] There is some evidence to suggest that in the 1780s and '90s there was a tendency for middle-class gardens to become slightly more 'naturalistic' and asymmetrical in their details, with serpentine paths and more irregularly shaped beds, but a geometric structure remained the norm.[36] Thus Francis Douce's garden in Gower Street, London in the 1790s had

46. *Middle-class gardening. This elaborate garden, laid out around the mill at Burnham Overy, Norfolk, is illustrated on a map of 1744.*

a simple, symmetrical and formal layout even if behind the box edgings to the paths the planting was varied and irregular.[37]

Like the middle classes, the rural gentry and even the great landowners were often enthusiastic gardeners. It was said in 1769 that the Dowager Duchess of Portland was 'exceedingly fond of gardening, is a very learned botanist, and has every English plant in a separate garden by themselves' at her seat in Bulstrode (Bucks).[38] Sir Martin Ffolkes, a prominent Norfolk landowner, is an extreme but perhaps not entirely atypical example. Ffolkes took over the extensive Hillington

47. Middle-class gardening. This detail from John Constable's painting of 1815 shows the flower garden created at East Bergholt, Suffolk by another miller: Constable's father, Golding. Note the essentially geometric arrangement of the flower beds.

estate in 1773, at a time when the mansion house was still surrounded by enclosed courts. He commissioned Samuel Driver to prepare a design for a landscape park, and if this had been implemented these would have been swept away. This did not happen, however, and the estate accounts for the years 1774 to 1780 show that there was intense activity within the walled gardens. In 1774 Ffolkes renovated and probably extended the orangery, putting in Dutch tiles, new water and heating systems and new glazing. Between 1774 and 1777 he purchased orange, lemon and lime trees, some from Holland, some from Norwich and some from the neighbouring town of Brandon. A new walled garden with a 'hott wall' was built in 1774, cucumber pits dug and frames and sashes bought for the hot beds. The year 1775 saw the building of a new pinery: walls were altered and repaired, and peaches, nectarines, apricots, cherries, plums, pears and apples were brought to line them. There was a hot house for forcing flowers and a succession house. The existing wilderness, established in the 1740s on an island in the park, was lovingly maintained throughout the 1760s and '70s; the large numbers of filberts and walnuts purchased in 1778 were probably planted there, together with the substantial quantities of bulbs mentioned in the estate accounts, and a summer-house was built at its centre in 1776.[39] Clearly, all these changes were carried out by a man who was a fanatic, and frenetic, gardener. Indeed, a friend wrote to him in 1777, complimenting him on his abilities, but warning: 'I am fearful, by your great success, you will be tempted to stay too long in the hot houses to the injury of your health.'[40]

Many gentlemen continued to be enthusiastic gardeners right through the century. But there is some evidence that gardening was increasingly regarded as an activity more appropriate for their wives. At this social level, women had been active gardeners for centuries – William Lawson's *Country Housewife's Garden* of 1617 was addressing an established audience. But the evidence suggests that as the park grew in importance in the course of the eighteenth century the garden, and especially the flower garden, was increasingly viewed as a female space. It is, for example, noticeable how often the flower gardens at great country houses were, in the second half of the century, explicitly associated by name with the owner's wife: the Duchess's Garden at Blenheim (Oxon), for example, or Lady Buckinghamshire's Garden at Blickling (Norfolk). And in the same period an interest in flowers and gardens seems, in general, to be more apparent in the diaries and tour journals of women than of men. Gardening was also increasingly seen as a suitably improving activity for young children, as in Maria Edgeworth's *Practical Education* of 1796.[41]

48. *The park at Chatsworth, Derbyshire.*

In a world dominated by adult males, we can see here one or two very good reasons why gardens should have been banished from public and prominent positions in front of the main façade of the country house. But more importantly, to live with gardens in full view was what the bourgeoisie did: just as to live with cabbages growing beneath the windows, or with muck heaps in sight, was the mark of the peasant. To be a gentleman was to live in a house set in parkland, and to enjoy views over open parkland from the windows of the house. And at the same time as the pleasure gardens were marginalized the kitchen garden, home farm, fish ponds, barns – all the things that had once clustered around the mansion – were also banished from sight. In a society increasingly geared to fashionable consumption, superior resources for production were no longer a particular mark of distinction. This was a revolution in landscape design, and its significance would not have been lost on contemporaries. The house was set free from all signs of industry, from all association with useful toil and activity.

Traditional food production facilities, all those things associated with direct involvement in husbandry, were indeed banished from proximity to the house. Yet at the same time, everyone knew that the parkland which replaced them was not in reality – and in spite of appearances – a useless and unproductive space. It too had economic functions, but of a particular kind: ones that for centuries had been especially associated with large landowners, ones that required an abundance of that most prestigious of all commodities – land. And while parks might appear to be chasms of inactivity yawning between the mansion and the surrounding world, they were in reality an arena for a whole range of recreational activities. These once again were ones long associated specifically with landed gentlemen, activities that depended on the ownership of broad acres. It is to the multifarious ways in which the landscape park was actually used that we must now turn.

CHAPTER SIX

'Beauty and Utility'

Landscape parks are usually considered as aesthetic artefacts, and their form explained through an analysis of the writings of aesthetes and intellectuals. Having decided that the park must be interpreted in aesthetic terms, that is, the evidence for its elucidation has been collected accordingly: evidence which, we should not be surprised to learn, confirms its essential status as a work of art. But parks can be profitably studied without this preconception. Indeed, such a simple approach to the gardens and grounds of country houses could never, in reality, have been shared by their owners. As members of the landed élite altered, amended, or simply ignored the suggestions of Brown, Woods, Richmond and the rest, or as they formulated their own ideas of parkland design, they were creating landscapes with a wide range of functions, landscapes which were far more than the setting for a country house, or a pretty prospect to be viewed from its windows. Parks were homes, farms, and forestry enterprises as well as being works of art. Moreover, these diverse activities were not simply fitted round or hidden away from the dominant aesthetic. They lay at the very heart of the landscape park, not simply modifying it but forming the very essence of its structure.[1]

THE MEANING OF GRASS

Parks were, ostensibly, 'natural' landscapes, divorced from agricultural production. But the landscape dissimulated. Pretending to shun the landscape of production, the park was, in fact, an integral part of it. Thus, in particular, the turf was systematically utilized with profit in mind. Sometimes the grazing was exploited directly by the home farm, sometimes it was leased out, in whole or part, to one or more local farmers. At least until the impact of 'picturesque' notions in the last decade of the century, there was broad agreement that turf should be grazed close. Stocking levels were, therefore, usually high: and so too, in consequence, the income derived from grazing. This went a long way towards offsetting the cost of parks, and thus ensured that they were an affordable luxury, available to any moderately wealthy gentleman. The landowner could have his cake and eat it, for economic exploitation – within sensible limits – did not run counter to the aesthetics of the landscape park, but on the contrary maintained and enhanced it.

There was, nevertheless, an inherent tension at the heart of this sensible combination of beauty and utility. Stocking at *too* high a density could disfigure

49. The meaning of turf: Studley Royal, Yorkshire. This painting by an unknown artist, c. 1750, shows the stable block proudly displayed across the park. Visitors out riding admire the grazing cattle.

the park. Bare muddy patches might be created, especially in the winter months and so estate accounts suggest that stock were usually turned out into parks a month or so later than was customary on other pasture lands. Even then, animal numbers were often only gradually increased, rising to a peak in the late summer. A more serious problem was the damage that stock, and in particular cattle, could cause to young trees, which thus had to be carefully protected with wooden fencing. Most important of all, however, was the fact that efficient control of grazing required some physical subdivision of the grass. The aesthetics of the landscape park demanded open, sweeping vistas. Yet contemporary maps suggest that parks were usually divided into a number of separately named subsections: the Hay Park, the Home Park, the North Lawn, the South Park, and so on. There was clearly potential for conflict here. If the boundaries of grazing compartments were too obvious they could erode the distinctive quality of the park, making it resemble the subdivided landscape of the surrounding agricultural countryside. It is hardly surprising, then, that owners went to considerable lengths to hide the necessary fences by (among other things) carefully incorporating the parkland

50. Parkland recreation: boating on the lake at Heveningham, Suffolk. An illustration from William Watts' The Seats of the Nobility and Gentry *(1779).*

plantations within the schemes of subdivision. This explains a number of otherwise puzzling things about the disposition of parkland woods. For example, when parks were extended sections of the earlier belts were frequently allowed to remain. These disrupted the vista, and prevented the new addition being brought into the overall scheme of the design: but they allowed the creation of a separate area of grazing without the intrusion of fencing into the open parkland. It was not just aesthetic considerations that determined the location of particular woods and clumps.

If care was taken there was no fundamental conflict here between aesthetics and economics. But even to make these neat distinctions is misleading. In reality we cannot easily isolate the economic function of the park from its social role, as a symbol of gentility. Everything in the landscape of the park had complex, overlapping functions. The animals grazing on the turf were more than lawn-mowers, more than machines for producing meat and wool. Members of the aristocracy and gentry alike took as keen an interest in the selective breeding of livestock as they did in the improvement of their horses and foxhounds.[2] In many aristocratic parks improved sheep breeds replaced deer as the prime symbols of patrician status: more rarely, as at Harewood (Yorks), it was improved cattle breeds that beautified the park.

As John Lawrence noted in 1801, 'There cannot be more interesting objects of view, in a park, than well-chosen flocks and herds, nor more appropriate to the rural scene, than their voices.'[3] The livestock grazing contentedly under the parkland trees – so ubiquitous a feature of contemporary engravings that we scarcely notice them – symbolized a peculiarly aristocratic form of husbandry (Figure 49). This was an association with a long pedigree, only partially engendered by concepts of pastoralism which the eighteenth-century élite inherited – like so much else – from the classical past. Grazing animals represented a form of leisured, effortless, 'natural' production which arable farming, involving a complex and laborious series of tasks (ploughing, harrowing, weeding, harvesting) did not. As Repton put it in 1792:

> Labour and hardship attend the operations of agriculture, whether cattle are tearing up the surface of the soil, or man reaping its produce; on the contrary a pasture shows us the same animals enjoying rest after fatigue, while others sporting with liberty and ease excite the pleasing idea of happiness and comfort annexed to a pastoral life. Consequently, such a scene must be more in harmony with the residence of elegance and comfort, and marks a degree of affluence, so decidedly that we never see a park ploughed up, but we always attribute it to poverty. . . .[4]

Repton's comment is slightly misleading, however. In 1801 John Lawrence urged that parks should, together with the home farm, be used as a 'theatre . . . for the display of *all* the notable varieties of experimental husbandry', and many of the larger parks did in fact contain areas of arable land within their belts. This was, in particular, a noticeable feature of those created by the great landowners most closely associated with the progress of agricultural improvement. Indeed, the connection between land improvement schemes and agricultural innovation on the one hand, and the creation of landscape parks on the other, deserves more emphasis. The term 'improvement' was used indiscriminately to describe both activities, and both involved not only economic power but a particular frame of mind: a breezy confidence, an ability to look at an existing piece of landscape and see its form not as God-given and inevitable but as provisional and changeable. Indeed, the two kinds of 'improvement' frequently went on side by side. Thomas Coke, perhaps the most famous agriculturalist of the century, transformed his estate at Holkham (Norfolk), establishing plantations, building new farms, intensively marling the land and rationalizing field boundaries. He held regular agricultural shows or 'sheep shearings' to propagate new techniques and ideas among his tenants, including the use of a new breed of sheep (first grazed, needless to say, in the park).[5] But he did not neglect his parkland, and when this was massively extended to the south in the 1780s and '90s only one new garden building – if we can call it that – was constructed: the Great Barn, designed by the country house architect Samuel Wyatt, which stood in a prominent location and was set off to great effect by decorative planting. The barn was intended, from the start, as a new venue for the 'sheep shearings', and it is not going too far to see it as the centrepiece of the park's new southern extension. The latter, it should be noted, was not put down to grass, but instead continued to be farmed as arable land by the home farm, Coke carefully recording the results of different methods of cultivation employed within it.

Arable farming could thus take place within the park. Conversely, aesthetic planting and other decoration often spilled out into the wider estate land, continuing a tradition which can be traced back, through the *fermes ornées* of the 1730s and '40s and the writings of Stephen Switzer, to the agricultural theorists of the mid-seventeenth century (and ultimately to classical writers). Home farms were often given fashionable embellishments, and connected by a path to the main areas of pleasure grounds around the house. Sometimes the aesthetic treatment was more widely applied, and one visitor to Harewood (Yorks) in 1777 described how 'the whole country forms a theatre of ornamented farms'.[6] As Whately put it in 1770, gardening 'Is no longer confined to the spots from which it borrows its name, but regulates also the disposition and embellishments of a park, a farm, or a riding'. He later explained that a 'riding' was an ornamental drive through the surrounding estate land, adorned with decorative planting, which was intended 'to lead from one beauty to another, and be a scene of pleasure all the way'.[7]

As a result of all this, the line between the 'aesthetic' landscape of the park, and the 'functional' landscape of demesne agriculture, often became blurred. Nevertheless, what Repton said in 1792 was still correct: a distinction remained between the landscapes of leisure and of arable production. It was only the more distant and secluded sections, of the more extensive parks, that contained crops. In the vicinity of the mansion the agricultural use of the park was limited, by definition, to livestock. If a landscape of arable toil should here triumph over one of pastoral ease, then the park had ceased to exist.

This association of the élite residence with open grassland long predated the rise of the landscape park. Since the fifteenth century turf had been the main component of the deer parks established beside élite residences. Moreover, seventeenth- and eighteenth-century estate maps leave no doubt that the manor houses of the gentry had usually – wherever possible – been surrounded by grass paddocks, rather than arable fields. These had often been planted up in a relatively ornamental fashion, and for this reason the line between pre-park landscape and the park itself is not always very clear-cut. This preference for a grassland setting was the consequence of a number of factors. To the kinds of long-established associations discussed by Repton the early decades of the eighteenth century had added another: in the discourse of garden design, turf came to have a patriotic significance. Switzer, Langley and others argued that it should form a major part of the gentleman's landscape because nobody in Europe grew it better than the English.[8] More important, however, were practical considerations. Grassland could be used for recreation and leisure in a way that ploughland could not. Thus the 4th Lord North thought that the pleasures of the deer park came not only from the presence of the deer themselves, but also from 'having so much pasture ground lying open for riding, walking or any other pastime'.[9] Riding was a particularly esteemed activity. It had held a special place in the lifestyle of the gentry and aristocracy since the early Middle Ages when horsemanship and knightly status had been inseparable. By the start of the eighteenth century, the thoroughbred racehorse was the aristocratic status symbol *par excellence.* The horse's 'strength, speed and courage symbolised the superior status of its owner'.[10] There were many parks in which the stables were fine buildings, proudly exposed to view, rather than being treated as necessary but ugly conveniences to be hidden away or screened by shrubberies and plantations, the usual fate of the kitchen garden (Figure 49). The open grass of the park provided an ideal place to ride fast, to enjoy a pastime restricted, in large measure, to the rich. The parkland turf was thus at one and the same time an important economic resource and a form of environment peculiarly associated with the landowning class.

A similar nexus of complex influences and associations informed the belts, clumps and plantations of the landscape park. Just as the park operated as a profitable grazing farm, so too was it a large-scale forestry enterprise. Estate accounts vividly portray the complexity and sophistication of estate forestry, both inside and outside the park. But they also reveal the way in which planting was an activity particularly suited to the lifestyle of a gentleman, and many landowners maintained detailed personal accounts of their forestry exploits which read like heroic struggles against the odds of nature. So important in the evolution of the landscape park were patrician attitudes towards trees and tree-planting that we cannot discuss these matters without a brief account of the more general development of forestry in the eighteenth century.

THE LANGUAGE OF TREES

Sylva's warnings about the strategic and economic implications of dwindling timber resources continued to be repeated into the eighteenth century. Batty Langley in 1728, for example, believed that if steps were not urgently taken to remedy the problem 'our nation will be entirely exhausted of building timber, before sixty years are ended'.[11] Phillip Miller in 1731, James Wheeler in 1747, Edmund Wade in 1755, and William Hanbury in 1758 all hammered home the same message, and most contemporaries shared the view that England's naval supremacy was at stake.[12] The navy certainly consumed a lot of timber. A first-rate ship of the line required 5,560 loads of oak, a second-rate 4,035: the annual consumption of timber at the six principal naval dockyards between 1730 and 1789 was around 30,000 loads a year, or about 1.5 million cubic feet.[13] Traditionally the dockyards had been supplied from the royal forests, but in England (unlike France) these had never been properly managed, at least in silvicultural terms. Many, of course, had never been very well wooded: technically speaking a forest was simply a tract of land over which Forest Law, a bundle of restrictions intended to conserve stocks of deer, was applied. The commons and wood-pastures that lay at the heart of these legal territories – the forests proper – had been under pressure since medieval times. The preservation of deer was not conducive to the preservation of timber. Their browsing prevented the replacement of felled trees by spontaneous regeneration – as did that of the sheep and cattle owned by commoners. Thus it was that Gilbert White was able to describe Woolmer Forest (Hants) in 1789 as 'entirely of sand covered with heath and fern; without having one standing tree in the whole extent'.[14] Not all were as bad as this, however, and the New Forest, and the Forests of Dean and Alice Holt, were able to provide a reasonable quantity of timber for the dockyards, although nothing like sufficient for their needs. Of the 30,000 loads a year required in the mid-eighteenth century they supplied only a fraction: in total around 77,000 loads of oak and 16,000 of beech were produced between 1730 and 1787.[15] The deficit was made up in part by imports from abroad but these were liable to interruption during wartime. There are, it should perhaps be said, grounds for believing that the scale of the problem was exaggerated in the discourse of forestry, but in the present context this matters little. Contemporaries *believed* that England faced a crisis in the supply of timber, and planting trees thus represented not only a patriotic act but also a shrewd financial investment.

So far as the evidence goes it was not until after 1750 that there was a significant expansion of forestry in England. Then, however, planting proceeded apace. The particularly outstanding examples of aristocratic enterprise are frequently quoted, but are worth repeating nevertheless: Thomas Johnes, who put in nearly 5 million trees between 1786 and 1816 at Hafod (Cardiganshire); the Earl of Selbourne, who planted over 150,000 trees every year in the 1770s and '80s at Bowood (Wilts); the Duke of Portland, who established between 60 and 100 acres (25–40 hectares) of trees each year on his estate at Welbeck (Notts); or Thomas William Coke, who planted no less than 2 million between 1782 and 1805 at Holkham (Norfolk).[16] These are the outstanding examples: but in fact, most landowners were busy with woods and plantations. It is sometimes suggested that the annual medals awarded for forestry between 1757 and 1835 by the Royal Society for the Encouragement of Arts were a significant influence in all this. Of greater importance, however, were more basic economic factors: the buoyancy in the timber market and, above all, the increasing pace of enclosure. Although, as we have seen, only a relatively small proportion of England was in fact enclosed during this period, a high proportion of the areas so affected comprised poor-quality heathland, moorland, and other 'waste'. Such marginal land had formerly been used as grazing by local communities. Appropriated by the aristocracy and gentry, it could now be used for large-scale schemes of afforestation.

Yet right into the nineteenth century people continued to warn that England was chronically short of timber. In part this was because many realized that at the same time as the new plantations were spreading over former wastes and commons, many ancient woods – especially those growing on the heavier soils of southern and eastern England – were being grubbed out, and turned over to arable cultivation.[17] Improvements in land drainage and high grain prices made this a sensible move, particularly given the character of these woods, and current perceptions of the likely development of the market.[18] Ancient woods were principally composed of coppices, and contained comparatively few timber trees. The coppice stools, generally cut at intervals of between ten and twenty years, produced massive quantities of straight, thin-sectioned 'poles' which were suitable for making hurdles and repairing buildings but were mainly used for firewood, or to make industrial charcoal. By the third quarter of the eighteenth century, however, agricultural writers were confidently predicting that the increasing importance of coal for domestic heating, and the decline in the use of charcoal for iron smelting, would soon reduce the value of such woods almost to zero: landowners should grub them out, and plough. In fact, the demise of coppice woods was not nearly so fast or so complete as many contemporary writers predicted, or as some recent writers have assumed. Indeed, new areas of coppiced woodland were established on many estates in the eighteenth and nineteenth centuries – even parkland belts can often be found to contain areas of coppice, usually composed of hazel or sweet chestnut. As late as 1851 some writers could argue the economic benefits to be derived from coppice woods.[19] Nevertheless, many ancient woods were grubbed out in this period, and the vast majority of estate plantations newly established after 1750 were composed entirely of standard trees.

To judge from estate accounts, such plantations were of varied composition. In most, conifers were a prominent feature, especially spruce, larch, silver fir, and Scots pine. The latter was especially popular for lighter, acid land (such as newly enclosed heathland) in the south and east of England. Larch, in contrast, was widely planted in upland areas. Its appearance in the vales of Cumberland appalled William Wordsworth, who regretted that 'those who plant for profit . . . are thrusting every tree out of the way to make room for their favourite, the larch' and had 'selected these lovely vales for their vegetable manufactory'.[20] Others took a different line. Bailey and Culley, for example, argued that the plantations of larch appearing all over northern England were 'adding greatly to the ornament of the country'.[21]

Sometimes the conifers were planted on their own, but they were often used in mixed plantations as 'nurses' for slower-growing hardwoods, especially oak and beech. Eighteenth- and early nineteenth-century plantations were generally planted more densely than is usually the case today, the young trees initially spaced at intervals of less than a metre. In consequence, they were generally thinned earlier, and more often, than is modern practice. The first conifers would be removed at perhaps five or six years. These young trees would not be wasted, however, for they could be used in similar ways to the products of traditional coppice woods, and indeed estate accounts often refer to them, somewhat confusingly, as 'poles'. Dense planting was intended to suppress competitive weed growth (always a problem before the widespread adoption of herbicides in the mid-twentieth century). It also reflects the fact that high losses of young trees were expected, especially from the depredations of rabbits. These were a serious problem, especially in the kind of sandy heathland environment in which many of these new plantations were being established, before the advent of cheap wire netting in the 1860s.

Woods and plantations were widely planted on eighteenth-century estates, but a quick glance at contemporary maps soon reveals that the majority were concentrated in and around the homes of landowners. There were a number of reasons for this. One was that woods needed to be closely watched and supervised in order to protect them against theft and vandalism. Given that many were established on former commons it is hardly surprising that local inhabitants felt that they still had a right to enter and take away firewood, although theft of wood and damage to trees were not new problems nor restricted to such places. In the late seventeenth century Moses Cook reported that three trees in the Earl of Essex's garden at Cassiobury (Herts) had been damaged 'by some base men or boys', and successive Acts of Parliament from the 1720s onwards laid down stiff penalties for damage to trees growing in plantations and pleasure grounds.[22] In 1773 William Chambers listed – among other recurrent crimes to which the 'common people' were prone – their propensity to cut down trees.[23] But woods and plantations were also established near to the mansion because they beautified it, and to some extent this perceived beauty derived from the fact that tree planting, and élite status, had long gone hand in hand (something which may in part explain the kinds of incidents of vandalism described by Cook). We have already seen how woods, groves and wildernesses had become steadily more important in gentlemen's gardens in the course of the seventeenth and early eighteenth centuries. Trees near a mansion gave it a certain cachet, especially in the more open, champion areas of England. Lord Caryll in 1699 refused to have the ash trees around his house felled because they were 'its chiefest ornament'.[24]

Yet woods and plantations were also established further out from the house and here they had an important significance, as statements of ownership. 'What can be more pleasant than to have the bounds and limits of your property preserved and continued from age to age by the testimony of such living and growing witnesses?' asked Joseph Worlidge in 1669.[25] We have already noted how avenues and plantations not only proclaimed that the land they grew upon was owned by a particular individual, but also the fact that it was owned absolutely and exclusively by them and was not subject to rights of common grazing. Planting was synonymous with complete *private* ownership: but also by implication with ownership by a gentleman. For while the yeoman farmer might plant some trees around his farmyard or in his hedges, only the larger landowner could put tens or hundreds of acres down to trees. No one else could afford to make this kind of long-term investment, locking up land from which more immediate returns could be derived. And precisely because it was a long-term investment, planting also symbolized confidence in the future, expressed an assumption that there would be heirs to enjoy the benefits of the planter's far-sighted actions.

Indeed, there was an easy connection to be made here between the longevity of particular woods and plantations, and the continuity of a certain family in a place or district. Such a connection was long-established, and partly explains the horror felt when, during the Commonwealth, there was large-scale felling in the sequestered parks of Royalists. Royalist propaganda after the Restoration exaggerated the extent of such depredations in order to foster an association between felling and republicanism, and – conversely – between tree-planting and loyalty to the restored monarchy.[26]

The oak tree had a particular place in this complex web of symbolism and association. Already in the seventeenth century its antiquity and spreading crown made it an obvious choice as a metaphor for established landed families: long associated with a particular locality, deeply rooted, stable, with branches sheltering the surrounding community. The increasing volume of literature urging the planting of this species for strategic reasons further elevated its importance, and by the end of the century the oak could become a metaphor for the British nation: in 1794 William Shenstone argued that 'Oaks are in all respects the perfect image of the manly character: in former times I should have said, and in present times I think I am authorised to say, the British one.'[27]

Some writers in the second half of the eighteenth century began to contrast the planting of oaks and other hardwoods – which they associated with long-established landed wealth – with the small-profits-quick-returns philosophy symbolized by softwood planting, which they associated with parvenus, upwardly mobile intruders into the ranks of landed society.[28] Of course, this literary trope had only a very tangential relationship to the actual practice of estate forestry. Long-established landowners were as happy as anyone to establish stands of pure conifers, at least in the outlying portions of their estates. But it was widely repeated. So too was the hostility to the pollarding of oaks and other indigenous trees. Pollards in hedges shaded out crops: better to plant standard trees in hedges, if you must have trees there at all, for the short boles of pollards meant they were of little value as timber. 'Let the axe fall with undistinguished severity on all these mutilated heads', urged Thomas Ruggles in 1786.[29] The practice had been attacked by Moses Cook as early as 1676.[30] In part this developing antipathy was due to the fact that the rich simply did not need the wood from pollards, using instead the produce of their coppices, or coal. The loppings from pollarded trees were usually reserved by custom for the use of the estate tenants. Pollarding was thus increasingly associated in the aristocratic mind with peasants and small farmers. But patrician hostility to the practice may also have been related to the growing antagonism towards topiary: both reflected a preference for the 'natural' form of the tree (in the modern, that is, rather than in any Neoplatonic sense).

Trees and tree-planting were thus loaded with symbolism in the eighteenth century. They represented the established order, the stability and security of great landed families and the monarchy, the defence of the realm, the British character. Little wonder, then, that trees were considered an essential part of the landscape of gentility. As Sir Alexander Dick put it in 1762, men of property 'should plant at proper places, and at proper distances, noble clumps of trees of all sorts, to dignify the look of the land'.[31] To plant was the very essence of gentility: to plant was to be a gentleman.

Now we cannot, of course, derive the landscape park in any obvious or direct way from the eighteenth-century's burgeoning love affair with trees. An enthusiasm for tree-planting does not in itself 'explain' the park. But there are several important pointers here. To begin with, the income to be derived from forestry in the medium or long term ensured that the 'natural' stands of woodland in the landscape park only *appeared* to be a form of conspicuous waste. On many soils, especially the more marginal, tree-planting could offer a better financial return in the medium term than agricultural rents, especially given that even oak trees (noted for their slow growth) could be considered ready for felling after only eighty or ninety years. The widespread practice of dense planting and repeated thinning also ensured a steady if comparatively small trickle of income in

51. An undated engraving of Caversham, Berkshire, showing a tree being felled in the park. This is an unusual picture: artists seldom depicted forestry activities in parks.

the shorter term. Forestry, like the exploitation of the parkland for grazing, thus meant that the park was an affordable luxury. Moreover, the landscape park was particularly well suited to the combination of the economic and the aesthetic in matters of woodland management. It was far better in this respect than the formal designs which it succeeded. Regular rows of trees, quincunxes and avenues would all be disrupted by thinning or felling, whereas 'natural' scatters of timber, or irregularly shaped stands of woodland, were much less drastically affected.

The trees most commonly used by Brown and his contemporaries naturally reflected the more general preferences emerging in the eighteenth century. Oak had pride of place in the landscape of the park, followed by other deciduous natives such as the beech and elm. Moreover, in the new style *trees* were increasingly valued as trees, rather than as parts of a more general design. Both topiary and pollarding were entirely forbidden (and formerly pollarded trees, incorporated from hedgerows when parks were laid out, were immediately allowed to grow as naturally as was possible from the damaged base of their 'mutilated heads'). Trees grew tall, with long straight boles: objects of beauty, but also objects of profit.

Some of the characteristic features of parkland woods may also derive, in part, from the needs of forestry. The carriage rides running through perimeter belts provided access when timber needed to be thinned or removed. Extraction was not a major problem in traditional woods, for their principal products were not tree trunks but faggots and coppice poles, and the timber trees they contained were generally rather widely spaced. Now that timber was the main crop it made sense to facilitate access. This may also have been one of the reasons why the characteristic parkland wood was a small clump or a thin belt, no part of which would be very far from the perimeter. In addition, some contemporary writers believed (probably wrongly) that woods like this – especially small clumps – also created the optimum conditions for the growth of timber. Henry Steuart praised the clumps of Brown and Thomas White (a landscape gardener who operated mainly in Scotland), emphasizing that they produced trees of 'great size and beauty':

> While in no part so deep as to impede the salutary action of the atmosphere, the circular or oval figure of the clumps, and their free exposure to the elements, furnished them with a far greater proportion of good outside trees.[32]

Of course, there was always a potential conflict between forestry and aesthetics. Indiscriminate felling would radically alter the structure and appearance of a design, but this was usually a sign that the owner was down on his luck. In general aesthetics and the economics of forestry could be reconciled by careful management. The more commercial areas of woodland were located in hidden or peripheral areas of the park, where clear felling and replanting could occur without ruining the view.

The apparent simplicity of parkland plantations thus disguises a remarkable complexity of function, purpose, and meaning. And we have not yet mentioned what was perhaps their main role – as game reserves.

THE GAME RESERVE

Foreign visitors frequently remarked on the English landed élite's addiction to hunting. 'One of the greatest pleasures of the English is that of the chase', noted the young Frenchman François de La Rochefoucauld in 1784: 'they are all mad about it.'[33] It was an obsession shared by almost all landowners, from local squire to national statesman. Robert Walpole, it was said, would always open letters from his gamekeeper before his parliamentary dispatches of the day. Hunting was pursued with a determined savagery. Towards the end of the century, in particular, estates vied with each other in recording the vast numbers of game birds mown down by visitors' guns. Otters, badgers and stags would be slaughtered with an easy conscience, as would the fox, an increasingly fashionable quarry as the century progressed.

Most garden historians ignore the impact of this love affair with hunting on the design of the landscape, although there are important exceptions. Robert Williams, in particular, has reminded us that the landscape park of Brown's day was still 'maintained as a private larder . . . a sylvan arena for blood sports'.[34] And

52. Coursing in Hatfield Park: an aquatint by James Pollard of 1824.

contemporary descriptions and illustrations make its importance in this respect
very clear (Figure 52). Numerous pictures of country house landscapes show
hares being coursed, hunts gathering on the turf before the mansion, or the
hounds running across the parkland in full cry in pursuit of the hapless fox. But
although the huntsmen tended to gather in parks (as they sometimes still do), the
hunt itself was not normally confined to their bounds and, at least by the second
half of the eighteenth century, fox earths were seldom encouraged within them.
There was a simple reason for this. The landscape park was above all a storehouse
for game birds, and every effort was therefore made to remove their principal
predators, including the fox.

Many eighteenth-century texts and documents show how the requirements of
game were carefully considered when parks were being designed. Thus Repton
argued against the creation of narrow belts with a wide drive through the centre
on the grounds that two narrow strips of plantation would not be 'such effectual
harbours of game, as deeper masses: especially where the game is likely to be
disturbed by a drive betwixt them'.[35] At Wimpole (Cambs) in 1801 the new east
drive ran to the north of Cobbs Wood because, as Repton's Red Book openly
states, 'this wood being one of the principal game covers ought not perhaps to be
disturbed'.[36] But the importance of hunting and shooting in the history of the
landscape park goes much deeper than such stray references would suggest.
Indeed, shooting was arguably *the* most important influence on the style of the

landscape park. To understand how, and why, we need to make another digression, and briefly investigate the development of game shooting in England during the course of the eighteenth century.

As we have seen, hunting had long been an important expression of social status. The late and post-medieval periods, however, saw a series of legislative changes designed to ensure that not just deer, but also other forms of game – hares, partridges, and pheasants – were reserved for the use and enjoyment of the rich. The framework of eighteenth-century game preservation was effectively established by the Game Act of 1671.[37] By its terms, game could only be taken by people possessing freehold property worth at least £100 per year; by those holding leaseholds of 99 years or longer or copyholds worth at least £150 a year; or else by those who were the sons or heirs apparent of esquires or others 'of higher degree'. Not only did the Act thus restrict the right to hunt to less than 1 per cent of the population (£100 per annum was, after all, fifty times the electoral franchise). It also (unlike earlier Acts) restricted it specifically to the established *landed* rich. Income, on whatever scale, from trades or professions was no longer in itself enough to qualify a man. It thus effectively proclaimed the superiority of land over all other forms of wealth.[38]

The 1671 Act maintained the penalties for hunting imposed by previous legislation, namely a fine of 20 shillings per head of game killed or three months imprisonment. Subsequent pieces of legislation raised the stakes. In 1707 the penalty was increased to a blanket fine of £5, or three months in prison. In 1723 the notorious Black Act, 'for the more effectual punishment of wicked and evil-disposed persons going armed, in disguise' – ensured that merely appearing in the vicinity of a game reserve, armed and with face blackened, was a hanging offence.

Poaching was only commercially viable if there was a ready market for game among poulterers and innkeepers. From the sixteenth century onwards there were thus sporadic attempts to limit the free market in game, and in 1755 all buying and selling of hares, pheasants and partridges, even by qualified sportsmen, was declared illegal.[39] These creatures had always been objects of élite gift exchange, conferred (like other exclusive or exotic products of the gentleman's domain) in return for political or other favours, cementing allegiances and defining social relationships. In the course of the eighteenth century this peculiar status was increased: game was removed entirely from the normal mechanisms of market exchange, and books or lists recording the favour of a hare or a partridge can be found in the archives of many landed families.

But it was not only game that could pass by gift outside the charmed circle of the élite. So too could the right to hunt it. For in spite of the terms of the 1671 Act large numbers of unqualified people did in fact go hunting, with the full knowledge and indeed permission of local landowners. Such 'indulgences' were one of the most important pieces of patronage bestowed by landowners, and were often used for political advantage, as when the Duke of Marlborough was trying to capture the borough of Marlborough from its political allegiance to Lord Bute, and offered the gentlemen of the corporation the tempting offer of permission to hunt over his land. Tenants too were often allowed some shooting, 'So long as they are kept within proper bounds. By such indulgences every farmer will himself become a zealous and faithful keeper.'[40]

But things were changing in the course of the eighteenth century. As Munsche, the leading historian of the game laws, has argued: 'the willingness of country gentlemen to "indulge" their tenants and neighbours with sporting rights slackened noticeably after 1750'.[41] This was principally because, in the second half of the eighteenth century, the hunting of game underwent profound and complex changes.

The hunting of game birds with hawks, once an essential part of a gentleman's accomplishments, was in decline by the early eighteenth century. This was largely the result of the increased efficiency of guns as the cumbersome and archaic matchlock was replaced in the armouries of the gentry by the safer, shorter, and more manageable flintlock.[42] Nevertheless, guns were still heavy and unwieldy by later standards – with a single barrel, and anything from 4 ft 6 in to 6 ft in length. Although one writer was able to complain in 1750 that 'The art of shooting flying is, within a few Years, come to such a Degree of Perfection, that few Fowls escape',[43] it is clear that the size and accuracy of firearms ensured that many if not most birds were shot on the ground, or else while flying close to it. The usual practice was to stalk the birds, accompanied by a friend or two, with setter dogs or spaniels. The former were trained to point silently to a bird in the grass or stubbles, or as it rested on a low branch; the latter would generally be used to flush them out of the hedgerows. Because of the casual, small-scale nature of shooting at this time, it was generally accepted that qualified gentlemen could stray on to each other's land, in pursuit of hares or game birds, with impunity. It was one of those neighbourly courtesies of polite society.

The indigenous partridge was well suited to this form of shooting. Partridges are essentially birds of open agricultural country. They do not perch high up in trees, preferring to rest (and nest) under hedges or bushes, or in the stubbles and long grass.[44] Game books, which began to appear in some numbers from the 1750s, attest to the pre-eminence of this quarry on most English estates. The appearance of these books, however, also signals the beginning of a significant shift in the practice of shooting, in part conditioned by changes in the pattern of landholding.

As the English landscape became more enclosed, and in particular as landed estates became increasingly consolidated, more strenuous attempts could be made to preserve game, safe in the knowledge that the birds would not simply wander off on to a neighbour's land. Game books show that the average size of the 'bag' steadily rose during the second half of the eighteenth century, especially on the larger estates, despite the repeated claims of contemporaries that game was becoming scarcer. An increase in the opportunities for game preservation was accompanied by improvements in firearm technology which ensured that ever larger numbers of birds could be shot. Through the 1750s, '60s and '70s guns continued to become lighter and shorter, and in 1782 William Watts, a Bristol plumber, discovered how to make 'drop shot', by pouring molten lead in a coarse spray from the top of a tower: this solidified into fairly accurate spheres as it descended, creating shot which penetrated further into the body of the prey. In

1787, the London gun maker Henry Nock invented the 'patent breech', which had a hole running right through the stock to the middle of the charge, rather than along its edge. Because it thus ignited the charge from the middle outwards, the explosion was much faster and considerably more powerful. These changes ensured further reductions in the length of gun barrels, dropping from an average of 3 ft 6 in in 1760 to 2 ft 6 in in 1790. Guns thus became lighter, more manoeuvrable, and so better suited to aerial slaughter.[45]

As the availability of game and the accuracy of guns increased, the ability of sportsmen increasingly came to be judged by their marksmanship, most conveniently measured by the number of birds that they could bring down. This in turn gave further encouragement to the idea that shooting flying birds – which involved greater personal skill – was of prime importance. In 1770 the idea that 'gentlemen shoot flying' was strongly propagated in the book *The Art of Shooting Flying*; by 1801 the author of the standard text on field sports noted that it was 'not exactly at present the custom for Gentlemen to shoot on the ground'.[46] By this time, the increasingly competitive nature of the sport meant that large numbers of players were often involved, frequently groups of guests invited to stay specifically to enjoy the pleasures of the shoot. Further improvements in firearms technology, and in particular the invention of the detonator in 1807, allowed further refinements in the sport: the development of true 'battue' shooting in which beaters would drive the birds out of the covert, and into sight of the waiting line of sportsmen.

The second half of the eighteenth century thus saw fundamental changes in the practice of game shooting. In 1750 it had been a casual, rather leisurely pastime involving two or three friends, accompanied by dogs, taking pot-shots at birds on the ground or near to it. By 1800 it was a far more organized activity, involving much larger numbers of people shooting large numbers of birds in full flight. The native partridge was not well suited to this new form of shooting: it spent much of its time on the ground and, when scared into flight, flew low across the fields. Nor was it well suited to being raised in large numbers, for it had (and has) large territories, as much as 4 hectares to a pair of birds in the winter. Far better suited to the new demands was the pheasant. Not only did this occupy much smaller territories; it also flew high: '*Phasianus colchicus* shot up over the tree-tops like a rocket, its long tail flaunting, its cocketing cry an incitement to the sportsman below.'[47] The pheasant, however, was only really at home in woodland, and where this did not exist it had to be planted. The need for pheasant cover was – along with all the other factors we have just discussed – a major factor in the general upsurge in tree-planting in England at this time.

Pheasants had long been reared on English estates, in special 'pheasantries'. Often these were erected within or beside gardens, and the feeding of the birds – like the feeding of fish in fish ponds – was the job of the gardener. A pheasantry was attached to the north side of the great garden at Wimbledon (Middx) in 1649, while in 1635 Sir William Brereton recorded in some detail the one constructed in the garden of Sir Arthur Ingram near York.[48] The inhabitants of these structures, however, were tame birds, raised to be eaten at the table, not to be shot in the field. Systematic attempts at rearing pheasants specifically for shooting began in

53. William Heath's comment on the Game Laws, 1823. A poacher, caught in a man trap, is fired on by a spring gun.

the early eighteenth century but only really took off after 1750. New kinds of pheasantry now appeared, particularly in the south and east of England: structures in which eggs found on the estate were hatched under domestic hens, and the young chicks then suitably pampered – fed on chopped boiled eggs, ants' eggs, and even toast soaked in urine. The brood was treated like this until ready to be set out in the woods. By the 1780s, on some estates in the south and east of England, the actual breeding and rearing was being moved out into the coverts. Thus at Blenheim in 1787 John Byng noted: 'In various parts of the park . . . clusters of faggots around a coop, where are hatched and reared such quantities of pheasants that I almost trod upon them in the grass.'[49]

But it was not just intensive breeding that increased the numbers of pheasants. Great efforts were now made to curb the bird's natural predators – hawks, owls, weasels, crows, stoats, magpies, polecats, while attempts to curb foxes in this context provided a source of constant conflict with the fox-hunting fraternity. Above all, systematic efforts were made to control a massive increase in the incidence of poaching, something made all the more worrying by the tendency, as one Yorkshire Justice of the Peace described in 1783, for poachers to 'assemble together in the night, in companies, armed with firearms, clubs, and other offensive weapons'.[50] This escalation had a number of causes. In part it was related to the general increase in rural poverty; in part it was the predictable outcome of the 1755 Act which, banning as it did all trade in game, naturally ensured a ready market in illegal birds. Above all, however, it was related to the massive increase in the scale of the temptation now offered to the poor, the hungry or the criminal by the gentry's well-stocked coverts.

The establishment's response was vicious. The Game Act of 1770 made poaching by night (armed or otherwise) punishable by six months imprisonment (twelve for a second offence), on the evidence of a single witness. This Act was ameliorated in 1773, when a new Night Poaching Act reinstated fines as the penalty, although now at a much higher level – up to £50, depending on the number of previous convictions. If the offender had more than two he could be imprisoned for twelve months and also publicly whipped. In the first decades of the nineteenth century yet more brutal legislation was brought in. A statute of 1800 gave gamekeepers the right to seize suspected poachers without warrant. If two or more were caught at night, away from the road with their customary tools of trade, they could be classed as 'incorrigible rogues' and thus liable to two years in jail with a whipping, or forced conscription into the armed forces. As the legislation became more savage, needless to say, poachers resisted arrest ever more violently. In 1817, as a further twist of the spiral, another Night Poaching Act prescribed seven years transportation to any person caught, suitably equipped for poaching, in 'any forest, chase, park, wood, plantation, close or other open or enclosed ground'. An even more Draconian Act replaced this in 1828. Most poachers, it is true, were still tried under the old game laws, and thus received the mandatory fine of £5. But the more extreme penalties were always available for persistent or violent offenders.[51]

All this legislative activity was to little avail. When in 1831 the archaic property qualifications for hunting were finally abolished (and the sale of game again

54. George Allen, Pheasant Shooting. *Scared into flight, the birds fly high, providing a challenge to the sportsmen beneath.*

legalized), around a sixth of all convictions in England were for game law offences. Most estates were in a state of permanent siege against poachers, and took their own measures to protect game: in particular by placing man-traps in the plantations, and mounting patrols by groups of keepers at night. Such measures were accompanied by an increasing reluctance to grant permission to more respectable neighbours to hunt over parts at least of the estate land. Apart from issues of security – it was easier to forbid all casual access than to vet favoured individuals – there was little point in stocking your coverts with pheasants if neighbours were then free to blast them out of the sky.

Eighteenth-century gentlemen were, then, obsessed with the pheasant: with breeding and killing it in ever larger numbers, and with preventing anybody else, except family and guests, from doing the same. It is hardly surprising that its needs had an immense effect on shaping their grounds. The gentry and their gamekeepers were keen observers of their quarry, and the particular preferences of the pheasant help to explain many of the features of eighteenth-century parkland plantations which we have already encountered. Contemporary opinion held that the best coverts were formed by young plantations between fifteen and

55. The Duke of Newcastle Returning from Shooting *by Francis Wheatley, 1788. The 2nd Duke of Newcastle in his park at Clumber (Notts). Clumber House, and the ornamental park bridge, can be seen in the background.*

twenty years old. Young conifers were thought to be particularly attractive to pheasants, especially those in which larch was a major element, 'on account of its branches growing nearly at right angles to the stem: this renders the sitting position of the birds very easy'.[52] We have already noted the importance of conifers in belts and clumps. Once these trees had grown to maturity, however, the suitability of the wood as a pheasant reserve declined dramatically: and a wood which lacked a well-developed shrub layer, such as that created by a stand of mature beech trees, was of little value to the game keeper.[53] Underplanting with some shade-resistant species was then required: hence the vast quantities of bird cherry which appear in many eighteenth-century accounts, and the great masses of rhododendron planted in belts and clumps in the nineteenth century ('the crowning plant for game cover', in the words of Alexander Forsyth).[54]

More important than all this, however, was the way in which the needs of the pheasant helped determine the characteristic disposition of park woodland.

Pheasants need woods but they do not live in their depths. As Blaine put it in 1858, pheasants 'are generally found in woody places, on the borders of plains where they delight to sport':[55] in other words they are essentially a creature of the woodland edge. Indeed, a modern study of radio-tagged birds revealed that they spend almost all their time within 20 metres of the boundary between woodland and open ground.[56] As the same study noted, this preference has an important effect on the holding capacity of woods of different size or shape. 'Small woods, by their very nature, have a higher "edge to area ratio"', and the optimum size for a covert would be less than a hectare. A large number of small woods would also allow the maximum number of pheasants to gain territories at breeding time. Large, continuous blocks of woodland, in contrast, 'often contain areas which are far from any woodland edge and thus of little use to pheasants'.[57] The only large woods suitable for intensive pheasant rearing are, therefore, ones planted in the form of a long thin strip, especially if provided with sinuous or scalloped edges.

Game coverts could be and sometimes were scattered across a gentleman's estate. But for reasons of security – but also, of course, for the convenience of owners and guests – it made more sense to concentrate the coverts relatively close to the mansion, effectively laying out its immediate surroundings as a game reserve. One logical arrangement would be to have a number of small blocks – let us call them *clumps* – scattered around the landscape. A more extensive area of woodland, planted in the form of a thin linear strip (perhaps with wavy or scalloped edges) could be placed on the periphery of the reserve: let us call it a *belt*. Where drives ran in from the outside world it would be sensible to erect a

56. *Eighteenth-century game card, Blenheim. Dead pheasants, woodcocks, and hare in the foreground; palace, park and the Column of Victory in the distance.*

lodge, to control access and to act – in effect – as a base for security guards engaged in permanent surveillance against the incursions of poachers. What we have just done, of course – almost without trying – is to construct the essential framework of the eighteenth-century landscape park.

But these landscapes were intended as much to regulate and articulate relations between members of the propertied class as they were to maintain or enforce the inequalities between that group and its social inferiors. For many relatively minor landowners, who shared their local area with others qualified to hunt, the need to raise ever larger numbers of game birds posed a tricky problem of etiquette. Given that it had long been customary, as we have seen, for sportsmen to hunt indiscriminately over each other's land, the development of systematic rearing required some way of excluding neighbours from the most important reserves without giving offence. The park was a particularly private space in which game could be preserved for the owner's use in a way that could not be considered unneighbourly. As de La Rochefoucauld put it in 1784:

> General custom . . . has established a mutual understanding between all those entitled to shoot that a man leaving his own property can go right ahead and shoot anywhere without getting into trouble with the owner provided he doesn't enter the owner's parkland. The rules of polite behaviour forbid this positively.[58]

The gentry's obsession with shooting cannot 'explain' the landscape park, any more than can their love affair with forestry, horse riding, or the selective breeding of livestock. The park does not have a single 'explanation': and that is because it did not have a single function. In Brown's own words, the landscape park supplied 'all the elegance and *all the comforts* that mankind wants in the Country'. Art, economics, and ideology were all expressed in its structure. In this increasingly divided world, the park was a landscape moulded by every aspect of the lifestyle of the class by whom it was owned.

CHAPTER SEVEN

Repton and the Picturesque

By the last decade of the eighteenth century the landscape park was triumphant: it was the essential symbol of gentility. Yet even as it reached the zenith of its popularity new patterns of social interaction, new concerns and new beliefs were bringing further changes in landscape design. Even before Brown's death in 1783 voices of protest had been heard against the bland simplicity of the landscape park, and the relegation of gardens and pleasure grounds to subordinate situations. As early as 1762 Lord Kames had advocated the establishment of more elaborate and extensive gardens near the house, while William Chambers, in his *Dissertation on Oriental Gardening* of 1772, had urged the creation of grounds with more complex and varied planting.[1] But it was not until the end of the century that such ideas really began to take hold.

HUMPHRY REPTON

The most important figure in the development of landscape design in the last years of the eighteenth century was Humphry Repton. Born at Bury St Edmunds in Suffolk in 1752, his father was a collector of excise and his mother the daughter of a minor Suffolk landowner (from whom Repton eventually inherited a small amount of land).[2] The family moved to Norwich in 1762, where Repton attended the grammar school. In 1764 he was sent to Helvoetsluys in Holland, in order to learn Dutch: it had clearly been decided that his future career lay in Norwich's still flourishing textile industry and, sure enough, on his return at the age of sixteen he was apprenticed to a textile merchant. In 1773, his apprenticeship completed, Repton married Mary Clarke and settled in Norwich. His father provided him with the capital to set up in business on his own, but initial success was followed by financial misfortune and, following the death of his parents, he gave up business and in 1778 bought a small country estate at Sustead near Aylsham (Norfolk). Here he lived a more congenial life, farming on a small scale, reading and sketching: some of his drawings were published as engravings in Armstrongs' *History and Antiquities of the County of Norfolk*, for which he also penned the sections on the hundreds of North and South Erpingham. More importantly, he now began to make some useful social connections, becoming friendly with the Lord of the Manor of Sustead, William Windham, who lived at nearby Felbrigg Hall. When the latter was appointed Chief Secretary to the Lord Lieutenant of Ireland in 1783 Repton went with him as confidential secretary. Windham resigned his post after only a few weeks, and on his return Repton served as his political agent

57. Humphry Repton's trade card, engraved after his own design in 1788.

in the 1784 election, in which he stood for Norwich as a coalition candidate closely allied with the Duke of Portland.[3]

These contacts were to become important when, in 1788, Repton decided to set up as a landscape gardener. By this time he had moved to Hare Street (Essex) and was in increasing financial difficulties: his decision to embark on a new career appears to have been a fairly impetuous one, although he had apparently already gained some experience in his chosen field, having designed gardens for his friends – including, probably, for William Windham.[4] He first touted for business by sending out 'circular letters addressed to former friends'. In these he states that 'Mason, Gilpin, Whately and Gerardin have been of late my breviary – and the works of Kent, Brown and Richmond have been the places of my worship.'[5] The expenses incurred in visiting the places in question are listed on the first page of his account book, opened in June 1788. They included landscapes designed by Kent (Oatlands (Surrey), Stowe, Holkham); Brown (Blenheim, Holkham, Redgrave (Suffolk)); and Richmond (Beeston St Lawrence (Norfolk) and probably Woolverstone (Suffolk)).[6]

Repton's first paid commission, in 1788, was to prepare a design for the grounds of a new villa at Catton, just outside Norwich. His client was a wealthy Norwich merchant, Jeremiah Ives. Other work in East Anglia, for members of the

58 and 59. Humphry Repton: 'before' and 'after' views from the Red Book for Hooton Park, Cheshire, 1802.

local radical/Whig connection, was followed by a clutch of commissions for Tory landowners in Nottinghamshire (Welbeck Abbey, Thoresby and Grove Hall) and elsewhere. By 1795, he had worked on more than fifty commissions, some for the most important members of the nobility. By the end of his career he had, he claimed, worked on more than four hundred properties.[7]

Repton's success, like that of Brown, depended in large part on his engaging personality and his abilities as a salesman. For most of his commissions he produced a Red Book consisting of a text accompanied by a number of water-colour sketches which, as Repton put it, 'will better serve to elucidate my opinion than mere words' (Figures 58–61). The text discusses the site and its 'improvement' under a number of categories such as Character, Situation, The Approach, The House, Walks and Drives, the Kitchen Garden, etc. The watercolours mostly have a slide or overlay which, when flat, shows the present appearance of the property and, when lifted, the results of the proposed improvements. It was the Red Book that clients initially purchased and paid for: that, in one sense, was the product. Repton would make further money from staking out the new work on the ground, and in some cases from undertaking more detailed supervision. But unlike Brown he was not primarily a contractor, did not head a large group of experts or employ a team of labourers.

The Red Book was a subtle device, which some contemporaries saw for what it was. William Mason described how Repton

> Alters places on Paper and makes them so picturesque that fine folks think that all the oaks etc he draws . . . will grow exactly in the shape and fashion in which he delineated them, so they employ him at a great Price; so much the better on both sides, for they might lay out their money worse and he has a numerous family of children to bring up.[8]

Repton differed in one fundamental way from Brown, and indeed from all other major landscape designers of the eighteenth century: he was a prodigious writer. Not only did he produce the texts for a large number of Red Books, he also wrote several volumes on garden design: *Sketches and Hints on Landscape Gardening* (1795), *Observations on the Theory and Practice of Landscape Gardening* (1803), *An Inquiry into the Changes in Taste in Landscape Gardening* (1806), *Fragments on the Theory and Practice of Landscape Gardening* (1816): books which ensured that his ideas were widely influential. And for modern historians there is a bonus: Repton makes a number of quite explicit connections between landscape design and social attitudes of the kind which, for earlier periods, we can usually only infer. These however, need to be interpreted carefully. Repton, like all of us, changed his ideas over time: and the Red Books were intended to please and entice his clients, and were therefore unlikely to present with any clarity or strength Repton's own views.

REPTON'S EARLY WORK

Repton consciously promoted himself as successor to Brown, and to begin with his landscapes were generally similar to his. Repton's early pleasure grounds, at

60 and 61. Humphry Repton: 'before' and 'after' views from the Red Book for Buckminster, Leicestershire, 1793.

places such as Langley (Kent) or Bulstrode (Bucks), were located to one side of the main façade and featured either shrubberies, threaded with serpentine paths and planted with cedars, cypresses, roses and honeysuckles; or (as at Courteenhall (Northants) in 1791) more regular arrangements of flower beds.[9] His early commissions, again like those of Brown, sometimes involved substantial feats of earth-moving, as at Welbeck in 1789, where the bill for contouring came to over £608.[10] Nor was he, at the outset, much of an innovator in the design of parkland. He used clumps which were much like those of Brown, although right from the start he tended to give them more irregular outlines and a denser understorey (usually composed of thorns). And he was keen on planting belts. Thus at Aston park (Cheshire) in 1793 he was fierce in his insistence that all sight of arable land should be rigorously excluded from the park;[11] while at Honing (Norfolk) in 1792 he was adamant that 'corn lands' and 'lawn' were 'incompatible with each other'. He explained to his client, Thomas Cubit, that

> If the park is divided from the farm only by a hedge, we know the breadth of a hedge, and its proximity is as offensive as if the pale made the line of separation; but if instead of a pale or hedge we substitute a wood of sufficient depth to act as a screen, the imagination gives still greater depth to that wood than it really has, and the park derives extent from what in fact is its boundary.[12]

Yet this quotation reveals a certain difference of emphasis, a certain subtlety of approach, which seems more original. This is evident from the very outset of his career, in his design for Catton park in 1788.[13] Repton's client, the merchant Jeremiah Ives, did not possess a country estate in the traditional sense. He owned, in fact, no more than a few fields, and the site chosen for the house (probably by Repton) lay at the northern end of the property, on a rise overlooking Norwich, with the park sloping away to the south. At first glance its design appears ordinary enough, with thick perimeter belts of beech, oak and sweet chestnut, extensive use of pre-existing hedgerow timber (prominent lines of ancient pollards still dominate the park), and a pleasure ground tucked away to the north of the house. What was novel was the care with which the wider countryside was integrated with the park. The layout of the perimeter belts was carefully contrived in order to allow selected views out from house and park. To the east there was a gap in the belt, with only some low shrub planting to obscure the line of a lane running along the perimeter of the park. This allowed views out into a pasture field beyond, the only one on this side of the park actually owned by Ives, and this Repton planted up in a suitably ornamental fashion. On the western side of the park there were further gaps in the belt, allowing views out across the few other fields owned by Ives: these were planted with clumps to give, once again, an impression of a large and continuous estate. The hall, as already noted, lay on the northern edge of the park, and the houses of the village (which Ives did not own) lay little more than 200 metres away. These were carefully screened from view by dense planting, although again there was a gap, to ensure that the tower of the parish church, picturesquely covered with ivy, was in full view of the pleasure ground. The drive to the hall did not strike out across the length of the park from the south, but instead ran only a short distance across the north of the grounds, leaving the main road near to the point where this entered Catton village. Here Repton erected a small picturesque thatched cottage – perhaps originally as a lodge, possibly merely as an embellishment. Again the belt was broken here, so that the building could also be seen from the interior of the park.

Turning into the drive and passing through the gates, views of the park were cleverly screened by shrubberies until the hall itself was reached. This device served to obscure the rather constricted northern extent of the park, and thus – like the gaps in the eastern and western belts – contrived to make Ives' domain appear much more extensive than it really was.

Now, few of these techniques were new. The careful placing of belts and plantations to make a property appear larger than its actual extent, for example, had been tried many times in the eighteenth century. The degree, however, to which visual symbol and illusion were here being subtly manipulated was novel: and it is particularly striking to find these devices already so well developed in Repton's first commission.

Of particular importance in all of Repton's early work was something he referred to as 'appropriation': the idea that the status of the landowner did not arise simply from the possession of an extensive park, but rather from the visible signs of his ownership spread throughout the whole area of the estate. Thus, as he wrote in the Red Book for Tatton Park (Cheshire),

> The first essential of greatness in a place, is the appearance of united and uninterrupted property. . . . There are various ways by which this effect is occasionally produced . . . viz. the church, and churchyards, may be decorated in a style that shall in some degree correspond with that of the mansion; – the market-house, or other public edifice, an obelisk, or even a *mere* stone, with distances, may be made an ornament to the town, and bear the arms of the family.[14]

Repton was acutely aware of what we might call the public image of a place, and the way that this redounded on the social prestige of the owner. Following the adage that first impressions last longest, he generally placed particular emphasis on the entrance to the park: as he put it in the Red Book for Tewin (Herts), 'the first object of improvement will be to prevent unfavourable first impressions'.[15] He thus generally preferred entrance drives which left the high road in a smooth curve rather than sharply, at a right angle: for the latter arrangement gave the impression that the road was continuing on 'to some object of greater importance . . . which is always if possible to be avoided'.[16]

Some of Repton's early clients were great landowners, but many were wealthy merchants or local squires of the kind who were increasingly laying out parks in the 1780s and '90s. Men with relatively small estates had to display their status in subtle ways, and in his commissions and writings Repton offered a sophisticated formula for achieving this.

THE 'PICTURESQUE CONTROVERSY'

By 1794 Repton was already a successful designer, and was beginning to assemble his ideas for publication in a book, *Sketches and Hints on Landscape Gardening*, when he suddenly became involved in a public controversy with two Herefordshire landowners, Uvedale Price and Richard Payne Knight. The latter's *The Landscape, a Didactic Poem* appeared in April 1794; Price's *Essay on the Picturesque* was published the following month.[17] Both Knight and Price were, in effect, developing ideas promulgated from the 1760s by the Revd William Gilpin concerning the beauties of natural scenery, and in particular the 'picturesque' scenery of the upland regions of Britain: cliffs, rocks, mountains, and cascades. In 1792 Gilpin transferred his attention to the field of abstract aesthetics and, by extension, to notions of landscape design. In the first of three essays on the appreciation of landscape and scenery, Gilpin argued that 'beauty' was a concept associated with the neat and the smooth, whereas *picturesque* beauty was a different category, implying roughness and ruggedness, qualities notably absent from the gentle swells of the Brownian park. 'How flat, and insipid is often the garden scene, how puerile, how absurd!' Gilpin wrote. 'The banks of the river, how smooth, and parallel! The lawn, and its boundaries, how unlike nature!'[18] Price and Knight took up where Gilpin left off, arguing that roughness and variety – in overall landforms and planting, as well as in the incorporation of such details as blasted trees, decaying cottages, and ivy-clad ruins – should play a prominent role in the design of the park (Figures 62 and 63). In addition, they suggested that landscape design should adhere to the principles of composition derived from painters of Italian landscapes such as Claude and Poussin, a concept which, as we have seen, had influenced the design of some élite grounds in the middle years of the eighteenth century. The composition – that is, the principle view from the house – should employ the same structural organization of the 'three distances': it should have a foreground, a middle ground and a far distance. 'And howso'er the view may be confin'd/Three mark'd divisions we shall always find', as Knight put it. Such a structure was lacking in Brown's designs which, with lawn sweeping up to the walls of the house, and a horizon often obscured by the encircling belt, were dominated by a kind of extended middle ground. More distant views, perhaps of high hills or (best of all) far mountains, ought to be included if possible. Conversely, some kind of foreground should be provided. At Payne Knight's own home at Downton Castle (Heref.) 'large fragments of stone were irregularly thrown amongst the briars and weeds, to imitate the foreground of a picture'.[19] In *The Landscape*, however, Knight appears to offer another alternative: the retention or even creation of terraces and formal gardens in front of the main façade of the mansion.[20]

Price and Knight did not limit their attacks to Brown and his 'imitators'. They also lambasted Repton, whose landscapes Knight described as 'designed and executed exactly after Mr Brown's receipt, without any attention to the natural or artificial character of a place'. Repton, in a hurriedly written appendix added to his *Sketches and Hints* of 1795, defended both the memory of Brown and his own position. But the real significance and substance of the somewhat bitter dispute that ensued remains a matter of debate. In some ways the two sides were less far

*62 and 63. A park in the style of 'Capability' Brown (62) given the picturesque treatment
(63). Illustrations by Thomas Hearne for Richard Payne Knight's* The Landscape: a
Didactic Poem *(1794)*.

apart than the violence of their disagreement would suggest. Repton himself, from a very early stage in his career, praised picturesque scenery of the kind admired by Gilpin, and professed 'that he sought the principles of his art, not in the works of Kent or Brown, but in those of the great landscape painters'. The differences between the two sides in the 'Picturesque Controversy' may, to some extent, have been more apparent than real, and related to the geography of patronage. Jay Appleton has pointed out that because Repton's commissions were overwhelmingly in the south and east of England, he had few opportunities to exploit the picturesque potential of rocky eminences, cascades, and other dramatic incidents offered by upland terrain.[21] There may be an element of truth in this suggestion. In those cases where Repton was provided by nature with the necessary raw materials, he could produce something almost as 'picturesque' as Knight's Downton. Thus at Mulgrave (North Yorks), Repton's treatment of the area to the south and south-west of Mulgrave Castle exploited to the full the possibilities provided by two parallel ravines and the sharp ridge between them.

Modern commentators, however, sometimes misunderstand, or oversimplify, the nature of the picturesque. It was not, in fact, simply the rocky scenery of the Highland zone which appealed to Price and Knight. The picturesque could be found in the rutted lane with its high hedgebanks, where

> The winter torrents, in some places wash down the mould from the upper grounds and form projections . . . with the most luxuriant vegetation; in other parts they tear the banks into deep hollows, discovering the different strata of earth, and the shaggy roots of trees.[22]

Similarly, the scenery of forests – more of a lowland than a highland form of landscape – was quintessentially 'picturesque'. When applied to garden design, the 'picturesque' was less about rugged grandeur, more about the creation of variety, surprise and interesting detail, in reaction to the formulaic simplicity of the Brownian park. Price and Knight found beauty in the details of the vernacular landscape, created by the toil of farmers and labourers: in ancient hedgebanks, old outgrown pollards – rather than in the empty contrived expanses of the landscape park, imposed insensitively on the local terrain. The picturesque landscape was, moreover, one to be explored, as well as to be enjoyed from the windows or the terrace: and when explored, it would reveal a succession of intriguing features and details not immediately visible from a distance.[23] Knight wrote how

> The stately arch, high rais'd with massive stone;
> The pondrous flag, that forms a bridge alone;
> The prostrate tree, or rudely propt-up beam,
> That leads the path across the foaming stream;
> May each the scene with different beauty grace.[24]

Human as well as natural features would litter the trail, admissible to the ranks of the picturesque if sufficiently hallowed by time: the 'quarry long neglected, and o'ergrown', the 'retir'd and antiquated cot'; but also rather plain and functional structures made of interesting local materials.[25] Such a succession of features was indeed created in the grounds of Downton, Knight's castle-like house in Herefordshire: Knight was a rich man and could afford such embellishments – including not only a dramatic bridge over the gorge there, but a number of less impressive features and buildings strung along the path beside it.

Repton was already, in 1794, using some of the features and details which might be considered necessary for a picturesque landscape, like the thatched cottage and church tower at Catton. Indeed, church towers feature prominently in almost all his early designs. But these were employed in a traditional way, as eye-catchers to improve, or focus, or lend interest to a more general prospect. Occasionally we find him trying to create walks with variety and surprises of a vaguely picturesque nature, as at Holkham (Norfolk) in 1789, where his design for the lakeside pleasure ground featured paths leading past buildings and features hidden in the woods. There was a 'snug thatched cottage . . . picturesquely embosomed in the trees', while more dramatic incident would be supplied by adapting a somewhat diminutive chalk-pit: a shallow cave was to be excavated in its side, whence visitors could relish 'this picturesque and awful spot'.[26] But the resemblances between this kind of thing and Downton are limited – and not simply because of the more muted nature of the local terrain. Knight's landscapes were about the evocative, about exploration and surprise. Repton's, in contrast, seem twee and predictable.

Repton himself, however, would have argued (not unreasonably) that landscapes such as those created at Holkham were more practical than those advocated by Price or Knight. Genteel visitors could there enjoy a healthy, amusing, but not threatening walk. Elsewhere he noted that

> While mouldering abbeys and the antiquated cottage with its chimney smothered in ivy may be eminently appealing to the painter, in whatever relates to man, propriety and convenience are not less objectives of good taste than picturesque effects.[27]

The Red Books generally exude the idea that the landscape around a country house needed to be lived in and used, not just looked at. They must combine 'beauty and utility'. Thus the spread of scrub and undergrowth across the parkland turf, something apparently advocated by Knight, would have reduced the density of stock which could be maintained and would thus have rendered the park a less affordable luxury for the average English gentleman.

To some extent, the differences in approach expressed in the writings of Repton on the one hand, and Payne and Knight on the other, were a manifestation of important ideological differences. The philosophy of the picturesque prophets seems complex and occasionally contradictory – the two men did not entirely share the same views or, at least, there were differences of emphasis. Knight emphasized ideas of individual freedom derived in part from Rousseau. The free spirit of man was to be embodied and expressed in the wildness and individuality of features in the landscape, and he thus praised the wild forest, where 'ev'ry shaggy shrub and spreading tree / Proclaimed the seat of native liberty'.[28] Some contemporaries certainly saw dangerous political implications in the picturesque. Repton's friend Anna Seward wrote to Dr Johnson about Knight's poem *The Landscape*:

> Knight's system appears to me the Jacobinism of taste; from its abusing that rational spirit of improvement suggested by Milton in his description of the primeaval garden; and realised and diffused by Brown . . . Mr Knight would have nature as well as man indulged in that uncurbed and wild luxuriance, which must soon render our landscape-island rank, weedy, damp and unwholesome as the incultivate savannahs of America . . . save me, good Heaven, from living in tangled forests and amongst men who are unchecked by those guardian laws, which bind the various orders of society in one common interest. May the lawns I tread be smoothed by healthful industry . . . and may the people, amongst whom I live, be withheld by stronger repelants than their own virtue, from invading my property and shedding my blood!! – And so much for politics and pleasure grounds.[29]

Yet Price and Knight were by no means intent on radical revolution, nor simply absorbed in obscure and impractical matters of philosophy and aesthetics. Knight was, as we have said, a wealthy landowner, and Price's beloved Foxley (Heref.) was no small estate. Its woods may have been picturesque incidents in the landscape, but they were also intensively managed, their coppiced underwood supplying poles for the local hop grounds. Price's land agent was Nathaniel Kent who – by a remarkable coincidence – also served Repton's friend and patron William Windham on the Felbrigg estate in Norfolk. Between 1770 and 1774 Kent raised the rental income of Foxley by some 21 per cent.[30] Careful estate management here included, however, a paternalist regard for tenants and labourers: and engendered an affection for the character of a place which the stereotyped quality and ruthless execution of Brown's 'improvements' seemed to negate. Such matters must have seemed particularly pressing in the 1790s, with France convulsed in violent revolution. When Price learnt that the French had landed on the coast of Pembrokeshire in 1797, he issued a pamphlet entitled *Thoughts on the Defence of Property* which argued that all local landowners in Herefordshire should be given arms, and training in how to use them. But the same pamphlet is also full of paternalist imagery and sentiment, stressing the need for 'attention and benevolence towards the labouring poor' to forestall social upheaval. He also emphasized the importance of maintaining smallholders, 'a bold yeomanry, their country's pride', against the expansion of large estates. Price talked a great deal about what he called 'connection', 'that great principal': 'from the beneficial mixture, and frequent intercommunication of high and low, that separation is happily disguised . . . '.[31] In general the proponents of the picturesque (like William Mason before them) opposed the complete seclusion of the country house, and favoured a less explicit separation of park and surrounding countryside.

Traditional paternalism went easily with a conservative local patriotism, and to some extent Price and Knight's aesthetic views can be read as an expression of enthusiasm for the scenery of their native Herefordshire, their hostility to Brown and Repton as a reaction against a school of landscape design which not only brought a stereotyped appearance to all country estates, but was based on the more muted countryside of the south-east. The spread of southern fashions into the more remote areas of England expressed the diffusion of more commercial, capitalist, social relations: relations which, as we have seen, were generally associated with the decline or demise of small landowners and farmers. 'Vast possessions give ambitious views, and ambitious views destroy local attachments', as Price put it.[32] Hardly surprising, then, that he and Knight took particular exception to Repton's concept of 'appropriation'. This they saw as no more than an expression of vanity, Price stating that

> There is no such enemy to the real improvement of the beauty of grounds as the foolish vanity of making a parade of their extent, and of various marks of the owner's property, under the title of 'Appropriation'.[33]

Repton at this stage seems to have thought rather less than Price about the ideological implications of landscape gardening. In the Appendix to *Sketches and Hints*, which formed an open letter to Price, he could do no better than reiterate the conventional line, insisting that the dominant landscape style represented:

> The happy medium between the wilderness of nature and the stiffness of art; in the same manner as the English constitution is the happy medium between the liberty of savages and the restraints of despotic government.[34]

Price, however, replied with a rather different and more sophisticated argument: that landscape gardening should be 'an art of peace', intended to dissipate social tensions. But by this time, under the sheer weight of experience, Repton's own ideas were beginning to change.

Repton's later writings betray an increasing degree of social awareness. Like Price and many other contemporaries he became more and more anxious about threats to the social order as the trend towards an increasingly polarized rural community, and an increasingly commercial society, was accelerated by the impact of the Napoleonic Wars. Noting in 1802 that he had earned just half the amount he had in 1799, Repton blamed the impoverishment of prospective clients on heavy war taxation.[35] He believed that established landed families were being forced to sell their estates to parvenus and speculators, to men who had grown rich on profitable wartime government contracts: 'I have seen upstart wealth trampling over all I have been accustomed to look up to with respect.' He believed that the 'new men' (many of whom in fact became Repton's clients) lacked any real understanding of, or any sense of responsibility towards, their estates. It was they, he became convinced – and the forces of commercialism which they represented – who were principally responsible for the quickening pace of enclosure, for the amalgamation of farms, and for the growing plight of the rural poor. France, engulfed in revolution, offered a model for what might happen in England if all this continued unchecked.

It was not so much that Repton's designs changed in the years around 1800 – although, as we shall see, they did. It was more that the kinds of effect he had long been creating were now being explained in new ways, more in tune with the times. Thus the extension of planting out into the surrounding countryside, the creation of links with the parish church and other prominent features in the locality, were no longer discussed solely in terms of *appropriation*, but also in terms of the landowner's paternalist care for the local community. Thus, in a famous quotation, he described how labourers' cottages can, if made 'a subordinate part of the general scenery . . . so far from disfiguring it, add to the dignity that wealth can derive from the exercise of benevolence'.[36] The country house should not stand 'solitary and isolated', detached from the village and the parish church, hidden away behind parkland belts which had become a barrier 'scarce less offensive than the pale'. There were, however, limits: the integration of estate and park could only go so far, for the park and farm were 'distinct objects, and ought never to be brought together in the same point of view'. Thus while Repton was now (like Price and Knight) reacting against the exclusivity of the Brownian park, he was not proposing a return to the kind of integration of husbandry and aesthetics advocated by Switzer earlier in the century.

Repton's paternalist sentiments found their fullest expression in the *Fragments* of 1816. By this time Repton was less willing to rush to the defence of Brown. What were becoming generally accepted defects of the landscape park he now often attributed to the man himself, rather than (as earlier) to his 'imitators'. Thus, 'Where a rattling turbulent mountain-stream passes through a rocky valley, like the Derwent at Chatsworth, perhaps Mr Brown was wrong in checking its noisy course, to produce the glassy surface of a slow moving river.'[37] Such an implied *rapprochement* with the prophets of the picturesque is elsewhere quite explicit, most notably in his comments on Knight's own domain:

> When I compare the picturesque scenery of Downton Vale with the meagre efforts of art, which are attributed to the school of Brown, I cannot wonder at the enthusiastic abhorrence which the author of *The Landscape* expresses for modern gardening.[38]

Above all, the practice of 'surrounding a house by a naked grass field' was, he could now openly acknowledge, a 'bald and insipid custom, introduced by Brown'.[39]

Yet when we look at Repton's solution to all this, we can also see the extent to which his ideas remained quite distinct from those of Price and Knight. For to remedy such defects by 'slovenly neglect, or by studied and affected rudeness', he argued, 'seems to be an opposite extreme not less offensive'. Instead, Repton increasingly emphasized one particular aspect of the picturesque package: he placed more and more emphasis on the foreground, on the gardens and pleasure grounds in the vicinity of the house.

THE RETURN OF THE GARDEN

By 1804, at Woburn Abbey (Beds), Repton was designing a complex sequence of pleasure grounds which included both an American garden and a Chinese garden. Two years later he was able to suggest that 'The gardens, or pleasure-grounds, near a house, may be considered as so many different apartments belonging to its state, its comfort, and its pleasure.'[40] In 1813 at Ashridge (Herts) no less than fifteen separate gardens were provided, including a rosarium, a 'Monk's Garden', a 'Mount Garden', and an American garden.[41] Equally significant, however, was the growing formality of some of his designs. Partly, perhaps, under the influence of his architect son John Adey, they became increasingly antiquarian in nature, even taking the form of geometric parterres:

>Close clipp'd box, th'embroider'd bed
>In rows and formal order laid.[42]

Such arrangements might even, as at Beaudessert (Staffs) in 1813, be placed across the main façade of the house. Even where such a drastic return to earlier traditions was not attempted, terraces – complete with balustrades and stone steps – were now regularly placed between house and park.

Repton was not a lone pioneer in all this. His increasingly prominent and geometric gardens were part and parcel of a more general shift in public taste

64. *The Return of the Garden: Repton's design for Lord Sidmouth's house in Richmond Park, from the* Fragments *of 1816.*

away from the open 'naturalistic' parkland setting for the house. In 1804 Archibald Forbes took over the neglected late seventeenth-century gardens at Levens (Cumbria) and recut the geometric topiary which had long since grown out of shape; four years later the writer Thomas Hope argued forcibly for the creation of new formal gardens in close proximity to the house; and by the 1810s there were many prominent designers such as Lewis Kennedy who were busy creating formal parterres for country houses. Repton was swimming with the tide as much as setting the stylistic pace.

As in earlier periods, a number of influences shaped the new fashion. To some extent, perhaps, the gentry were simply bored with the blandness of the Brownian park, and wanted something new: a desire which professional designers and contractors, ever in need of new work, were keen to encourage and exploit. But there were other, more specific reasons for the change, and Repton himself gives us two of them. The first relates to developments in architecture. Repton dabbled in architecture and wrote a good deal about its relationship with landscape design. Although he sometimes advocated the construction of a house in the classical style – the 'Grecian' or 'Modern' style, as he called it – he became a keen supporter of the new fashion for the gothic. From the start of his career he favoured the retention of existing, genuine examples of ancient manor houses. As early as 1789 he had argued against the demolition of the ancient Shrubland Hall (Suffolk), and in the Red Book for Lamer (1792) he affirmed his belief that 'There is so much picturesque beauty and importance even in the worst species of what is called gothic architecture that I am always an advocate of preserving its character wherever possible.'[43]

As the years passed he began to recommend the construction of entirely new houses in what he termed 'Manor House Gothic', by which he meant a vaguely Tudor or Elizabethan style. Here Repton was, once more, part of a more general trend – and by 1816 he was able to refer to the 'prevailing taste for the Gothic style' in England.[44]

Yet again, to some extent the new fashion simply represented a desire for something novel after a century of erecting buildings in a broadly classical style: and gothic fitted in well with the contemporary enthusiasm for the romantic, dramatic and picturesque evident in the writings of Gilpin and others. But the new taste was also a manifestation of the social anxieties we have already mentioned. It represented an escapist yearning for a supposedly more harmonious and stable age, before the Industrial Revolution and the emergence of agrarian capitalism. Repton wrote nostalgically of the days when the 'old manor House' was the centre of an organic rural community, where 'the lord of the soil resided among his tenants'.[45] In addition, gothic fitted in well with new demands being placed on gentlemen's residences. The age of the country house party was well under way. As standards of road transport steadily improved, larger numbers of visitors had to be accommodated in country houses, together with a more diverse range of rooms for entertaining. Moreover, larger numbers of servants were now being maintained by the rich (who could now better afford them, given the fall in the value of wages); yet in this increasingly polarized society there was a growing desire to keep them, and all that they did, discreetly hidden away from family and visitors. These diverse

65. *The Return of the Garden: Repton's design for Ashridge Park, Hertfordshire, from the* Fragments *of 1816.*

demands could best be fitted into the asymmetrical, rambling form of the pseudo-medieval castle or manor house rather than the compact plan of the classical residence. Thus at Wyatt's great gothic pile of Ashridge, high in the Hertfordshire Chilterns, long wings allowed a proliferation of rooms for entertaining and permitted the servants to be kept well away from the main body of the house (and sexually segregated: another growing concern). The invention of the bell pull allowed them to be easily summoned when required.[46]

Whatever the precise explanation for the change in architectural taste, it had important implications for garden design. The clean, compact lines of Palladian or Neoclassical houses had been complimented by the smooth simplicity of the landscape park. The more elaborate and asymmetrical edifices now being erected demanded more detail and structure in front of their main façades. They needed gardens, and preferably gardens of a suitably antiquarian nature: as at Ashridge, where Repton 'ventured boldly to go back to those ancient trim Gardens, which formerly delighted the venerable inhabitants of this curious spot'.[47]

But even more important in the return to prominence of the garden were changes in the clientele of designers such as Repton, in the new social and economic climate of the early nineteenth century. As Repton himself noted in 1816:

> It seldom falls to the lot of the improver to be called upon for his opinion on places of great extent . . . while in the neighbourhood of every city or manufacturing town, new places as villas are daily springing up, and these, with a few acres, require all the conveniences, comforts, and appendages, of larger and more sumptuous, if not more expensive places. And . . . these have of late had the greatest claim to my attention. . . .[48]

66. Even when country houses were not provided with elaborate gardens, a balustraded terrace was increasingly interposed between house and park. From Repton's Fragments *of 1816.*

An increasing concentration of these more lowly, or at least more circumscribed properties inevitably engendered a change in style. Small properties needed, as Repton noted, more careful attention than larger grounds. Villa owners lacked the resources for large-scale manipulation of the landscape. It was not by 'adding field to field, or by taking away hedges, or by removing roads to a distance' that the surroundings of a villa were to be improved. Instead, this was to be done by exploiting 'every circumstance of interest or beauty within our reach, and by hiding such objects as cannot be viewed with pleasure': a yet more intimate and refined version of the treatment which, since Catton in 1788, Repton had been meting out to small country estates. The approach of the Brownian school could never be made to work on grounds which extended over only a few hectares. In particular, it was impossible to surround grounds of small extent with a continuous belt, because this would simply serve to emphasize their limited size, and would create an offensively confined space. Above all, working on a smaller scale meant designing with greater attention to detail, and hence giving more emphasis to the garden: to the cultivation of flowers and bushes, rather than to the establishment of great sweeps of turf, and the planting of woods and plantations.

Changing patterns of wealth and power thus, once again, had their effect on the development of landscape design. The landscape park had, in the increasingly fluid social conditions of mid-eighteenth-century England, helped to mark out the superiority of the landed rich and define them as a group apart. But in the early nineteenth century, as Britain emerged as an industrial nation and an imperial power, wealth increasingly flowed to the middling ranks of society. And as the century progressed it was to this group that writers on garden design increasingly turned their attention.

CHAPTER EIGHT

Postscript: Beyond Georgian England

INTO THE NINETEENTH CENTURY

The picturesque controversy created a great deal of interest in the final decades of the eighteenth century. What is less clear is the extent to which picturesque notions were actually put into practice in the parks and gardens of the gentry. Neither Price nor Knight operated as professional designers, although Price in particular offered informal advice at a number of places, including Bentley Priory (Middx) and Cassiobury (Herts). By 1837 a description of the latter house noted how

> Immediately beyond the lawn, to the east, is a part of the park, abounding with large and grand forest-trees, interspersed with furze, thorn &c., forming a striking contrast to the dressed scenes adjoining the house.[1]

It is possible that in the years around 1800 a number of parks were given a rather wilder, rougher appearance in this way, by planting thorns and other scrub in the turf and, perhaps, by reducing the stocking levels in order to encourage the growth of longer and lusher grass. But when, in the first decades of the nineteenth century, professionals arrived on the scene who consciously described themselves as 'picturesque' designers, their style was both more sophisticated and more formulaic than this. One was John Claudius Loudon, who claimed in 1805 that he was 'The first who has set out as a landscape gardener, professing to follow Mr Price's principles', adding 'How far I shall succeed in executing my plans, and introducing more of the picturesque into improved places, time alone must determine.'[2] Another was William Sawrey Gilpin, twenty-one years Loudon's senior and William Gilpin's nephew and pupil, who began work as a designer around 1806. Although there was much to distinguish the landscapes of these two men, and of others working in the picturesque mode, there was also much that they had in common.

Picturesque parks were more densely and irregularly planted than those of Brown or Repton – two or more trees were frequently planted in a single hole in order to create a dense and irregular outline. More use seems to have been made of conifers, especially the Scots pine, with its rapid growth and romantic, twisted head. Less easy to define is the somewhat amorphous structure of the planting, with clumps and trees scattered profusely, in order to give an overall feeling of variety and luxuriance, rather than being carefully positioned to frame vistas and views (Figures 67 and 68). Lakes, too, were now provided with more busy detail, their shores made increasingly irregular, their surface broken up with a profusion of islands. And, following the advice and precept of Knight and Price, primitive and rustic buildings and other features of interest were sometimes scattered through the landscape, often in such a way that they had to be discovered through exploration, rather than being enjoyed immediately from the windows of the house.

These designers continued to emphasize the importance of gardens and pleasure grounds as the immediate setting of the house. Loudon (especially in the middle of his career) was interested in formal gardens, but he also developed the pleasure-ground styles of the previous century, making extensive use of the wide range of exotic plants now available in order to create environments which looked as different as possible from 'wild nature'. By 1832 he had coined a term – 'gardenesque' – for the kind of planting he considered suitable for such areas, in which individual specimens were carefully placed so as to be displayed to best advantage.[3] Gilpin's designs likewise featured extensive pleasure grounds, formal parterres, and in particular prominent terraces: these were often extended in an asymmetrical fashion far beyond the façade of the house. Gravel paths wandered through interminable shrubberies, provided with a bewildering range of exotics.

By this stage, of course, we are leaving the age of Brown far behind, and are arriving in the England of Victoria: a world in which the wealth and political influence of middle-class managers and administrators was increasing with every passing decade, in which entrepreneurs and industrialists were amassing fortunes to rival those of traditional landed families. The changed circumstances are well illustrated by the career of Loudon himself. For in spite of his stated ambition in 1805, he did not in the event work primarily as a designer of country house landscapes nor, in fact, as a designer at all. It was as a writer that he was most important. His *Encyclopedia of Gardening* of 1822 was phenomenally successful, and was followed by further volumes on agriculture, trees and shrubs, and plants: in all, it is said, he penned more than 60 million words. His books sold well, principally to the expanding middle class: and it was to this group, above all, that his advice was increasingly directed. His first major work was entitled the *Treatise on Farming, Improving and Managing Country Residences*; his last was significantly entitled *The Suburban Gardener and Villa Companion*.[4] It was as a designer of public, urban parks and cemeteries, rather than of country house grounds, that Loudon made his direct mark on the English landscape, although his ideas for garden design continued to find their way into the grounds of the rich.

THE SURVIVAL OF THE PARK

The return to prominence of the garden to the country house landscape, while inexorable, was nevertheless gradual. Many country houses continued to look out

67 and 68. *The picturesque in practice: note the busy detail shown in these sketches of William Sawrey Gilpin's proposed improvements to the lake at Wolterton, Norfolk,* c. *1830.*

directly on to open parkland until the second half of the century: and even at its end there were many that continued to do so. More importantly, the rise of the *garden* was not accompanied by any diminution in enthusiasm for the *park*. Formal gardens, even knots and parterres, might return but there was no strong desire to reinstate the kinds of walled enclosure within which these had once been set. Instead, the increasingly flamboyant displays were placed on broad open terraces of a loosely Italianate inspiration, terraces which in the middle decades of the century – under the influence of designers such as William Andrews Nesfield and Charles Barry – grew ever more extensive and elaborate (Figure 69). Leaning against their low balustrades, the owner his family and friends could enjoy unrestricted views over the expanses of parkland below.[5]

For all houses of any note had a park. Indeed, these continued to proliferate in the middle decades of the nineteenth century. Wealth and power might flow to new men, successful capitalists; but as in the previous century, a personal fortune made in mines and factories was soon invested in a rural estate, complete with a mansion – and a park. The gulf between rich and poor continued to widen in the early years of the nineteenth century, and remained vast: and the park continued, above all, to provide the gentleman and his family with seclusion and privacy. In spite of Repton's strictures against the continuous belt, and the picturesque predilection for the distant prospect, parks were now if anything *more* enclosed than they had been in the previous century. In 1834 Tallyrand's niece, the Duchess de Dino, observed with disappointment that

English people . . . hate to be seen, and to secure privacy are quite willing to dispense with an extended view. . . . You need not hope to amuse yourself by watching the movements of passers-by, the travellers, the peasants working in the fields, the villages or the surrounding country. Green lawns, and flowers round about the house, and splendid trees which block all vistas – these are what they love and what you find almost everywhere.[6]

The appearance of the park did not radically change in Victoria's England. The picturesque ideas of Loudon and Gilpin had their effect, it is true, in the increasing variety of parkland planting. Horse chestnut and lime now rivalled oak and beech in many parks, and exotic conifers were more widely planted (although, as we have seen, pines and larches were by no means unknown in the Brownian park). The tall Wellingtonia, blocking the vistas of an earlier design like some vast alien toilet brush, is one noted legacy of the period. There was also a proliferation of features intermediate between the structure and detail of the garden and the open expanses of parkland. Woodland gardens and arboreta were particularly popular, and walks running through the perimeter belts, bordered by box, yew and laurel, abounded. Yet the essential structure of the landscape park survived, with comparatively little alteration: irregular, naturalistic, with its clumps and belts and lake. And – albeit colonized still further by 'gardenesque' detail – it was this distinctive landscape, created by and for a leisured élite, that came to form the basic aesthetic of public parks when these began to be created in towns and cities during the middle and later decades of the nineteenth century.

69. Italianate terraces created by William Burn and William Andrews Nesfield at Lynford, Norfolk, around 1860.

Their casual scatter of trees, open water, and meandering paths, owed more to the designs of Repton and Brown than to any other inspiration.

The landscape park may have been the product of a particular time and place, the consequence of a specific constellation of social, political and economic forces in eighteenth-century England. Yet just as it had a prehistory, an ancestry, in the aesthetic deer parks of the fifteenth and sixteenth centuries, so too did it have an afterlife in the Victorian era. Like all artefacts, landscapes and buildings, the landscape park could change its meaning within the society which had given it birth, as time passed and circumstances altered.

The Landscape Park in the Twentieth Century

The landscape park continued to be the quintessential expression of wealth and status until the twentieth century. Only then did it suffer an eclipse. The park was an integral part of a landed estate, and as agriculture moved into recession from the 1880s and the rental income from farmland declined, those landowners who lacked alternative, non-agricultural sources of income found themselves in increasing financial difficulties.[7] Many were forced to sell up following the end of the First World War: as much as 25 per cent of the land area of England is supposed to have changed hands in the four years between 1918 and 1922. This land was bought by tenant farmers, by developers, by the Forestry Commission. Many country houses were demolished or converted into schools and hotels: their parks were ploughed or engulfed in conifer plantations or, if in the vicinity of a major city, were gobbled up by housing developments (usually rather up-market ones) and golf courses.

Where country estates survived intact in the interwar years so too, in general, did their parks (there was little incentive to plough these up with agriculture in a state of continued depression): but the elaborate gardens created in Victorian times were progressively simplified, to save on escalating wage bills. The Second World War brought further problems, however. Many country houses and their grounds were taken over by the military, much of their woodland clear-felled to meet the wartime timber shortage, and large areas of parkland ploughed as part of the 'Dig for Victory' campaign. And in the immediate postwar years, while the fortunes of agriculture began to revive, those of the landscape park did not. The days when a country seat set in a vast and seemingly useless park inspired awe and respect, brought status and political advantage, were long gone. In the political circumstances of 1945, such things seemed an embarrassment: a pressing reminder of the wealth of the owners, a symbol of a passing age of privilege, an invitation to tax. Moreover, with many country houses (and their grounds) now reaching a respectable age, they were becoming increasingly expensive to maintain. In 1945 or 1950 the days of the country house must have appeared numbered: and even when the mansion was retained, the park was increasingly regarded as an unnecessary encumbrance. Better to plough it up for cereals, plant it with conifers, or excavate it for gravel.

Yet contrary to predictions, from the late 1950s the country house and its landscape experienced a revival. The National Trust – originally established to protect wild places and other rural landscapes – first began to acquire country houses and their estates in the 1930s, but in the postwar decades these acquisitions proceeded apace. The public flocked to visit them. At the same time, many private owners began to open their properties, partly to make money but partly as a condition of tax exemptions and repair grants. These, in various forms, were made available by successive postwar administrations of every political persuasion: for one aspect of the postwar political consensus was that the public purse should provide money to preserve the architectural treasures of a bygone age, buildings which rightly or wrongly were deemed part of the British heritage. Country houses were thus valued once again, and their owners were more confident of their future. Those that survived intact into the 1960s have generally continued to exist: where private owners have been obliged to sell, they have generally found new uses as health clinics or research centres and their grounds, at least in part, have been maintained.

Why it should be that the British people have become increasingly concerned with the conservation of the country house is a vast subject which cannot be examined in any depth here. The development was, and is, closely bound up with the more general growth of the 'heritage industry' in Britain, with the tendency for a nation in political and economic decline to become obsessed with its past.[8] In the 1970s and '80s the number of museums in Britain increased inexorably, many of them presenting for popular consumption a past of contented simplicity which, in reality, never existed. The country house has a particular place in all this: a symbol of stability and continuity, of wealth with taste, of an 'upstairs–downstairs' world of privilege tempered by social duty. They are the homes of the families who ruled when Britain was top nation: family homes, private places, somehow like our own yet on a grander and nobler scale. And they are quintessentially *rural*: by definition, you do not find country houses and parks in run-down inner-city areas, an important consideration in a culture which continues to prioritize the life of the countryside over that of the town.

Whatever the reasons for the British obsession with preserving these signs of a privileged past, the conservation of a country house of necessity implies the preservation of its setting, its garden and park: together they form a unified composition of power and beauty – 'The portico of a Palladian mansion seen across a lake at sunset, deer grazing by the water's edge'.[9] Yet the preservation of the building is a much simpler matter than the preservation of the landscape in which it stands, and it was probably for this reason that concern for parks and gardens grew more slowly than that for the houses they surrounded, during the 1970s and early '80s, as it became apparent that many were in a state of terminal decline.

THE FUTURE OF HISTORIC LANDSCAPES

Gardens and parks are not like buildings. Restoration is never enough; long term management plans, and the funding to go with them, are required. For landscapes continue to change, to grow and alter and decay. The more structured and unnatural the design, in general, the sooner neglect becomes apparent: but even the naturalistic planting of the landscape park eventually goes the way of all natural things. We may think of these places as 'historic landscapes' but unlike history, unlike the past, they are not dead but living, and thus always in the process of dying. Yet 'historic landscapes' is itself an illuminating term. Its currency implies something important about how we perceive the role of these parks and gardens, suggesting that their artistic development is over, has been frozen. This has important implications – not least for their owners, who might wish (not surprisingly) to leave their own mark on a property perhaps held by their family for generations. More importantly it raises the question: if such landscapes are to be preserved then what phase in their history should we enhance through restoration and future management? The avenue of flowering cherries recently planted obliquely across the Bridgeman vista, the Leyland cypress hedge established in front of the main entrance – these are features all garden historians could happily dispense with. But what of the Victorian terraces so wilfully destroying the impact of one of Brown's designs? Few enthusiasts for the Georgian Age would wish to let them decay, still less intentionally sweep them aside. And if they did, what of the claims of those who – employing the most sophisticated archaeological techniques, the most detailed documentary research – might wish to reconstruct the old formal gardens around the house which were destroyed by that great vandal Brown? There are, it is true, some country house landscapes which date to a single period, but most are complex, multi-period palimpsests. Garden restorers often side-step such awkward questions by returning the landscape to some arbitrary point in time, such as the late nineteenth or early twentieth century, as it is depicted on first or second edition Ordnance Survey 25 inch or 6 inch: 1 mile maps. This is all right as far as it goes, but it generally results in a landscape very different from anything experienced (or intended) by eighteenth-century designers, often, for example, creating strange mixtures of original but overmature planting and youthful replacements.

How we restore thus raises a host of difficult questions; what we preserve raises others. Britain is cursed with too much history, laden with decaying buildings and landscapes rendered redundant by social and economic change. In spite of what the most ardent conservationists might suggest, it is only possible to preserve a tiny proportion of eighteenth- and nineteenth-century parks and gardens, and *if* public money is to be used for this purpose it ought to be carefully targeted at a group of gardens selected not only for their supposed artistic importance, but as representatives of particular periods, localities and social levels.

To some people, of course, even this course of action is suspect, for ideological reasons. It has become fashionable in certain circles to decry the preservation of parks and gardens because of their supposed role in the manufacture of a largely mythical past, used to bolster the inequalities of the present. It will be apparent from the arguments presented in this book that I would agree that landscapes had, and have, social and political roles. But obliterating the signs of an unequal past will not in itself change general notions of history. The past is a battlefield of conflicting interpretations, and to destroy its most tangible and immediate evidence will do nothing to change popular views one way or the other. Above all, a desire to maintain traces of the past in the environment around us need not imply any necessary acceptance of the values of the societies that have left them. I can enjoy the tracery in the windows of a parish church without subscribing to the medieval Catholic ideology that inspired its creation: and much the same applies to the pleasure I derive from the sweeping grandeur of one of Brown's landscapes, or the more intimate pastoralism of a small country park. To recognize the social and economic factors that created these landscapes adds to their interest and relevance, but need not destroy the more basic sensory pleasures that we can derive from them.

This book has emphasized the social, the political, and the economic aspects of garden design, as opposed to those aesthetic and philosophical perspectives which are often prominent in accounts of the eighteenth-century landscape. Rather than see a steady, inexorable progression from formality to informality, from 'art' to 'nature', I have argued for a more complex pattern, and one related to broader currents of social change. Styles of landscape design were pushed in this direction, or in that, by a whole bundle of interrelated forces. These changed from decade to decade, and from place to place, as England developed first as a capitalist, and then as an industrial, society. Of course, by concentrating on economics, lifestyles and ideologies I have neglected other factors which were perhaps no less important in the formulation of successive styles. I have said little in this volume about the changing roles of men and women, about the progress of philosophy and aesthetics, or about developments in horticulture. For there is only so much space in a book, and there are many stories that can be told about the landscapes of eighteenth-century England. But someone else must tell them.

Notes

Chapter One

1. The best traditional accounts of eighteenth-century garden history can be found in: M. Hadfield, *A History of British Gardening* (London 1960); C. Hussey, *English Gardens and Landscapes 1700–1750* (London 1967); and above all in D. Jacques's excellent *Georgian Gardens: the Reign of Nature* (London 1983).
2. H. Walpole, *The History of the Modern Taste in Gardening* (Garland Edition, New York 1982).
3. T. Turner, *English Garden Design: Landscape and Styles since 1660* (Woodbridge 1986), especially pp. 5–27.
4. See, in particular, K. Thomas, *Man and the Natural World* (London 1983), especially pp. 260–9.
5. J.C. Loudon, *The Suburban Gardener and Villa Companion* (London 1838), p. 162.
6. J. Dixon Hunt, *Garden and Grove: the Italian Renaissance Garden in the English Imagination 1600–1750* (London 1986), p. 182.
7. See in particular J. Phibbs, 'An Approach to the Methodology of Recording Historic landscape', *Garden History* 11, 2 (1983), pp. 167–75; A. Taigel and T. Williamson, *Parks and Gardens* (London 1993), pp. 11–29.
8. C. Taylor, *The Archaeology of Gardens* (Aylesbury 1983).
9. Hertfordshire Record Office, D/ER Z 12.
10. H. Repton, *Fragments on the Theory and Practice of Landscape Gardening* (London 1816), p. 75.
11. A. Bermingham, *Landscape and Ideology: The English Rustic Tradition, 1740–1860* (London 1987), especially pp. 9–14; S. Pugh, *Garden–Nature–Language* (Manchester 1988).
12. Bermingham, *op.cit.*, pp. 13–14.
13. T. Williamson and L. Bellamy, *Property and Landscape* (London 1987); M. Turner, *English Parliamentary Enclosure* (Folkstone 1980); J.A. Yelling, *Common Field and Enclosure in England 1450–1850* (London 1977); R. Wordie, 'The Chronology of English Enclosure 1500–1914', *Economic History Review* 36 (1983).
14. M. Turner, *op.cit.*
15. H.A. Clemenson, *English Country Houses and Landed Estates* (London 1982); J.P. Cooper, 'The Social Distribution of Land and Men in England, 1436–1700', *Economic History Review* 20 (1967), pp. 419–40; J.V. Beckett, *The Aristocracy in England 1660–1914* (Oxford 1986), pp. 43–90.
16. P. Langford, *A Polite and Commercial People* (Oxford 1992), pp. 389–461.
17. *Ibid.*
18. B. Hill, *The Growth of Parliamentary Parties, 1689–1742* (London 1976); J.C.D. Clark, *English Society 1688–1742: Ideology, Social Structure, and Political Practice During the Ancien Régime* (Cambridge 1985); J.C.D. Clark, *Revolution and Rebellion: State and Society in the Seventeenth and Eighteenth Centuries* (Cambridge 1980).
19. Langford, *op.cit.*, pp. 710–25.
20. J. Barrell, *An Equal Wide Survey* (London 1984).
21. Bernard Mandeville, *The Fable of the Bees: or, Private Vices, Public Benefits* (London 1714); John Locke, *An Essay Concerning Human Understanding* (London 1690); David Hume, *A Treatise of Human Nature* (London 1739).
22. N. McKendrick, J. Brewer and J.H. Plumb, *The Birth of a Consumer Society* (London 1982).
23. Langford, *op.cit.*, p. 709.
24. *Ibid.*, pp. 59–124; M. Girouard, *Life in the English Country House* (Yale 1978), pp. 188–93.
25. Hertfordshire Record Office, D/EP P21 & 21A.

Chapter Two

1. M. Laird, *The Formal Garden: Traditions of Art and Nature* (London 1992); R. Duthie, 'The Planting Plans of Some Seventeenth-Century Gardens', *Garden History* 18, 2 (1990), pp. 77–102; A. Taigel and T. Williamson, *Parks and Gardens* (London 1993), pp. 30–47.

2. See T. Williamson and A. Taigel, 'Some Early Geometric Gardens in Norfolk', *Journal of Garden History* 11, 1 & 2 (1991), pp. 1–10.

3. The best discussions of the Renaissance garden in England are: J. Dixon Hunt, *Garden and Grove: the Italian Renaissance Garden in the English Imagination 1600–1750* (London 1986); and R. Strong, *The Renaissance Garden in England* (London 1979).

4. P. Everson, 'The Gardens of Campden House, Chipping Campden, Gloucestershire', *Garden History* 17, 2 (1989), pp. 109–21.

5. Royal Commission on Historical Monuments, *An Inventory of the Historical Monuments in the County of Northamptonshire*, Volume 3: *Archaeological Sites in Northamptonshire* (HMSO, London 1981), pp. 105–11.

6. C. Taylor, P. Everson, and R. Wilson-North, 'Bodiam Castle, Sussex', *Medieval Archaeology* 34 (1990), pp. 155–7.

7. O. Rackham, *The History of the Countryside* (London 1986), p. 123.

8. *Ibid.*, pp. 122–9; Paul Stamper, 'Woods and Parks', in G. Astill and A. Grant (eds) *The Countryside of Medieval England* (Oxford 1988), pp. 128–48; Jean Birrell, Deer and Deer Farming in Medieval England', *Agricultural History Review* 40, II (1993), pp. 112–26.

9. R. Hoppitt, 'A Study of the Development of Parks in Suffolk from the Early Eleventh to the Seventeenth Century' (Unpublished PhD Thesis, University of East Anglia, 1992), pp. 132–3.

10. Stamper, *op.cit.*, pp. 146–7; Frank Woodward, *Oxfordshire Parks* (Woodstock 1982); H. Prince, *Parks in England* (Isle of Wight 1967), pp. 4–5; K. Thomas, *Man and the Natural World* (London 1983), pp. 202–3.

11. W. Bray (ed.), *Memoirs Illustrative of the Life & Writings of John Evelyn Esq FRS Comprising his Diary 1641 to 1705/6* (London 1870), p. 346.

12. T. Turner, *English Garden Design: History and Styles since 1650* (Woodbridge 1986); M. Hadfield, *A History of British Gardening* (Harmondsworth 1985), pp. 106–78; J. Dixon Hunt and Erik de Jong (eds) 'The Anglo–Dutch Garden in the Age of William and Mary', *Journal of Garden History* 8, 2 & 3 (1988); D. Jacques and A. Jan Van Der Horst, *The Gardens of William and Mary* (Kent 1988).

13. F. Hopper, 'The Dutch Classical Garden and André Mollet', *Journal of Garden History* 2, 1 (1982), pp. 25–40.

14. E.B. MacDougall and F. Hamilton Hazlehurst (eds) *The French Formal Garden* (Third Dumbarton Oaks Colloquium on the History of Landscape Architecture, Washington, 1979); R.G. Saisselin, 'The French Garden in the Eighteenth Century: from Belle Nature to the Landscape of Time', *Journal of Garden History* 5, 3 (1985), pp. 284–7.

15. E. de Jong, 'Virgilian Paradise: a Dutch Garden near Moscow in the Early Eighteenth Century', *Journal of Garden History* 1, 4 (1981), pp. 305–44.

16. L. Knyff and J. Kipp, *Britannia Illustrata* (1707; reprinted London 1984, ed. John Harris and G. Jackson-Stopps, London).

17. S. Switzer, *Ichnographia Rustica* (London 1718), Vol. 1, p. 76.

18. *Ibid.*, p. 331.

19. B. Langley, *New Principles of Gardening* (London 1728), p. 201.

20. M. Girouard, *Life in the English Country House: a Social and Architectural History* (Yale 1978), pp. 119–60.

21. H. Green, *Gardener to Queen Anne: Henry Wise (1635–1738) and the Formal Garden* (Oxford 1956).

22. Switzer, *op.cit.*, p. 81.

23. R. North, *A Discourse of Fish and Fish Ponds* (London 1713), p. 27.

24. J. Evelyn, *Sylva, or a Discourse of Forest-Trees and the Propagation of Timber in his Majesties Dominions* (London 1679).

25. Switzer, *op.cit.*, p. 52.

26. Turner, *op.cit.*, pp. 22–4; D. Leatherbarrow, 'Character, Geometry and Perspective: the Third Earl of Shaftesbury's Principles of Garden Design', *Journal of Garden History* 4, 4 (1984), pp. 332–58; R.T. Wallis, *Neoplatonism* (London 1972), pp. 160–4.

27. Berkshire Record Office, D/ED F 14.

28. Duthie, *op.cit.*, p. 85.

29. R. North, 'Cursory Notes on Building Occasioned by the Repair, or Rather Metamorphosis of an Old House in the Country', in H. Colvin and J. Newman (eds), *Of Building: Roger North's Writings on Architecture* (Oxford 1981), p. 87.

30. W. Lawson, *The Countrie Housewife's Garden* (London 1617), p. 10.

31. Duthie, *op.cit.*, p. 94.

32. Williamson and Taigel, *op.cit.*, pp. 5–9.

33. J. Thirsk, 'Making a Fresh Start: Sixteenth-Century Agriculture and the Classical Inspiration', in M. Leslie and T. Raylor (eds), *Culture and Cultivation in Early Modern England: Writing and the Land* (Leicester 1992), pp. 15–34.

34. Unpublished draft of pamphlet on doves and dove houses by Hamon le Strange of

Hunstanton: Norfolk Record Office, Le Strange ND 22.34.

35. *Ibid.*

36. North, *Fish and Fish Ponds*, p. 21.

37. *Ibid.*, p. 56.

38. *Ibid.*, pp. 72–3.

39. Judith Roberts, *Yorkshire Gardens: An exhibition of Documents at the North Yorkshire Record Office* (York 1993), pp. 6–7.

40. Kip and Knyff, *op.cit.*; C. Campbell, *Vitruvius Britannicus or the British Architect* (London 1725).

41. Switzer, *op.cit.*, p. 83.

42. The Journals of Sir John Clerk of Penicuik. Scottish Record Office, GD 18/2107. I would like to thank John Phibbs for drawing this important document to my attention.

43. T. Hamilton (6th Earl of Haddington), *Forest Trees: Some Directions about Raising Forest Trees* (ed. M.L. Anderson, London 1953), p. 58.

44. Raynham Hall (Norfolk), Muniments Room, uncatalogued.

45. Langley, *New Principles*, p. viii.

46. Norfolk Record Office, Hare 5532 223 × 5.

47. Bedfordshire Record Office, CRT 130 SIL 19.

48. Laird, *op.cit.*, pp. 96–7.

49. G. Sheeran, *Landscape Gardens in West Yorkshire 1680–1880* (Wakefield 1990), pp. 24–5.

50. *Ibid.*, pp. 25–9.

51. K. Bilikowsky, *Hampshire's Countryside Heritage 5: Historic Parks and Gardens* (Southampton 1983), pp. 16–17.

52. Langley, *op.cit.*, pp. 203–7; Switzer, *op.cit.*, pp. 311–17.

53. Hertfordshire Record Office, D/ER Z 12.

54. H. Walpole, *The History of Modern Gardening* (Garland edn, New York 1982), p. 53.

55. *Ibid.*

56. Switzer, *op.cit.*, p. 34.

57. Charles Perry's tour of northern England: Norfolk Record Office, MC 150/49.

58. M. Hoyles, *The Story of Gardening* (London 1991), p. 46.

59. Berkshire Record Office, D/EX 258/9.

60. D. Cruikshank, *A Guide to the Georgian Buildings of Britain and Ireland* (London 1985), pp. 2–23.

61. *Ibid.*, p. 10.

62. Laird, *op.cit.*, pp. 121–2; J. Caree, 'Lord Burlington's Garden at Chiswick', *Garden History* 1, 3 (1973), pp. 23–30.

63. Laird, *op.cit.*, p. 121.

64. B. Langley, *Practical Geometry Applied to the Practical and Useful Arts of Building, Surveying, Gardening and Mensuration* (London 1729), p. 33.

65. Sheeran, *op.cit.*, p. 23.

66. Langley, *New Principles*, p. 196.

67. Quoted in M. Hadfield, *A History of British Gardening* (London 1960), pp. 160–3.

68. Switzer, *op.cit.*, p. xix.

Chapter Three

1. A. Ashley Cooper, 3rd Earl of Shaftesbury, 'The Moralists', in *Characteristics of Men, Manners, Opinions, Times* (London 1711: ed. J.M. Robertson, New York 1964); treatise 5, part 3, section 2, p. 125.

2. *Spectator*, 414, 25 June 1712.

3. A. Pope, 'Epistle to Burlington', in H. Davies (ed.) *Poetical Works* (Oxford 1966), p. 318.

4. S. Switzer, *Ichnographia Rustica* (London 1718), pp. 338–9.

5. *Ibid.*, pp. xviii, xix, 346.

6. D. Leatherbarrow, 'Character, Geometry and Perspective: the Third Earl of Shaftesbury's Principles of Garden design', *Journal of Garden History* 4, 4 (1974), pp. 332–58, 334.

7. *Ibid.*, pp. 336–45.

8. *Ibid.*, pp. 354–6.

9. Leatherbarrow, *op.cit.*

10. Switzer, *op.cit.*, pp. v–vi.

11. *Ibid.*, p. xii.

12. *Ibid.*, p. 40.

13. *Ibid.*, p. 317.

14. *Ibid.*, p. 274.

15. *Ibid.*, p. xviii.

16. *Ibid.*, p. xix.

17. *Ibid.*, pp. xxx, xxxvii.

18. D. Jacques, 'The Art and Sense of the Scriblerus Club in England 1715–1735', *Garden History* 4, 1 (1976), pp. 30–53.

19. A. Taigel and T. Williamson, 'Some Early Geometric Gardens in Norfolk', *Journal of Garden History* 11, 1 & 2 (1991), pp. 59–65; D. Yaxley, 'Houghton, Documentary Evidence', in A. Davison, 'Six Deserted Villages in Norfolk', *East Anglian Archaeology* 44 (1988), pp. 83–94.

20. The visitor was Matthew Decker. John Cornford, 'The Growth of an Idea', *Country Life* 14 May 1987, pp. 162–5.

21. Historic Manuscripts Commission *15th Report*, Appendix, part 6, p. 85.

22. G. Jackson-Stops, *An English Arcadia 1600–1990: Designs for Gardens and Garden Buildings in the Care of the National Trust* (Washington 1991), pp. 46–8.

23. Taigel and Williamson, *op.cit.*, pp. 100–4.

24. Wolterton Hall, Norfolk, archives: WOLT 8/20.

25. *Ibid.*, 8/12.

26. T. Hamilton (6th Earl of Haddington), *Forest*

Trees: Some Directions About Raising Forest Trees, ed. M.L. Anderson (Edinburgh 1953), p. 58.

27. M. Laird, 'Ornamental Planting and Horticulture in English Pleasure Grounds 1700–1830', in J. Dixon Hunt (ed.) *Garden History: Issues, Approaches, Methods* (Washington 1992), pp. 243–77.

28. Hamilton, *op.cit.*, p. 54.

29. K. Bilikowsky, *Hampshire's Countryside Heritage 5; Historic Parks and Gardens* (Southampton 1983), p. 17.

30. R. Fausset, 'The Creation of the Gardens at Castle Hill, South Moulton, Devon', *Garden History* 13, 2 (1985), pp. 102–25.

31. Jackson-Stops, *op.cit.*, p. 46.

32. A. Taigel and T. Williamson, *Parks and Gardens* (London 1993), pp. 72–4.

33. J. Dixon Hunt, *William Kent Landscape Garden Designer* (London 1987).

34. Historic Manuscripts Commission, *Carlisle*, pp. 143–4.

35. A. Young, *The Farmer's Tour Through Eastern England*, Vol. 1 (London 1771), pp. 34–42.

36. M. Batey, 'The Way to View Rousham by Kent's Gardener', *Garden History* 11, 2 (1983), pp. 125–32.

37. A. Tinniswood, *A History of Country House Visiting* (London 1989), p. 75.

38. K. Rorschach, *The Early Georgian Landscape Garden* (New Haven 1983), pp. 39–45.

39. R.W. King, 'Phillip Southcote and Woburn Farm', *Garden History* 2, 3 (1974), pp. 27–60.

40. J. Dixon Hunt, *Garden and Grove: the Italian Renaissance Garden in the English Imagination 1600–1750* (London 1986), pp. 192, 222.

41. H.T. Dickinson, *Walpole and the Whig Supremacy* (London 1973).

42. G. Clarke, 'Grecian Taste and Gothic Virtue: Lord Cobham's Gardening Programme and its Iconography', *Apollo* 97 (1973), pp. 56–67.

43. Rorschach, *op.cit.*, pp. 27–34.

44. *Ibid.*, pp. 17–26.

45. *Ibid.*, pp. 35–7.

46. P. Edwards, 'The Gardens at Wroxton Abbey, Oxfordshire', *Garden History* 14 (1986), pp. 50–9; A. Hodges, 'Painshill Park, Cobham, Surrey 1700–1800', *Garden History* 2, 2 (1973), pp. 39–68: Rorschach, *op.cit.*, pp. 39–46.

47. D. Jacques, 'On the Supposed Chineseness of the English Landscape Garden', *Garden History* 18, 1 (1990), pp. 180–91.

48. Rorschach, *op.cit.*, pp. 59–64.

49. M. Charlesworth, 'Sacred Landscape: Signs of Religion in the Eighteenth-Century Garden', *Journal of Garden History* 13, 1 & 2 (1993), pp. 56–68.

50. N. Penny, 'The Macabre Garden at Denbies and its Monument', *Garden History* 3, 3 (1975), pp. 58–61.

51. L. Stone, *Family, Sex and Marriage 1500–1700* (Harmondsworth 1979).

52. E. Harwood, ' Personal Identity and the Eighteenth-Century English Landscape Garden', *Journal of Garden History* 13, 1 & 2, pp. 36–48.

53. Tinniswood, *op.cit.*, pp. 63–108.

54. R. Dodsley, *A Description of the Leasowes the Seat of the Late William Shenstone Esq* (Reprinted by Garland Press, New York 1982), p. 374.

55. Harwood, *op.cit.*

56. Norfolk Record Office, MC 40/101.

57. The Hon. James Bucknall Grimston, 'An Account of a Northern Town in 1768'; Hertfordshire Record Office, D/EV F 14.

58. P. Willis, 'Capability Brown in Northumberland', *Garden History* 9, 2 (1981), pp. 157–83.

59. Charles Perry MD, 'A Tour of Northern England', 1725; Norfolk Record Office, MC 150/49.

60. Norfolk Record Office, MC 40/101.

61. Tinniswood, *op.cit.*, p. 75.

62. *Ibid.*, p. 91.

63. N. Scarfe (ed.), *A Frenchman's Year in Suffolk: French Impressions of Suffolk Life in 1784* (Ipswich 1988), p. 198.

64. Norfolk Record Office, MC 40/101.

65. This important point – on which much of the following argument is based – was first made by John Phibbs in his article 'Pleasure Grounds in Sweden and their English Models', *Garden History* 21, 1 (1993), pp. 60–90.

66. George Mason, *An Essay on Design in Gardening* (London 1770), p. 25.

67. Phibbs, *op.cit.*

68. Young, *op.cit.*, p. 35.

69. *Ibid.*, pp. 72–6.

70. *Ibid.*, pp. 36–7.

71. *Ibid.*, p. 33.

72. Berkshire Record Office, D/ELL C1/240.1.

73. Hertfordshire Record Office, D/EB 1622 P3.

74. Taigel and Williamson, 'Some Early Geometric Gardens', pp. 88–9.

75. R. Williams, 'Sir John Dalrymple's "An Essay on Landscape Gardening"', *Journal of Garden History* 3, 2 (1983), pp. 144–56.

76. H. Stevenson, *The Gentleman Gardener's Recreation* (revised 11th edn, London 1769).

77. H. Repton, *An Inquiry into the Changes of Taste in Landscape Gardening* (London 1806), p. 33.

78. *The World*, No. 15, 12 April 1753.

Chapter Four

1. R. Williams, 'Making Places: Garden Mastery and English Brown', *Journal of Garden History* 3, 4 (1983), pp. 382–5.

2. E.J. Climenson (ed.), *Passages from the Diaries of Mrs Phillip Lybbe Powys 1756–1808* (London 1899), p. 115.

3. For the characteristics of Brown's style, see in particular D. Stroud, *Capability Brown* (London 1965); R. Turner, *Capability Brown and the Eighteenth-Century English Landscape* (London 1985); and T. Hinde, *Capability Brown: the Story of a Master Gardener*.

4. Quoted in Stroud, *op. cit.*, pp. 156–7.

5. W. Roberts, *Memoirs of the Life and Correspondence of Mrs Hannah More*, 3rd edn, 4 vols (1835), Vol. 1, p. 267. Mrs More to her sisters, December 1782. Punctuation modernized.

6. P. Willis, 'Capability Brown in Northumberland', *Garden History* 9, 1 (1981), pp. 157–83.

7. Willis, *op.cit.*, p. 159.

8. Quoted in Stroud, *op.cit.*, pp. 117–18.

9. Williams, *op.cit.*

10. W. Chambers, *Dissertation on Oriental Gardening* (London 1772), p.v.

11. J.C. Loudon, *Observations on the Theory and Practice of Landscape Gardening &c* (Edinburgh 1804), p. 210; G. Jeykll, *A Gardener's Testament* (London 1937), p. 30.

12. Stroud, *op.cit.*, p. 13.

13. Information from David Brown of the Centre of East Anglian Studies, who has been working on Brown's bank account as part of his research into Nathaniel Richmond and other 'imitators'.

14. This suggestion was made to me by David Brown.

15. W. Taylor and J. Pringle (eds), *The Chatham Correspondence* (London, 1838–40), Vol. 4, p. 430.

16. D. Stroud, *Humphrey Repton* (London 1962), p. 27.

17. F. Cowell, 'Richard Woods (?1716–93). A Preliminary Account'. Part 1, *Garden History* 14, 2 (1986), pp. 85–120; Part 2, *Garden History* 15, 1 (1987a), pp. 19–54; Part 3, *Garden History* 15, 2 (1987b), pp. 115–35.

18. Quoted in Stroud, *Repton*, pp. 27–8.

19. Cowell, *op.cit.*, 1987b.

20. *Ibid.*

21. A. Tinniswood, *A History of Country House Visiting* (London 1989), pp. 93–5.

22. The Hon. James Bucknall Grimston, 'An Account of a Northern Tour in 1768'; Hertfordshire Record Office, D/EV F 14.

23. Private Collection: Beeston Hall (Norfolk) archives.

24. Climenson, *op.cit.*, p. 121.

25. Red Book for Tewin: Hertfordshire Record Office, D/Z 42 Z 1.

26. H. Prince, 'Parkland in the Chilterns', *Geographical Review* 49 (1959), pp. 18–31.

27. Grimston, 'Northern Tour': Hertfordshire Record Office D/EV F 13–14.

28. Stroud, *op.cit.*, p. 103.

29. H. Moggridge, '"Capability" Brown at Blenheim', in J. Bond and K. Tiller (eds) *Blenheim: Landscape for a Palace*, (Gloucester 1987), p. 94.

30. H. Repton, *Fragments on the Theory and Practice of Landscape Gardening* (London 1816), p. 94.

31. W. Watts, *The Seats of the Nobility & Gentry in a Collection of the Most Interesting and Picturesque Views* (London 1799).

32. M. Laird, *The Formal Garden: Traditions of Art and Nature* (London 1992), p. 92.

33. Bedfordshire Record Office, L/30/9a/6/117.

34. *The Autobiography and Correspondence of Mary Delaney* (London 1862), Vol. 3, p. 285.

35. Richard Woods, 'A Design for the Improvement of Little Linford'; Buckinghamshire Record Office, MA 275 R.

36. Stroud, *op.cit.*, pp. 68–9.

37. *Horace Walpole's Journal of Visits to Country Seats 1751–84* (Walpole Society, 1927–8), p. 45.

38. U. Price, *Essays on the Picturesque*, Vol. 2 (London 1810), p. 148.

39. Bedfordshire Record Office, CRT 100/27/4 p. 32.

40. T. Jefferson, *Memoranda of a Tour of the Gardens of England*, quoted in Bond and Tiller, *op.cit.*, p. 123.

41. N. Scarfe (ed.), *A Frenchman's Year in Suffolk: French Impressions of Suffolk Life in 1784* (Ipswich 1988), pp. 34–5.

42. H. Walpole, *The History of Modern Taste in Gardening* (Garland edn, New York 1982), p. 272.

43. Repton, *Fragments*, p. 167.

44. Journal of a Tour by Edward Watts, 1777; quoted in D. Lambert, *Record of Documentary Sources* (Centre for the Conservation of Historic Parks and Gardens Report No. 4, York 1991), p. 81.

45. The importance of this passage was first emphasized by Robert Williams in his seminal article, 'Rural Economy and the Antique in the English landscape Garden', *Journal of Garden History* 7, 1 (1987), pp. 73–96, esp. p. 86.

46. Williams, *op.cit.*, p. 86.

47. Buckinghamshire Record Office, D/DR, 5/96/52 & 53.

48. A. Pope, 'Epistle to Burlington', l. 62, in H. Davis (ed.), *Pope: Poetical Works* (Oxford 1966), p. 316.
49. Repton, *Fragments*, p. 104.
50. Bucknall Grimston, 'Northern Tour'; Hertfordshire Record Office, D/EV F13.
51. A. Orum-Larsen, 'The Old North European "Meadow Copse" and the English Landscape Park', *Garden History* 18, 1 (1990), pp. 174–9.
52. E.g. Stroud, *op.cit.*, p. 177.
53. Holkham Hall (Norfolk) estate archives: A/39.
54. See, e.g., the pictures of Cassiobury in Hertfordshire or Badminton in Gloucestershire.
55. P. Miller, *The Gardener's Dictionary* (London 1731), p. 45.
56. J. Phibbs, 'Groves and Belts', *Journal of Garden History* 19, 2 (1991), pp. 175–86.
57. Ibid., p. 186.
58. Houghton Hall (Norfolk), muniment room: map 23.

Chapter Five

1. K.D.M. Snell, *Annals of the Labouring Poor: Social Change and Agrarian England 1660–1900* (Cambridge 1983); P. Langford, *A Polite and Commercial People: England 1727–1783* (Oxford 1992), especially pp. 435–59; M. Turner, *English Parliamentary Enclosure* (Folkestone 1980).
2. F. Brooke, *History of Lady Julia Mandeville* (2nd edn, London 1763), Vol. I, pp. 222–3.
3. For the development of lodges see, in particular, T. Mowl and B. Earnshaw, *Trumpet at a Distant Gate: the Lodge as Prelude to the Country House* (London 1985).
4. G. Sheeran, *Landscape Gardens in West Yorkshire 1680–1880* (Wakefield 1990).
5. *Ibid.*, p. 128.
6. *Ibid.*
7. E.J.Climenson (ed.), *Passages from the Diaries of Mrs Phillip Lybbe Powys 1756–1808* (London 1899), p. 175.
8. O. Goldsmith, *A Prospect of Society, Being the Earliest Form of His Poem The Traveller* (ed. B. Dobell, London 1902), ll. 405–10.
9. B.A. Holderness, '"Open" and "Closed" Parishes in England in the Eighteenth and Nineteenth Centuries', *Agricultural History Review* 20 (1972), pp. 126–39; D.R. Mills, *Lord and Peasant in Nineteenth-Century Britain* (London 1980).
10. M. Batey, 'The Way to View Rousham by Kent's Gardener', *Garden History* 11, 2 (1983), p. 128.
11. H. Repton, Red Book for Tewin Water, Hertfordshire; Hertfordshire Record Office, D/Z 42 Z1 P 21 A.
12. L. Lewis (ed.), *Hird's Annals of Bedale.* North Yorkshire Record Office Publications No. 2 (1990), stanzas 675–6. I would like to thank Judith Roberts for drawing this document to my attention.
13. D. Stroud, *Capability Brown* (London 1965), pp. 70, 77, 91.
14. J. Rosenheim, *The Townshends of Raynham: Nobility in Transition in Restoration and Early Hanoverian England* (Connecticut 1989), p. 188.
15. Stroud, *op.cit.*, pp. 234, 243.
16. Norfolk Record Office, HEA 489 256 × 4.
17. For the development of 'polite society' see, in particular, Langford, *op.cit.*, pp. 59–124; M. Girouard, *Life in the English Country House* (Yale 1978), pp. 188–93; M. Girouard, *The English Town* (Yale 1990), pp. 76–80.
18. *Ibid.*, pp. 76–7.
19. N. MacKendrick, J. Brewer and J.H. Plumb, *The Birth of a Consumer Society* (London 1982), p. 1.
20. S. Daniels and S. Seymour, 'Landscape Design and the Idea of Improvement 1730–1900', in R.A. Dodgshon and R.A. Butlin (eds), *An Historical Geography of England and Wales* (London 1990), pp. 487–520; p. 497.
21. Girouard, *Life*, pp. 125–6.
22. D. Cruickshank, *A Guide to the Georgian Buildings of Britain and Ireland* (London 1985), pp. 62–4.
23. Girouard, *Life*, p. 210.
24. Climenson, *op.cit.*, p. 25.
25. *Ibid.*, p. 72.
26. Langford, *op.cit.*, pp. 61–79, 116–21.
27. H. Fielding, *Enquiry into the Causes of the Late Increase in Robbers* (Oxford edn 1988), p. 77.
28. N. Forster, *An Enquiry into the Recent High Price of Provisions* (London 1767), p. 41.
29. T. Williamson and L. Bellamy, *Property and Landscape: A Social History of Land Ownership and the English Countryside* (London 1987), pp. 124–5; J.G.A. Pocock, *The Machiavellian Moment: Florentine Political Thought and the Atlantic Republican Tradition* (New Jersey 1975); J. Barrell, *An Equal Wide Survey* (London 1984).
30. W. Marshall, *Planting and Rural Ornament* (2nd edn, 1796), Vol. I, pp. 283–4.
31. MacKendrick *et al.*, *op.cit.*, p. 66.
32. R. Duthie, 'Florists' Societies and Feasts after 1750', *Garden History* 12, 1 (1984), pp. 8–38.
33. T. Fairchild, *The London Gardener* (London 1722), p. 35.
34. Quoted in K. Thomas, *Man and the Natural World* (London 1983), p. 229.
35. R. Bell, 'The Discovery of a Buried Georgian

Garden in Bath', *Garden History* 18, 1 (1990), pp. 1–21.

36. D. Cruickshank and N. Burton, *Life in the Georgian City* (London 1990), p. 202.

37. R.T. Longstaffe-Gowan, 'Proposals for a Georgian Town Garden in Gower Street: the Francis Douce Garden', *Garden History* 15, 2 (1987), pp. 136–44.

38. Climenson, *op.cit.*, p. 121.

39. Norfolk Record Office, NRS 8380 (A) 24D.

40. Revd Lord to Martin Ffolkes, Jan. 1777; Norfolk Record Office, MC 50/25, 503 × 7.

41. H. Colvin and C. Nelson, '"Building Castles of Flowers": Maria Edgeworth as Gardener', *Garden History* 16, 1 (1988), pp. 58–70.

Chapter Six

1. Much of the argument in this chapter was first presented in my paper 'The Landscape Park: Economics, Art and Ideology', *Journal of Garden History* 13, 1 and 2 (1993), pp. 49–55. See also S. Daniels and S. Seymour, 'Landscape Design and the Idea of Improvement 1730–1900', in B.A. Dodgshon and R. Butlin (eds) *An Historical Geography of England and Wales* (London 1990), pp. 488–520.

2. K. Thomas, *Man and the Natural World* (London 1983), pp. 59–60.

3. J. Lawrence, *The Modern Land Steward* (London 1801), p. 100.

4. H. Repton, Red Book for Honing (Norfolk) (private collection).

5. R. Parker, *Coke of Norfolk: a Financial and Agricultural Study 1707–1842* (Oxford 1975).

6. Journal of a Tour by Edward Witts, 1777: quoted in D. Lambert, *Record of Documentary Sources (Centre for the Conservation of Historic Parks and Gardens Report No. 4* (York 1991), p. 81.

7. T. Whately, *Observations on Modern Gardening* (London 1770), pp. 1, 164–5.

8. See, e.g., S. Switzer, *Ichnographia Rustica* (London 1718), p. 336.

9. Quoted in Thomas, *op.cit.*, p. 202.

10. *Ibid.*, p. 59.

11. B. Langley, *A Sure Method of Improving Estates, by Plantations of Oak, Elm, Ash, Beech and Other Timber Trees, Coppice Woods &c.* (London 1728), p. 1.

12. P. Miller, *The Gardener's Dictionary* (London 1731); J. Wheeler, *The Modern Druid* (London 1747); E. Wade, *A Proposal for Improving and Adorning the Island of Great Britain: for the Maintenance of Our Navy and Shipping* (London 1755); W. Hanbury, *An Essay on Planting* (London 1758).

13. D. Sayer, 'The Oak and the Navy', *Quarterly Journal of Forestry*, 86, 1, pp. 40–3.

14. G. White, *The Natural History of Selbourne* (Everyman edn, London 1906), p. 17.

15. Sayer, *op.cit.*, p. 41.

16. H. Prince, 'The Changing Rural Landscape', in G.E. Mingay *The Agrarian History of England and Wales*, Vol. VI (1750–1850), pp. 7–83; p. 69. For the best discussion of the significance of forestry in élite culture see S. Daniels, 'The Political Iconography of Woodland in Later Eighteenth-Century England', in D. Cosgrove and S. Daniels (eds) *The Iconography of Landscape* (Cambridge 1988), pp. 51–72.

17. O. Rackham, 'The Ancient Woods of Norfolk', *Transactions of the Norfolk and Norwich Naturalists Society* 27, 3 (1986), pp. 161–77; 169–70.

18. E.J.T. Collins, 'The Coppice and Underwood Trades', in Mingay, *op.cit.*, pp. 485–500.

19. E.g. Henry Woods, 'The Management of Underwood', *Irish Farmer's Gazette*, June 1851.

20. W. Wordsworth, *Guide to the Lakes of Westmoreland and Cumberland* (1810), p. 120.

21. J. Bailey and G. Culley, *General View of the Agriculture of Cumberland* (London 1794), p. 202.

22. M. Cook, *The Manner of Raising, Ordering and Improving Forest Trees* (London 1676), p. 32.

23. Sir W. Chambers, *An Explanatory Discourse by Tan Chet-Qua* (London 1773: Augustan Reprint Society 1978), pp. 139–40.

24. Quoted in Thomas, *op.cit.*, p. 208.

25. J. Worlidge, *Systema Agriculturae* (London 1669), p. 72.

26. Daniels, 'Iconography of Woodland'.

27. W. Shenstone, *Essays on Man and Manners* (London 1794), p. 68.

28. Daniels, 'Iconography of Woodland'.

29. T. Ruggles, 'Picturesque Farming', *Annals of Agriculture* 7 (1786), p. 23.

30. Cook, *op.cit.*, pp. 58–9.

31. Quoted in Thomas, *op.cit.*, p. 208.

32. H. Steuart, *The Planter's Guide* (Edinburgh 1828).

33. N. Scarfe (ed.), *A Frenchman's Year in Suffolk: French Impressions of Suffolk Life in 1784* (Ipswich 1988), p. 39.

34. R. Williams, 'Rural Economy and the Antique in the English Landscape garden', *Journal of Garden History* 7, 1 (1987), pp. 73–96.

35. H. Repton, *Fragments on the Theory and Practice of Landscape Gardening* (London 1816), p. 175.

36. Red Book for Wimpole: quoted in G. Jackson-Stops, *An English Arcadia: Designs for Gardens and Garden Buildings in the Care of the National Trust* (Washington 1991), p. 118.

37. P.B. Munsche, *Gentlemen and Poachers: the English Game Laws 1671 1831* (Cambridge 1981), p. 19.
38. *Ibid.*, pp. 15–17.
39. *Ibid.*, pp. 8–27.
40. P. Delabere Blaine, *An Encyclopaedia of Rural Sports: or a Complete Account . . . of Hunting, Shooting, Racing &c.* (London 1838), p. 808.
41. Munsche, *op.cit.*, p. 32.
42. C. Chenevix Trench, *A History of Marksmanship* (London 1972), pp. 103–26; M. Brander, *The Hunting Instinct: the Development of Field Sports Over the Ages* (London 1964), pp. 87–101.
43. Anon., *Thoughts on the Present Laws for Preserving Game* (London 1750), p. 12.
44. H. Hopkins, *The Long Affray* (London 1985), p. 68.
45. M. Hastings, *Sporting Guns* (London 1969).
46. T. Page, *The Art of Shooting Flying* (5th edn, London 1784); W. Daniel, *Rural Sports* (2 vols, London 1801–2).
47. Hopkins, *op.cit.*, p. 54.
48. M. Hadfield, *A History of British Gardening* (Harmondsworth 1960), pp. 68, 86.
49. C.B. Andrews (ed.), *The Torrington Diaries* (London 1934), Vol. I, p. 395.
50. H. Zouch, *An Account of the Present Daring Practices of Night-Hunters and Poachers* (London 1783), p. 1.
51. Munsche, *op.cit.*, pp. 76–105.
52. Blaine, *op.cit.*, p. 856.
53. D. Hill and P. Robinson, *The Pheasant: Management and Conservation* (London 1988), pp. 38–45.
54. A. Forsyth, 'Game Preserves and Fences', *Journal of the Horticultural Society* 1 (1846), p. 201.
55. Blaine, *op.cit.*, p. 854.
56. Hill and Robertson, *op.cit.*, p. 43.
57. *Ibid.*, p. 44.
58. Scarfe (ed.), *op.cit.*, pp. 40–1.

Chapter Seven

1. H. Home, Lord Kames, *Elements of Criticism* (London 1762), p. 85; W. Chambers, *A Dissertation on Oriental Gardening* (London 1772).
2. D. Stroud, *Humphry Repton* (London 1962); K. Laurie, 'First Years', in G. Carter, P. Goode and K. Laurie (eds) *Humphry Repton, Landscape Gardener* (Norwich 1982), pp. 5–9.
3. S. Daniels, 'The Political Landscape', in Carter *et al.*, *op.cit.*, pp. 110–21.
4. J. Phibbs, 'A Reconsideration of Repton's Contribution to the Improvements at Felbrigg,

Norfolk', *Garden History* 13, 1 (1985), pp. 33–44.
5. Laurie, *op.cit.*, p. 12.
6. Norfolk Record Office.
7. S. Daniels and S. Seymour, 'Landscape Design and the Idea of Improvement, 1730–1900', in R.A. Dodgshon and R.A. Butlin (eds) *An Historical Geography of England and Wales* (London 1990), p. 497.
8. William Mason to William Gilpin, 26 December 1794. Bodleian Library MS (Eng, misc. d.571.f.224). Quoted in M. Batey, 'William Mason English Gardener', *Garden History* 1, 1 (1973), p. 23.
9. K. Laurie, 'The Pleasure Ground', in Carter *et al.*, *op.cit.*, pp. 50–61.
10. K. Laurie, 'Working Methods: Earth Moving', in *ibid.*, p. 16.
11. Red Book for Aston park, Cheshire, 1793. Mrs Paul Melon Collection, Garden Springs Library, Upperville, Virginia.
12. Red Book for Honing Hall, Norfolk, 1792. Private collection.
13. No Red Book was apparently produced for the site, but two watercolours by Repton showing the intended effects of the improvements are in the Castle Museum, Norwich.
14. Quoted in Patrick Goode, 'The Picturesque Controversy', in Carter *et al.*, *op.cit.*, p. 34.
15. Hertfordshire Record Office, D/Z 42 Z1 P21A.
16. Red Book for Honing Hall, Norfolk, 1792. Private collection.
17. R.P. Knight, *The Landscape: a Didactic Poem, in Three Books. Addressed to Uvedale Price Esq.* (London 1794); U. Price, *An Essay on the Picturesque, as Compared with the Sublime and the Beautiful* (London 1794).
18. W. Gilpin, *Three Essays on Picturesque Beauty, on Picturesque Travel and on Sketching Landscape* (London, 1792), p. 57.
19. J.C. Loudon, *The Landscape Gardening and Landscape Architecture of the Late Humphry Repton Esq.* (London 1840), p. 354.
20. T. Turner, *English Garden Design: History and Styles since 1650* (Woodbridge 1986), p. 124.
21. J. Appleton, 'Some Thoughts on the Geography of the Picturesque', *Journal of Garden History* 6, 3 (1986), pp. 270–91.
22. Price, *op.cit.*, Vol. I, p. 24.
23. This important aspect was emphasized to me by John Phibbs.
24. Knight, *op.cit.*, p. 51, ll. 236–40.
25. Points again emphasized by Phibbs: see his short but seminal paper, 'The Picturesque Movement', in *Architectural Association Conservation Newsletter* 3 (1992), pp. 3–4.

26. Red Book for Holkham, 1789. Private collection.

27. J.C. Loudon (ed.), *The Landscape Gardening and Landscape Architecture of the Late Humphry Repton Esq.* (London 1840), p. 105.

28. Knight, *op.cit.*, p. 33, ll. 39–40.

29. *The Letters of Anna Seward, 1784–1807*. (6 vols, Edinburgh 1811), Vol. 4, pp. 10–11.

30. S. Daniels and C. Watkins, 'Picturesque Landscaping and Estate Management: Uvedale Price at Foxley 1770–1829', *Rural History* 2, 2 (1991), pp. 141–70. Much of what follows is based on the arguments presented in this important article.

31. Price, *op.cit.*, Vol. III, p. 177.

32. *Ibid.*, fn. to p. 217.

33. H. Repton, *Sketches and Hints of Landscape Gardening* (London 1795), p. 61.

34. Again, the arguments here draw heavily on the work of Stephen Daniels. See, in particular, 'Political landscape'; and S. Daniels, 'Cankerous Blossom: Troubles in the Later Career of Humphry Repton Documented in the Repton Correspondence in the Huntingdon Library', *Journal of Garden History* 6, 2 (1986), pp. 146–61; p. 146.

35. Repton, *Observations on the Theory and Practice of Landscape Gardening* (London 1803), pp. 10–11.

36. *Ibid.*, p. 119.

37. *Ibid.*, p. 33.

38. *Ibid.*, p. 39.

39. Loudon, *op.cit..*, pp. 330–1.

40. K. Laurie, 'The Pleasure Ground', in Carter *et al.*, *op.cit.*, p. 60.

41. *Ibid.*, p. 58.

42. Red Book for Shrubland Hall. Private collection. Red Book for Lamer, 1792: quoted in K. Laurie 'Architecture', in Carter *et al.*, *op.cit.*, p. 77.

43. Repton, *Fragments*, p. 15.

44. Repton, *Inquiry into the Changes in Taste*, p. 66.

45. M. Girouard, *Life in The English Country House* (Yale 1978), pp. 229–32, 268–318.

46. Repton, *Fragments*, p. 139.

47. *Ibid.*, p. 69.

48. *Ibid.*

Chapter Eight

1. J. Britton, *A History and Description of Cassiobury Park in Hertfordshire* (London 1837), p. 45.

2. J.C. Loudon, *Observations on the Formation of Useful and Ornamental Plantations . . .* (Edinburgh 1804), pp. 214–15.

3. T. Turner, 'Loudon's Stylistic Development', *Journal of Garden History* 2, 2 (1982), pp. 175–88.

4. M.L. Simo, *Loudon and the Landscape* (London 1988).

5. For an account of English garden design in the nineteenth century see, in particular, B. Elliot, *Victorian Gardens* (London 1986); and M. Laird, *The Formal Garden: Traditions of Art and Nature* (London 1992), pp. 141–73.

6. Princess Fryderyk Wilhelm Anton Radziwill (ed.), *Memoirs of the Duchess de Dino* (London 1909), pp. 56–7.

7. H.A. Clemenson, *English Country Houses and Landed Estates* (London 1982); A. Taigel and T. Williamson, *Parks and Gardens* (London 1993), pp. 134–46.

8. R. Hewison, *The Heritage Industry: Britain in a Climate of Decline* (London 1987); Patrick Wright, *On Living in an Old Country: the National Past in Contemporary Britain* (London 1985).

9. G. Jackson-Stops (ed.), *The Treasure Houses of Britain: 500 Years of Private Patronage and Art Collecting* (Yale 1985), p. 10.

Index

Figures in italic indicate illustrations.